Lesson Plans for Developing Digital Literacies

Lesson Plans for Developing Digital Literacies

Edited by

Mary T. Christel
Adlai E. Stevenson High School, Lincolnshire, Illinois

Scott Sullivan
National-Louis University

National Council of Teachers of English
1111 W. Kenyon Road, Urbana, Illinois 61801-1096

Manuscript Editor: Bonny Graham

Production Editor: Carol Roehm

Interior Design: Doug Burnett

Cover Design: Jody A. Boles

Cover Images: iStockphoto.com/Stratol
iStockphoto.com/daboost
iStockphoto.com/pablohart

NCTE Stock Number: 27971

It is the policy of NCTE in its journals and other publications to provide a forum for the open discussion of ideas concerning the content and the teaching of English and the language arts. Publicity accorded to any particular point of view does not imply endorsement by the Executive Committee, the Board of Directors, or the membership at large, except in announcements of policy, where such endorsement is clearly specified.

Every effort has been made to provide current URLs and email addresses, but because of the rapidly changing nature of the Web, some sites and addresses may no longer be accessible.

Library of Congress Cataloging-in-Publication Data

Lesson plans for developing digital literacies / edited by Mary T. Christel, Scott Sullivan.
     p. cm.
   Includes bibliographical references and index.
   ISBN 978-0-8141-2797-1 (pbk)
   1. Internet in education—United States.   2. Internet literacy—Study and teaching (Secondary)—United States.   3. English literature—Study and teaching (Secondary)—United States.   I. Christel, Mary T.   II. Sullivan, Scott, 1966–
   LB1044.87.L48 2010
   373.133'44678—dc22

                                                             2010036434

I define Web 2.0 as the design of systems that harness network effects to get better the more people use them, or more colloquially, as "harnessing collective intelligence." This includes explicit network-enabled collaboration, to be sure, but it should encompass every way that people connected to a network create synergistic effects.

Tim O'Reilly
radar.oreilly.com
September 2008

The term "Web 2.0" (2004–present) is commonly associated with web applications that facilitate interactive information sharing, interoperability, user-centered design, and collaboration on the World Wide Web. Examples of Web 2.0 include web-based communities, hosted services, web applications, social-networking sites, video-sharing sites, wikis, blogs, mashups, and folksonomies. A Web 2.0 site allows its users to interact with other users or to change website content, in contrast to non-interactive websites where users are limited to the passive viewing of information that is provided to them.

Wikipedia, Web 2.0 entry
March 4, 2010

Contents

Acknowledgments

Creating a collection of twenty-six lessons that represents the efforts of thirty contributors has been a daunting task, despite our experience assembling and editing the first collection, *Lesson Plans for Creating Media-Rich Classrooms* (2007). In that inaugural foray, we never anticipated the myriad details and delays that we faced when we depended on thirty busy contributors to maintain our deadline schedule. In taking on this second project, we have appreciated the continued support of the Commission on Media and members of the Assembly on Media Arts, two arms of the National Council of Teachers of English (NCTE) that are finding new directions in a changing climate of 21st century literacies. We also accepted the charge to assemble this volume of lessons at the request and behest of Bonny Graham, our staff editor for the first volume. And we appreciated her faith in our work and how tentatively she made the initial query, knowing the challenges this project presents for two educators who still need to hold down day jobs, not to mention maintaining personal and family responsibilities.

The scope of contributors represented in this collection would not have been possible if we hadn't had the support of the NCTE IT staff to deploy a call for proposals that reached targeted members of the Council who had attended and presented at the Annual Convention in San Antonio, which featured a robust Web 2.0 strand, as well as a summer institute in Indianapolis that focused on emerging 21st century literacies.

The IT staff at Adlai E. Stevenson High School, Charlene Chausis and Patricia Guillette, went above and beyond in moments of technical crises that spanned remedying stubborn files, formatting nightmares, and hardware disasters.

And once again, we need to thank the fine folks at the Borders café in Highland Park, Illinois, for informally hosting—or rather, tolerating—our editorial meetings over the course of the last year or so. We were pleased that we could continue our tradition of meeting there, and we tried to spend a bit of the royalties from the first book on coffee, sweets, books, and DVDs.

Introduction: What's on the Other Side, When You Finally Cross the Digital Divide?

Scott Sullivan
National Louis University

> *Most young Americans possess little of the knowledge that makes for an informed citizen, and too few of them master the skills needed to negotiate an information-heavy, communication-based society and economy. Furthermore, they avoid the resources and media that might enliven them and boost their talents.*
>
> Mark Bauerlein, *The Dumbest Generation*

"Do you like this Olde English font? Or should I use Wingding?"

It must have been in the late 1990s, just after the much misinterpreted comment by Vice President Al Gore that he invented the Internet, that the term *digital divide* became, as many phrases do, one of the buzzwords to infiltrate educational circles as well as the culture at large. This divide seemed to name a socioeconomic issue, the fact that some groups, the middle and upper classes, had an easier time accessing the Internet and using it to their advantage, and others, the poor and disenfranchised, did not have that ability. It was thought that access was the key—if there were just computers in classrooms and an active Internet connection, everything would be fine. Legislation was introduced, bills passed, money appropriated, and computers were finally in schools. Those schools then got online access and, apparently, educators simply waited for the miracles that technology would bring.

The ensuing decade, and research by people like Larry Cuban in *Oversold and Underused: Computers in the Classroom*, would show that teachers did not really change their instruction, despite having access to computers and the Internet. The reasons for this lack of adoption are likely many, but one that seems logical is that teachers were never students in a classroom that effectively used technology, so they didn't have a frame of reference to effectively use technology in their own teaching practice. Computers were treated as glorified typewriters that allowed students with bad handwriting to turn in papers that were easier to read, though most teachers quickly learned that every writing assignment needed a "Times font, size 12 ONLY" admonition, or there was a risk of students spending most of the lab time playing with fonts for the title of the paper.

Teachers who introduced students to PowerPoint in the mid- to late 1990s were treated to letters that spun about, were typed onto the screen with an authentic-sounding typewriter noise, or raced across the screen before screeching to a halt. Lost in all the bells and whistles was the content: Did the words make meaning? Or did the students work on the production more than their thoughts? Ultimately, was it really worth class time to teach these skills to kids at the expense of other, seemingly more important, content? It seemed that technology was mostly good for delivering flashy-looking products that masked mundane thinking, with the added burden of teacher unfamiliarity with the tools themselves. Many teachers sat in their schools' new computer labs and endured professional development on how to use the programs already loaded onto the computers. Long on technical talk about slides, documents, and hypertexts, and short on immediate practical concerns ("How *do* I shut off that screeching tire sound when the title slide plays?"), professional development was often a slow vehicle to changing the mindsets of teachers and their use of technology in the classroom.

The "Classroom without Walls"

It was within this technological environment of experimentation, shoddy implementation, and nascent visual interface to the Internet that I began my career in teaching English. On the first day of orientation at my first job, one of the first things my mentor told me to do was to go to the computer lab to reserve dates for students to compose their papers. Never mind that, as a brand new teacher, I had no idea what my students would be writing *about*; the key was to get those sacred Fridays in the lab so the students could type their papers and deliver them to me for grading over the weekend. Being a dutiful learner, or at least pretending to be at that point, I signed up my classes for the computer lab every Friday for the school year, because that was what I *should* do.

The learning curve in using technology is steep, but here are a few hard-earned insights should you find yourself in a similar situation: First, coming up with writing assignments that are worth students' effort to write and type every Friday for the school year is not nearly as easy as it sounds. Second, if kids are forced to type something, they fully expect to get that something back, completely graded, the following Monday morning. Sure, I know better now, but then? I thought I was doing what every English teacher did—grade papers all weekend. The technology that was supposed to be making my life easier was, in fact, making it harder. Though, to be fair, it wasn't the technology's fault that I decided to assign a typed essay due every Friday, but it did make that task easier for kids, and I made an attempt to do what I thought was right. The effort was an academic failure, but at least I tried.

In this environment, I was introduced to Nicenet.org, which bills itself as "the Internet Classroom Assistant." A very apt name, as it turns out, since it really did become an assistant of sorts for how I started to run my classroom. Nicenet is, of this writing, more than eleven years old, elderly by Internet standards, and while it was cutting edge and helpful in its day, its limitations have prompted me to move on to Google groups as a way of handling many of the chores I once accomplished through Nicenet; Google also conveniently allows me to integrate these activities with my Gmail account. But Nicenet still exists, providing a free, easily usable platform from which I learned one of the most valuable lessons I'd ever get on how to deal with the crushing flow of student written work: let students grade one another first. Of course, it's not that simple, and I'm being a bit facetious, but Nicenet gave me the ability to truly implement peer editing teams, a compositional strategy I knew to be helpful but that took so much time to implement fully that I was rarely able to use it effectively.

Nicenet was perfect—students could be online asynchronously and could read and respond when their schedules permitted (but within deadlines established with the peer editing team). Best of all, I didn't have to dedicate so much in-class work time to peer editing team meetings. If I'd had the skill and insight at the time, I would have tracked more closely the writing that my students workshopped in peer editing teams and compared it to the writing done in an "on-demand" setting. My experience now tells me that giving students the time and space to spend more quality time with one another's writing really helped improve their writing skills.

What I am sure of is that the tools of Nicenet began migrating into other aspects of my teaching. The Documents section of the site became the repository for missed assignments. The Links page let me connect to annotated sites my students could visit for context to support whatever we were discussing in class at the time. I posted assignments that required students to post extended short-answer essays to a prompt, then craft 125-word responses to two other classmates' work. We held threaded discussions that could be used as data points for essays because the archived conversations were easily searchable. The Nicenet platform became, then, our classroom without walls. Every teacher dreams that his or her students are thinking and discussing the issues raised in class after they leave each period, but with Nicenet, that was almost guaranteed. Students enjoyed going online, they knew they had work to do, and they did it in cyberspace, not within the physical confines of my classroom. And the pile of papers I took home each weekend diminished considerably. Not because we weren't writing— we were writing more than ever—but because the interactive nature of Nicenet allowed the students to carry their own weight. They didn't simply wait for my decree on the quality of their work; instead, they were getting extensive, ongoing feedback from peers that was, quite possibly, more important to them than my opinion.

Gone were discussions about why Lucida Calligraphy wasn't an acceptable font for an academic paper, replaced by conversations that centered on the work itself and whether it resonated with an audience of peers. This was a liberating experience. Student writing measurably improved, not because of the technology, but because the technology became an integral vehicle for teaching what I already knew: when kids talk about their writing with people whose opinion they value, the writing improves. Nicenet facilitated and enhanced those discussions, and pointed me toward the understanding that technology isn't a means to an end; it's a tool for achieving ends that I, as a teacher, already had in mind. It showed me that technology is a pedagogical tool, like any reading strategy, and that some things are better served without the Internet, word processing, or any other tech-related tool. Socratic seminars, for example, can happen online, but in my experience they happen more effectively in a face-to-face environment. Learning to fit the tool to the task and adapt it as the needs of individual courses demanded took a while, but the lessons were definitely worth the effort.

Web 2.0? Did I Miss 1.0? And Whatever Happened to the Internet?

Clearly, the roles of technology, media, and content are constantly evolving in the English language arts (ELA) classroom. Using the Web today is an entirely different experience than it was even at the turn of the millennium. In fact, the term *the Web* has a different meaning from that of *the Internet* of old. The Internet is no longer seen as an unknowable entity that exists in some unknowable place. Kids of all ages create "product" for the Internet all the time, and the production of knowledge and its dissemination is one of the fundamental differences between the Internet, the Web, and its newest incarnation, the Web 2.0. In the beginning, the Internet referred to a system of information available if you knew where to find it. A URL (uniform resource locator) was mandatory, because searching the Web for a site was a time-eating chore; there was no easy way to categorize, to sort, or to make sense of the results of early search engines, which limited the Internet's efficacy and appeal to the casual user.

As the Internet grew, it underwent several distinctive phases, but the most prominent change was a switch from text-based information, where all material on the Web was in fact text, to a graphic interface, where the now seemingly ubiquitous idea of clicking an icon became the norm for operating on the Web. Now information really was at the fingertips of students. The application of the Internet as an educational tool and pedagogical strategy, though, has come along much more slowly, though many teachers now incorporate the Web in their lessons, their planning, and their teaching lives.

The switch to Web 2.0—the current name of the latest phase of Internet development—is a logical extension of the nature of the Internet. First named by Darcy DiNucci (according to *Wikipedia* [gasp!]), Web 2.0 encompassed the idea that the Internet would be a common platform not only providing information, like Web 1.0, but also allowing interactivity and productivity to increase. The platform of Web 2.0 would support all software applications, making virtually obsolete the necessity of purchasing programs. It would allow for endless variation and customization for each user. Most important, however, Web 2.0 marked the rise of the individual as participant on the Web, not simply the consumer. With the advent of blogs, wikis, and social networking sites, people no longer go on the Web just to grab information: they create it and post it. The Web is no longer the domain of only those who have the coding skills needed to build a webpage. The Web has the capacity to become an extension of the self.

"Mom? Is that *you*?"

We seem to be living in a moment of another type of digital divide, though one that is closing rather rapidly, and that is the divide between creators and consumers on the Web. Social networking sites like Twitter and Facebook have been on the leading edge of Web 2.0 with their exceptionally fast growth, but nearly all sites now have adapted to incorporate the Web 2.0 sensibility.

In years past, a user who read a story on a news site had no technological capability for expressing his or her thoughts on the piece. Now, articles can be tagged, posted to Digg, incite active discussion forums where people can share opinions, and be shared, embedded, or emailed to others.

The story is no longer stuck on the page, or in this case, the screen; it is a potential piece of information that can be used or dismissed by the user with a few clicks of the computer mouse. News, or any other article posted on the Web, is no longer the province of the person or corporation who created and posted it; it is a unit of knowledge that can be manipulated as users wish—posting it to their own blogs, cutting and pasting it into a newsletter, or any other of a wide variety of applications. The uniform platform of Web 2.0 allows for the nearly seamless movement of information between destinations.

In addition to the appropriation and personalization of existing content, the uniform platform allows easy creation of new material. Websites are so easily created that, by some estimates, there are billions of them now on the Internet. No one really knows for sure. What is certain is that the role of the Web is increasing in the lives of nearly everyone, as evidenced by a 2009 article on CNN.com: "All in the Facebook Family: Older Generations Join Social Networks" outlines how the fastest-growing demographic on Facebook, women over the age of fifty-five, uses social networking sites to remain connected to their far-flung families (Sutter).

Facebook originally started as a college campus–based program that existed to keep students in touch with friends on campus and those who attended different universities. It has evolved, along with Twitter, into one of the most traveled-to destinations on the Web. The interconnection made possible by social networking sites is fundamentally changing the way people interact with online content, the way they perceive the roles of producers and consumers of media, as well as the way they view the role of the Internet in their lives.

To children who are "growing up digital," a phrase coined by Dan Tapscott in the late 1990s, connection with others via the Web is simply a matter of daily life; there's nothing at all unusual about using your phone to take pictures of your friends and then posting those photos on your social network site page. It's an expectation—if an event occurs but isn't blogged about, it may as well not have happened. For many students, life is lived online, the virtual reactions and conversations as real as any that take place face to face. The dangers of online life, too, are as real as those in "real" life. Stories of predators, cyber bullies, and stalkers abound, and students today, though they are perceived as being technologically savvy, are as naïve about online issues as they are about real-life dangers. They depend on the adults in their lives to help guide them through the thickets of life, both real and virtual, and it's the responsibility of the schools to add online skills to students' repertoires.

If we subscribe to the belief that schools should prepare students for the world they are about to enter, it is incumbent upon us to recognize the importance of the digital world and begin formulating a pedagogy that frames for students the shifting roles of information production and consumption, how to evaluate sources of information, and how to effectively use technology to communicate. Many of those skills lie squarely in the domain of the ELA teacher, so incorporating Web 2.0 technology into the everyday pedagogy of a school is a logical fit for English departments. The National Council of Teachers of English (NCTE), the International Reading Association (IRA), and many business organizations, like the Partnership for 21st Century Skills (P21), all recognize the need for schools to integrate technology training at a far deeper level than currently exists. Issues such as teacher readiness to embrace a more digitized world and the lack of a coherent pedagogy for teaching these new technologies effectively, as well as fitting them into the existing mission of the English department, remain obstacles.

Lesson Plans for Developing Digital Literacies is framed as a resource for teachers who find themselves in that transitional state between having a passing knowledge of Web 2.0 tools and bridging them into a more sophisticated understanding of how to integrate them into day-to-day instruction. One of the risks faced in creating a text like this is the timeliness of the information. Many of the websites and programs named in this text may, due to the fickle nature of the Web and its users, disappear overnight. Therefore, what we've attempted to do is to create pedagogy around a site or program that will allow teachers to implement the same lesson using a different site or program that does something similar; the tools might be slightly different but the process and results should be equivalent. Asynchronous chat programs, graphics programs, picture aggregating sites—all will evolve over time, and some of the sites named specifically in these lessons will disappear. But the information on how to use these ideas instructionally will sustain the relevance of these lessons regardless of the life or death of a single program. If the Web 2.0 world teaches us anything, it teaches us to be nimble and adaptive with the tools at hand.

Finally, this book seeks to address a pressing issue in every ELA classroom—that of reading skills. With the introduction of every new technology, people lament the lost skills the prior generation valued. Reading is a skill that, through wave after wave of technology, detractors of new technologies lament as lost. While some of these complaints feel true—it does seem, for example, that our students read less and have less interest in reading for enjoyment—in many ways, the issue is moot. The Internet and its role in people's lives is more than a passing fad. If Sutter's CNN.com article is any indication, the connections being made via social networks seem to be replacing the social interactions we've experienced in the past.

The issue, then, is to figure out the place of the ELA teacher in this milieu. Do we embrace new technology and integrate it into our instructional practice? Or lament the loss of reading skills in our students, do what we can to remediate that, and continue on as we have in the past? At the risk of using an outdated cliché, it would seem the choice is clear— ELA teachers should not be the new buggy whip makers. We should be proactive in teaching our students to compose text with clarity, communicate with purpose, and read for understanding, all skills reinforced in any ELA classroom. To that effort, this text attempts, as much as possible, to build bridges between literature and the Web and between student composition around print texts and electronic resources, and to engage students in a wide variety of composition strategies.

The need for this engagement is pressing, as Mark Bauerlein points out in *The Dumbest Generation*. He discusses how the Nielsen Corporation, in an April 2006 "Alertbox," posted an article titled "F-Shaped Pattern for Reading Web Content" that explored how people scan a webpage widely at the top, then in gradually narrowing scopes of reading as they hunt for the most useful information. It seems that technology really is changing the ways people read and process information, just as each new introduction of technology has in the past.

Strategies for integrating technology require the same sound pedagogy that focuses on more "traditional" texts. Good teaching is, we believe, still good teaching, and the responsibilities of the ELA teacher haven't changed. We are still preparing students to read and write their world in ways that empower, change, and fulfill them.

Works Cited

Bauerlein, Mark. *The Dumbest Generation: How the Digital Age Stupefies Young Americans and Jeopardizes Our Future (Or, Don't Trust Anyone Under 30).* New York: Tarcher, 2008. Print.

Cuban, Larry. *Oversold and Underused: Computers in the Classroom.* Cambridge: Harvard UP, 2003. Print.

Sutter, John. "All in the Facebook Family: Older Generations Join Social Networks." *CNN.com.* Cable News Network, 13 Apr. 2009. Web. 28 May 2009.

Tapscott, Don. *Growing Up Digital: The Rise of the Net Generation.* New York: McGraw-Hill, 1997. Print.

"Web 2.0." *Wikipedia: The Free Encyclopedia.* Wikimedia Foundation. Web. 28 May 2009.

Beyond Web 2.0 Tools: Understanding Evolving Digital Interaction

Joseph J. Geocaris
Adlai E. Stevenson High School, Lincolnshire, Illinois

When many of us hear the term *Web 2.0*, we associate it with an ever-expanding repertoire of Internet-based, open-source programs, many of which are discussed in this book. However, focusing too much on Web 2.0 tools can lead us to overlook their cultural meaning. After all, it's inevitable that wikis will evolve into something new and that Facebook will eventually be replaced. The point has never been the program, but the way Web 2.0 technology alters the ways we gain access to and interact with information as well as each other—just like Gutenberg's printing press did so many centuries ago.

If you are reading this book shortly after its publication, you will likely find the same programs still available in the forms discussed here. If you are reading it some time later, you may know of other, more advanced programs. Regardless, think of this collection of lessons as more than a how-to guide; think of it as a series of artifacts illustrating how teachers on the forefront of the Web 2.0 evolution have begun integrating the digital culture into their classrooms. Each lesson will have certain common tenets and assumptions about student learning in this emergent world. Pay close attention and you will see the following principles—which have also shaped much of our society and culture in the early twenty-first century—illustrated within:

1. *Creating relevance by expanding beyond the classroom:* The Internet expands our interactions. Using Web-based technology opens doors to new audiences and creates opportunities for authentic experiences. Paradoxically, it is also a portal through which students can work in ways that interact directly with their sense of identity, one reason for the success of Facebook.

2. *Incorporating "play":* If you have ever watched a kid play a video game, you have seen how she will experiment with techniques

and style, failing frequently only to try again and again until she has achieved mastery and won. Failure is not a threat in the Web 2.0 world, but a necessity. The Web 2.0 world encourages experimentation. It is active learning in its truest form.

3. *Varied types of collaboration:* Collaboration methods expand in digital culture. They may involve drawing on preexisting documents for ideas and forms, moving a project through a system in which individuals have clear roles, or building something by consensus (Jones). In Web 2.0 classrooms, teachers also become collaborators in the process.

4. *Shared authority:* In *Drive*, Daniel Pink describes the new world of work in which management and the workforce share a great deal of power in deciding how to engage a task. Likewise, shared power over task is central to developing learning communities.

5. *Incorporation of multimodal communication:* A quick browse through the Web demonstrates the variety of representational forms that writers and designers use. Web 2.0 classrooms give students practice in both decoding and creating these forms.

6. *Critical awareness of technology:* A strong Web 2.0 classroom asks students to consider all of the factors that go into evaluating technology, including infrastructure, policy, platform, intellectual property, and rhetorical effect of a program. Critical awareness focuses on the "how" and the "why" behind technology use (DeVoss, Cushman, and Grabill).

As these underlying themes illustrate, digital technologies shape the ways we think, the ways we interact, and the ways we understand. They represent a cultural movement. While digital culture seems to shift and change rapidly, these six themes are consistently present. With a closer look, teachers will see that they are evolutions of long-established best practice principles. So it is exciting for me, as a teacher, to see that digital culture emphasizes the thing I value the most—learning in a community.

Works Cited

DeVoss, Danielle Nicole, Ellen Cushman, and Jeffrey T. Grabill. "Infrastructure and Composing: The When of New-Media Writing." *College Composition and Communication* 57.1 (2005): 14–44. *JSTOR*. Web. 16 Feb. 2009.

Jones, Scott. "From Writers to Information Coordinators: Technology and the Changing Face of Collaboration." *Journal of Business and Technical Communication* 19.4 (2005): 449–67. *JSTOR*. Web. 30 May 2010.

Pink, Daniel H. *Drive: The Surprising Truth about What Motivates Us*. New York: Riverhead, 2009. Print.

Recommended Resources

Baron, Dennis. "From Pencils to Pixels: The Stages of Literacy Technologies." *Passions, Pedagogies, and 21st Century Technologies*. Ed. Gail E. Hawisher and Cynthia L. Selfe. Logan, UT/Urbana, IL: Utah State UP/NCTE, 1999. Print.

Gee, James Paul. *What Video Games Have to Teach Us about Learning and Literacy*. Rev. & updated ed. New York: Palgrave Macmillan, 2007. Print.

Selfe, Cynthia L., and Gail E. Hawisher. *Literate Lives in the Information Age: Narratives of Literacy from the United States*. New York: Erlbaum, 2004. Print.

Turkle, Sherry. *Life on the Screen: Identity in the Age of the Internet*. New York: Simon & Schuster, 1995. Print.

Yancey, Kathleen Blake. "Made Not Only in Words: Composition in a New Key." *College Composition and Communication* 56.2 (2004): 297–328. *JSTOR*. Web. 30 May 2010.

Companion Website: Directory of Supplemental Materials

A book that focuses on using the Internet and its vast resources in the classroom would not be complete without a Web-based resource of its own. The following lessons are linked to a series of digital handouts and samples of student work located at a companion website that can be accessed at http://www.ncte.org/books/lpfddl; these resources are signaled throughout the text with references to specific handouts, as well as the marginal "website" icon you see here. On the site you will find a number of other resources that will help you to connect with the contributors of this book and share your experiences implementing these lessons, as well as share lessons that you have developed. The website will also continue to update resources to keep pace with the developing and evolving nature of the Internet and Web 2.0 tools.

Part I: Web Basics: Getting Started

Chapter Title	List of Supplemental Materials
1. Wikipedia Is Not the Enemy: Training Students in Evaluation and Participation in Wiki Culture	1.1 Wikipedia Survey 1.2 Wikipedia Project: Understanding the Critical Process 1.3 Student Reflection 1.4 Grading Rubric for Wikipedia Project
2. How Did That Get on My Facebook Page? Understanding Voice, Audience, and Purpose on Social Networking Sites	2.1 Prewriting Activity for Reflective Essay
3. Stop. Shoot. Send: Using Phone Cameras to Find Meaning and to Engage Students	3.1 Evaluation Rubric 3.2 Student Self-Evaluation
4. It's a Comic Life: Creating Information-Based Comics	4.1 Student Sample.pdf 4.2 Student Sample.pdf 4.3 Student Sample.pdf 4.4 Creating Digital Info Comics

Part II. A Classroom without Walls: Collaborating with Web-Based Applications

Part III: The 21st Century Essay: Researching, Collaborating, and Composing

16.What's in a Wordle? Using Word Clouds to Teach Reading, Writing, and Revision	16.1 Wordles of Excerpts from the Three Scaffold Scenes in *The Scarlet Letter*
17. Building Rubrics Collaboratively with Google Docs	17.1 Let's Build a Rubric on Google Docs!
18. Networked Research Reporting: Using Ning to Report Student Research	18.1 Hypermedia Writing Overview 18.2 Facebook Social Group Analysis
19. Photo Essays: Bring Literary Themes to Life	19.1 Digital Photo Essay

Part IV: Interactive Literature Study: The Paperback vs. the Computer Screen

20. *Macbeth* Mystery: An Interactive Approach to Challenging Language	20.1 *Macbeth* iMovie Assignment 20.2 Rubric for *Macbeth* Movie Trailer 20.3 Solve the Mystery 20.4 Essay: Have You Solved the Mystery?
21. Podcasting the Traditional Book Review	21.1 Rubric 21.2 ISP Podcast Rubric
22. Would Ralph "Friend" Piggy? Using Social Networks to Study Character	22.1 Character Study Activity 22.2 Instructions for Creating a Ning
23. Dear Emma, Just Tweet Me: Using Microblogging to Explore Characterization and Style	23.1 Jane Austen Style Features 23.2 Historical Tweet Samples
24. Symbolic Analysis of *One Flew Over the Cuckoo's Nest*: Literature, Album Art, and VoiceThread	24.1 Charting the Meaning behind Motifs 24.2 Symbolic Analysis Assignment Sheet
25. Macbethbook: Synthesizing Research and Literary Analysis to Create a Social Networking Environment	25.1 Model Social Networking Profile 25.2 Macbethbook Rubric
26. A New Media Pilgrimage: Chaucer and the Multimodal Satire	26.1 Storyboard Form 26.2 Chaucerian Pilgrimage Rubric

I Web Basics: Getting Started

What's the Use? Making Sense of Fair Use, Copyright, and Free Use in the Age of Mashups, Remixes, and Open Educational Resources

Mark B. Dolce
Media Literacy Consultant

Fair Use

For most of us, the legal doctrine of fair use is a bit like that vaguely recognizable student who returns to visit after graduating. You remember the face, sort of, but that's about it. After the name is reunited with the face, more of the details come back to you (or not). In the case of fair use, however, you probably know more about it than you think. After all, it is the centerpiece of free speech under the First Amendment that allows for the proper functioning and growth of our educational system, to say nothing of cultural advancement and the dissemination of cultural information. That is not hyperbole, as you'll see later on.

In somewhat less dramatic terms, NCTE has defined fair use as

> [t]he right to use copyrighted material without permission or payment under some circumstances—especially when the cultural or social benefits of the use are predominant. It is a general right that applies even in situations where the law provides no specific authorization for the use in question—as it does for certain narrowly defined classroom activities (National Council of Teachers of English Media Commission).

This first part of NCTE's definition refers to legal protection of copyright, created by the United States Constitution. The clause allows Congress "to promote the Progress of Science and useful Arts, by securing for limited Times to Authors and Inventors the exclusive Right to their respective Writings and Discoveries" ("The Constitution of the United States," Article 1, Section 8, Clause 8.). The intention of copyright was not simply to confer ownership rights on writers and inventors—for a limited time—but to foster the creation of culture as well (Aoki, Boyle, and Jenkins). Over time, this clause has led directly to a growing body of copyright, patent, and now intellectual property law. However, it wasn't until recently that Congress attempted to provide guidance on how a copyrighted work could be used without infringing on or violating the rights of a copyright holder.

The Copyright Act of 1976 placed specific limitations (fair use) on these "exclusive rights" (i.e., copyright) and defined four criteria to determine if a particular use of a copyrighted work is covered under fair use (Aoki, Boyle, and Jenkins 36):

1. whether the intended use of the material is for commercial or educational purposes;
2. the nature of the copyrighted work itself;
3. the portion of the copyrighted work used in relation to the totality of the copyrighted work; and
4. the commercial or other impact on the use of the copyrighted work.

One of the most important aspects of fair use is that it applies across all media. The preceding criteria apply whether the copyrighted material is a Web 2.0 application, a Google map, or a map from a hardbound encyclopedia. It's also important to remember that these criteria are not hard-and-fast rules or "bright lines," but merely suggested ways in which the public might apply fair use when using copyrighted material or creating something new, be it a work of art, an online video documentary, or a podcast. Therefore, whether or not something falls under fair use is rightly evaluated on a case-by-case basis. For example, not all educational uses constitute fair use and some commercial uses are covered under fair use. In its "Code of Best Practices in Fair Use for Media Literacy Education," NCTE provides guidelines and examples of how teachers can stay within the protection of fair use in developing and sharing curriculum that includes copyrighted material (NCTE Media Commission).

In broad terms, the teaching profession and our democratic society would be very different indeed without fair use. As suggested earlier, fair use gives you the freedom to do your job as an English teacher. Among other things, it allows you to do things like

- use the introduction of the five child characters in *Willy Wonka and the Chocolate Factory* as a discussion-starter about archetypes;
- show a clip from the Pixar animated film *The Incredibles* as a comparison and contrast to one of the main themes of Kurt Vonnegut's short story "Harrison Bergeron";
- air a home recording of the episode of *The Oprah Winfrey Show* during which Oprah interviews Elie Wiesel as they walk through Auschwitz;
- show your American Literature class the recent Levi jeans commercial that features a recitation of "Pioneers! O Pioneers!" by Walt Whitman;
- make Glogster posters in a class and post them online (see De Abreu's lesson in Chapter 5);
- offer classes in media literacy and film analysis in which your texts for the class are feature films, commercials, news broadcasts, television programs, websites, online videos, and podcasts; and
- append a published John Updike essay on Herman Melville as part of an ACT-style reading exercise—don't have too much fun!

(Notice that there's nothing in this list about photocopying an entire textbook and distributing it to students, which is roughly equivalent to downloading pirated music files or movies from peer-to-peer networks.) For a moment, consider all the materials similar to those listed that you use in your own classroom. Now, consider a prohibition on those materials and how their absence would impact your curriculum. The following example from my own experience illustrates the freedom that fair use extends and the limitations exercised by corporate copyright holders.

A few years back, two colleagues and I created a senior-level media literacy course that included the news documentary *Control Room* (2004), which chronicled the first independent news network in the Middle East, Al Jazeera, and its staff (and the visiting foreign correspondents) and how they covered the American invasion of Iraq in the spring of 2003. We thought it was important for students, most of whom were in early middle school when the war began, to understand the media environment in the United States during precisely the same period covered in *Control Room*. You may recall that Ted Koppel, then the host of *Nightline*, was embedded with American soldiers advancing on Baghdad. His nightly reports from the "front lines" of the advancing American forces were central to the program for about two months. However, the ABC News website included few if any copies of *Nightline* from the spring of 2003. A customer support representative explained that most of the *Nightline* episodes of that period were available through a third-party vendor, not as full episodes, but by the minute—anywhere from $80 to $300 per minute! It didn't matter to ABC that the intended use was noncommercial and educational. I ended up purchasing one of the few episodes available, but I wondered how academics or historians would be able to access pre-Tivo material such as this in the years to come.

Fair Use in Action

In the world beyond the classroom, we see fair use in action everywhere: in columns where critics quote from the books they're reviewing; in television programs such as *60 Minutes* and *Frontline*; in film and video documentaries like Robert Greenwald's *Outfoxed* (see sidebar); and in parodies of all kinds, be it a send-up of *My Fair Lady* or a takeoff on the green screen, virtual sand-and-sandal extravaganza *300*. If you really want to see fair use in action on the Internet, go to YouTube and type "mashup" into the search box. Among the more than 100,000 search results, you'll probably still find "DJ Earworm—United State of Pop 2009 (Blame It on the Pop)—Mashup of Top 25 Billboard Hits." In this video, DJ Earworm remixes the music videos and audio tracks of twenty-five different pop songs, which are all individually copyright protected. However, what he's created is something transformative (in that it repurposes or adds value to a preexisting work), and to many media critics, his work might even be termed educational. DJ Earworm's mashup, with more than 12,000,000 views so far, is as much a testament to fair use—and one man's monomania!—as it is a commentary, most certainly unintended, on

The thesis of Robert Greenwald's 2004 documentary, *Outfoxed: Rupert Murdoch's War on Journalism*, is that Fox News, owned and operated by Murdoch and his media conglomerate News Corp., represents a new "yellow journalism" that is guided by sensationalism, extreme political bias, and fear-mongering. To support his thesis, Greenwald used hundreds of clips of actual Fox News broadcasts. If Greenwald had attempted to get permission or license the use of the clips from Fox News, the prohibitive cost, which is usually priced per minute, would have made it impossible to make the film. He went ahead and used the clips and released the film, confident that the use was covered by fair use. Despite vociferous protests from Fox News, the documentary was never challenged in court. It stands today as an example of how fair use acts as a counterweight to copyright when the public interest supersedes the commercial interest of the copyright holders (Aoki, Boyle, and Jenkins 23).

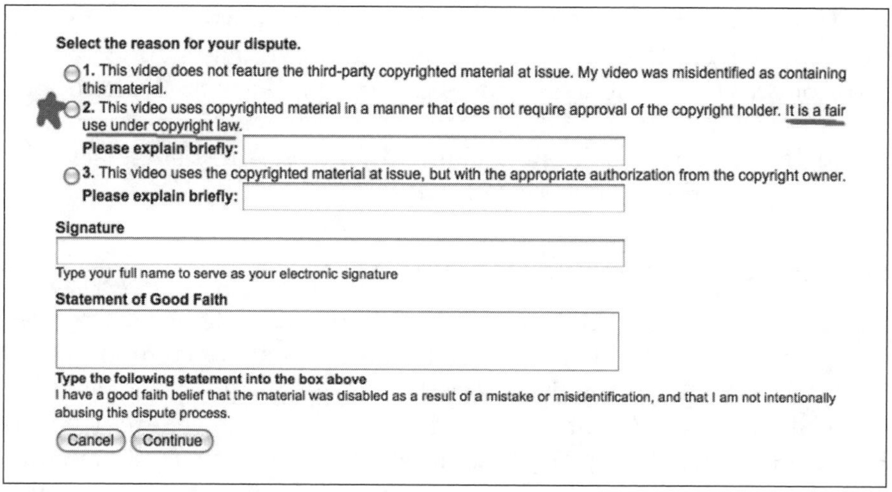
Select the reason for your dispute.

1. This video does not feature the third-party copyrighted material at issue. My video was misidentified as containing this material.

2. This video uses copyrighted material in a manner that does not require approval of the copyright holder. It is a fair use under copyright law.

Please explain briefly:

3. This video uses the copyrighted material at issue, but with the appropriate authorization from the copyright owner.

Please explain briefly:

Signature

Type your full name to serve as your electronic signature

Statement of Good Faith

Type the following statement into the box above

I have a good faith belief that the material was disabled as a result of a mistake or misidentification, and that I am not intentionally abusing this dispute process.

Cancel Continue

Figure I.1. This is the dispute form that YouTube has users fill out when it blocks a video because it has detected copyrighted material. The second choice invokes fair use.

the banal commonality of popular music. Obviously, DJ Earworm relied on copyrighted material to create his video mashup. Depending on how he formatted the video when it was uploaded, he might have had to complete a dispute form to unblock some or all of the video content (see Figure I.1). If he did, and the website tried to block the video, he could have claimed that the video mashup is fair use.

Earlier I suggested that fair use is key to the exercise of free expression under the First Amendment. If you think about it, where would our educational system and our democracy be without the ability to comment on, draw from, and transform works protected by copyright? This is especially important given the current term limits for copyright holders. You will recall that the Constitution states that "authors and inventors" have "exclusive rights" for a "limited time." Copyright used to expire after a mere fourteen years, meaning that copyright holders could control how their work was used for only the fourteen years specified by law. However, that limited time has been expanding rapidly, especially in the last forty years. In 1977 the copyright term was twenty-eight years, with an option to renew for an additional twenty-eight years. Currently, the copyright term has been extended to seventy years past the death of the author, and ninety-five years for corporate authors.[1] In practical terms, this means that most works created in the twentieth century are off limits; only those published before 1923 are most likely in the public domain and free to be used by anyone for any purpose. What is clear from the recent extension of copyright term limits is that the pendulum has swung back in favor of copyright holders, thus reducing the robustness of the public domain. While fair use counteracts the exclusivity of these rights, the reality is that a weak public domain weakens our democracy as a whole (Aoki, Boyle, and Jenkins 9).

Free Use and the Public Domain

Fair use does not cover the material that is free for us to use in any way we see fit. This kind of material is found in what we commonly call the public domain. Many of us already take advantage of this material, especially on government websites like the Library of Congress, which includes a trove of historical photographs, recordings, maps, and manuscripts. As previously noted, works created before 1923 are now (with some exceptions) in the public domain. It is sometimes confusing to distinguish between what constitutes free use and what is covered under fair use. In general, free use covers all works produced by the government, works whose copyright terms have expired, and also certain situations involving the creation of new works. For example, if your students are shooting a video on a street corner and they happen to film a crowd of people in the background of certain shots, they are free to use that footage without obtaining permission from those individuals. People on the street have no expectation of privacy except in circumstances where they are focused on specifically. Free use also covers most depictions of corporate logos or other trademarked graphic or textual elements. (For more specifics on these aspects of free use, see Jaszi.)

Creative Commons

In 2001 a group of committed academics, entrepreneurs, and artists formed a nonprofit called Creative Commons (http://creativecommons .org), which works "to increase the amount of creativity (cultural, educational, and scientific content) in 'the commons'—the body of work that is available to the public for free and legal sharing, use, repurposing, and remixing" (Creative Commons). To accomplish this, Creative Commons (CC) created standardized tools easily accessed on their website that allow individual creators, teachers, companies, and institutions to grant permission to use their creative work. This allows the creator to reserve all, most, or some of their exclusive rights. CC even provides tools to assist creators in relinquishing all rights to the extent possible under copyright law. CC licenses (see Figure I.2) are adaptable according to

Figure I.2. This example of a CC license lets the user know that the creator allows use of the work by attribution for noncommercial purposes and that the user can share the work, but only if the user employs an identical share-alike CC license.

how much or how little control the creator of the work wishes to retain. It's important to note that CC is not an alternative to copyright, but instead an accessible tool that works alongside copyright. It is in fact a direct response to the myriad modes of expression enabled by digital devices and emerging Internet applications (Creative Commons).

Open Educational Resources (OER) and OpenCourseWare

Not surprisingly, Creative Commons has also been at the forefront of the Open Educational Resources (OER) movement, which seeks to use the Internet to place educational resources for teachers *and* students in the public domain. This movement is still in its infancy, but it is gaining acceptance and accessibility, especially at the university level. According to the William and Flora Hewlett Foundation, one of the most committed proponents of OER, open education "is the simple and powerful idea that the world's knowledge is a public good and that technology in general and the Worldwide Web in particular provide an extraordinary opportunity for everyone to share, use, and reuse knowledge" (Atkins, Brown, and Hammond). This movement is working to provide educators with the means to create curricula from free and publicly available (downloadable) sources in collaboration with colleagues all over the world. Eventually, as the tools are developed and more educators contribute work, we will be able to access a repository of resources or seek out a colleague to create an entire curriculum, revamp a unit, or simply find a lesson on a particular topic. Whether OER will put traditional textbook publishers out of business remains to be seen, but open source textbooks are already out there, and it is only a matter of time before cash-starved or innovative school districts look to cost-effective alternatives when buying materials or assessing fees for textbooks. The OER as proposed on the CC website also goes beyond mere networking, licensing, and collecting; it explores such things as changing pedagogies to adapt to a digital world that no one could have predicted twenty or even ten years ago.

Related to OER is something called OpenCourseWare (OCW), which is the "free and open digital publication of high-quality educational materials, organized as courses" to "advance education and empower people worldwide through opencourseware." These courses typically include all or most of the course materials. They are not offered for credit, but they are free to anyone with Internet access. Right now, for example, you can go to MIT's OpenCourseWare site (see "Online Resources" below) and pick a class, such as Reading Poetry. The course includes all materials, including assignments and readings. Although geared toward college-age students, the ideas and materials can be freely adapted to fit your needs. You may find something to refresh your poetry unit or just to refresh your poetry-reading skills.

Online Resources

American University's Center for Social Media
http://www.centerforsocialmedia.org/

One of the best places to find resources for everything related to media, technology, and their intersection with the law and society. You'll find an impressive array of codes for best practices, guidelines, videos, white papers, etc.

Creative Commons
http://creativecommons.org/

Nonprofit organization dedicated to providing tools that allow individuals, organizations, and companies to share their creative work in a way that acknowledges the versatility of digital creation, publication, and dissemination.

Duke University's Center for the Study of the Public Domain
http://www.law.duke.edu/cspd/

Founded in 2002, the center is dedicated to research and to publicizing the contributions of the public domain to speech, culture, science, and innovation, and to transforming that research into sound public policy.

Massachusetts Institute of Technology (MIT) OpenCourseWare
http://ocw.mit.edu/index.htm

Perhaps the largest source of free and open course work—syllabi, readings, assignments—available for education, edification, and adaptation.

National Council of Teachers of English (NCTE)
http://www.ncte.org/

NCTE has produced clear and effective guidelines for teachers regarding fair use in the classroom: http://www.ncte.org/positions/statements/fairusemedialiteracy and http://www.ncte.org/cccc/committees/ip/ipreports/fairuse.

Public Knowledge
http://www.publicknowledge.org/

A Washington, DC–based public interest organization that works to "stop any bad legislation from passing that would slow technology innovation, shrink the public domain, or prevent fair use."

Note

1. Corporate authorship includes written and audiovisual material published by for-profit and nonprofit corporations. However, according to most, if not all, terms of service posted at the bottom of corporate websites, anything posted—comments, videos, iReports for CNN—become the property of the corporation for the copyright term limit from the date of publication. So think twice before posting your thoughtful ideas on any website.

Works Cited

Aoki, Keith, James Boyle, and Jennifer Jenkins. *Bound by Law? Tales from the Public Domain*. Durham: Duke UP, 2008. Print.

Atkins, Daniel E., John Seely Brown, and Allen L. Hammond. "A Review of the Open Educational Resources (OER) Movement: Achievements, Challenges, and Opportunities." *OERderves* [Blog]. Marshall Smith, Catherine Casserly, and Phoenix Wang. Feb. 2007. Web. 15 Sept. 2010.

Creative Commons. About/What Is CC? *Creative Commons*. N.d. Web. 2 Feb. 2010.

Jaszi, Peter. "'Yes, You Can!' Where You Don't Even Need 'Fair Use'." *Center for Social Media*. American University, School of Communication. 1 Aug. 2006. Web. 20 Jan. 2010.

National Council of Teachers of English (NCTE) Media Commission. "NCTE Guideline: Code of Best Practices in Fair Use for Media Literacy Education." *National Council of Teachers of English*. Nov. 2008. Web. 14 Jan. 2010.

William and Flora Hewlett Foundation, The. Education/Open Educational Resources. *The William and Flora Hewlett Foundation*. N.d. Web. 21 July 2010.

Recommended Resource

Hobbs, Renee. *Copyright Clarity: How Fair Use Supports Digital Learning*. Thousand Oaks, CA/Urbana, IL: Corwin/NCTE, 2010. Print.

1 Wikipedia Is Not the Enemy: Training Students in Evaluation of and Participation in Wiki Culture

M. Elizabeth Kenney
Adlai E. Stevenson High School, Lincolnshire, Illinois

Context

Stevenson High School is a large, public high school located in the outer suburbs of Chicago. Since the mid-1990s, we have offered a one-semester elective course in media analysis for regular-level college-prep seniors. When the course was first introduced, teachers still got their news from a newspaper, watched television on a television, and used computers solely for work-related activities. Our curriculum has evolved rapidly to reflect the media landscape, and our Media Analysis course has become among the school's most popular electives. We tend to attract students who feel they have had enough of the standard literature-and-composition curriculum and are hungry for something different, something they consider relevant to their lives. Our course aims to introduce these students to the study of mass communication through units focused on news and information, advertising, and entertainment. Our goal is to train them in habits of critical reflection, and to avoid cynicism about the media in favor of the empowerment that comes through critical consciousness.

Rationale

Teachers' attitudes toward Wikipedia reflect more general attitudes toward the Internet. Rarely does a day go by that I don't use Wikipedia to look something up, but teachers tend to raise their eyebrows when anyone cites Wikipedia as a source. Some teachers and departments actually ban Wikipedia from the research process, though my informal research suggests that such bans only prevent students from admitting that they've used it. We should help students use Wikipedia the way professionals use it: with appreciation for its usefulness as a quick starting point but with a keen awareness of its limitations. Media Analysis is the perfect place for students to explore beyond warnings about the danger of overreliance on Wikipedia and for teachers to help young people develop the analytical skills they will use to assess the usefulness and proper purpose of sources such as Wikipedia. This lesson takes students through the process of describing, analyzing, and evaluating a media message. But it can be more than simply a lesson in conducting research or analyzing a media message: it can serve as an invitation to participate in online culture.

I strongly recommend that you complete this assignment alongside the students. It is enormously helpful to encounter the challenges of the assignment at the same time the students are. Completing the project with them will also help you stay abreast of changes to Wikipedia; as I taught the project most recently, significant changes were made to Wikipedia's editing policies, reducing the number of entries that we—as infrequent Wikipedia users—would be allowed to edit. Each year I begin this project with an expectation that things will be different.

Objectives

Students will be able to

- Describe and analyze the features of a Wikipedia article that they select on their own, following teacher models
- Conduct independent research to verify the accuracy of information in a Wikipedia article
- Revise and improve a Wikipedia article by correcting inaccurate information, providing missing documentation, or creating a new section
- Optional: Execute changes to a Wikipedia article, following Wikipedia's own guidelines for what makes a strong article

NCTE/IRA standards addressed: 1, 3, 5, 7, 8, 11, 12

Materials/Preactivity Preparation

- You will need one complete, current Wikipedia article for group analysis. This may be printed and photocopied for the class or projected on a screen.

- Students will need access to computers, either in class or at home.
- One news article that informs students about how Wikipedia works and highlights some of the questions regarding its use. (See Works Cited for suggestions.)
- Optional: You may wish to develop a survey about students' experiences and attitudes regarding Wikipedia, or you may wish simply to lead an informal discussion at the beginning of the sequence.

Before beginning the lesson, select a Wikipedia article and model the sequence students will follow. Articles that work well for this sequence are relatively short (three to five pages if printed out) and have inherent interest for students: a controversial subject the class has been discussing, a notorious celebrity who has recently been in the news, or perhaps even an article about the school itself. Celebrities are always interesting to students; Lady Gaga seems to fascinate everyone at the moment, whereas David Letterman's entry became more interesting after he was accused of sexual misconduct. It may be difficult to find a musical group that everyone in the class will be engaged with, but one that has emerged fairly recently will be more manageable than a group with a long history: as I write this, the entry for Taylor Swift is about half as long as the entry for the Rolling Stones. For more civic-minded students, the entry for a local congressperson or mayor might be interesting; for a school engaged in a censorship controversy, perhaps the Supreme Court decision in *Hazelwood v. Kuhlmeier* would be an appropriate topic. Although topics need not be particularly timely, breaking news can be a draw. For example, I found myself teaching this lesson in the fall of 2008, two days after Sarah Palin had been announced as John McCain's running mate, sending millions of Americans running to Wikipedia to find out more about her. We were able to look at her entry, as well as the last-minute changes that had been made to her website just before the announcement was made. But the best discussions I've ever had have been about the entries for our school itself and for Tupac Shakur. Students would rather talk about Tupac than Palin any day.

Time Frame

The lesson will require one to two 50-minute class periods for you to introduce the subject, model the process, and launch the students on their projects. The rest of the sequence can be conducted outside of class, over a week or so, depending on how much research you expect students to do. For a course in which the primary objective is to develop research skills, or in which the students need more direct supervision of the research process, you might find that spending three to four hours of class time is time well spent. If you expect students to actually edit the Wikipedia articles they are studying, you need to allow more time to accommodate the learning curve.

Description of Activity

Before starting the lesson, I survey students about their use of Wikipedia, asking them how they use it and what they think about it, either in a formal, written survey a week before beginning the unit or in an informal discussion on the first day (see Handout 1.1). It's important to gather this information every year, because knowledge and attitudes toward interactive resources evolve quickly; the assumptions and experiences of one group of students might be very different from those of the group the year before. Usually my seniors tell me and each other how they used Wikipedia in their junior research papers, sometimes in cheerful contradiction of their teachers' explicit instructions. In sharing their experiences, however, students quickly raise two key points: (1) they have found Wikipedia useful for getting an overview of a topic and pointing them to further sources, but (2) they never felt fully confident that what they were reading was accurate because, after all, *anyone* can edit Wikipedia.

I also assign students an article to read that explains how Wikipedia works, either before beginning the lesson or to follow up the first day's activities. "All the News That's Fit to Print Out" by Jonathan Dee is perfect for my Media Analysis course. The real purpose of this article is to sketch the changing role of the gatekeeper as the news-gathering function shifts across different media, but it also includes an informative description of the editorial hierarchy of Wikipedia, as well as a thoughtful discussion of the value and limitations of Wikipedia as a news source. One important aspect of Wikipedia Dee discusses is the neutral point of view (or "NPOV") as one of the five pillars of Wikipedia. The neutral point of view is an essential aspect of Wikipedia that students need to understand before proceeding with the lesson. In another class, I might bring in an article describing a school or teacher's policy of banning Wikipedia for student use (see, for instance, Olanoff) and lead a discussion on the advantages and disadvantages of such a policy. If the article I used did not mention the neutral point of view, I would show students the Wikipedia page that explains this ("Five Pillars"; "Wikipedia: Neutral Point of View").

I begin the lesson with some previewing questions before sharing the article I've selected. I tell students the topic and ask them: If you were responsible for writing an article on this topic for Wikipedia,

- How would you break it down? What would the different sections be?
- What sorts of images would you include in your article?
- What parts of the article might be potentially controversial? Why?
- Where would you go to find and verify information for your article?

Students share their responses with a partner or small group, highlighting which points they agreed on and where their ideas differed. Then I lead a whole-class discussion in which they share their thoughts. To keep this from being a dry activity, you must select a topic that has inherent interest for students. Although I find the debate about the newest Supreme Court nominee to be fascinating, my students are more engaged if I bring up Tupac Shakur and ask them how a neutral writer would handle the conspiracy theorists who believe that Tupac is alive.

We then examine the article, projected from my computer on to a screen (you could also photocopy the article for the class), and I lead a discussion:

- How has the article been broken down into parts? Do these seem like the most logical divisions?
- What effect do the images have on the article? What impression do they give of the subject? What impression would a different image (or set of images) have made? (You might want to pull some alternate images ahead of time and then share these so that students can speak concretely about the effect of different images.)
- Are there aspects of this issue that some users are likely to find controversial? If so, how does the article handle these areas? Is the article itself likely to offend anyone?
- How thoroughly is the information in the article documented? What sources of information are included at the end? Does the citation of sources enhance the credibility of the article?
- Overall, how well does this article conform to Wikipedia's goal of the neutral point of view? How reliable does the information appear to be? To whom would this article be useful? How would someone use it? To whom might this article be a disappointment? What limits the usefulness of the article? Where would a person need to turn to get more or better information?

Then I give students their assignment: Now it's your turn. Choose a subject about which you consider yourself knowledgeable, find the Wikipedia entry on that subject and print it out, and then use questions I've provided to help you develop a thorough description, analysis, and evaluation of the article (for the full assignment, see Handout 1.2).

A note on low-tech versus high-tech tools: it is certainly helpful to have access to such technology as computers in the classroom and the ability to project from the teacher's computer, but these tools aren't necessary. In fact, I have found it helpful to use low-tech tools in conducting this lesson. I like to have students print out their articles so that they have a stable form of the text to analyze. (Some Wikipedia articles don't change much from day to day, but some do.) Students find it useful to read their articles with a highlighter in hand. Sometimes I'll provide highlighters in a variety of colors and ask students to color-code their reading: one color for information that everyone would agree on and another color for information that needs to be verified. Students sometimes use sticky notes to indicate areas where a new section should be added. Such low-tech tools can be used alongside more advanced technology to make the process of description, analysis, and evaluation more concrete.

Once I have approved all topics, students work alone or in groups to describe, analyze, and evaluate their chosen articles. I spend one full 50-minute period modeling the process, then another full period letting students browse and choose their topics and get started on their description. My students complete the rest of the project outside of class. However, if they needed more direct instruction in the research process or in using technology, I would spend another two days supervising their activities, letting them work in pairs or in groups. Students should answer the following questions:

Description

- Why is this person, event, invention (or whatever) of such significance that it merits inclusion in an encyclopedia?

- How long is the entry? Does the length seem surprising? (Compare the length to entries of similar subjects.)

- How is the entry divided into subtopics? List them.

- When was the entry last updated? See the very last page for this information.

- What information seems to be the most recent? How can you tell?

- What kind of visual information (photos, graphs, tables, etc.) is included? List visual elements and explain what each adds to the entry.

- Who are the experts cited in the body of the entry (if any)? List them.

Analysis

- Identify three pieces of information that ought to be "fact-checked"—pieces of information that are not universally known and that are not documented in the article.

- Find independent sources to either support or contradict these "facts." Include full bibliographic information (including URLs for online resources) for all sources.

- What information in the article did you find the most surprising or enlightening?

- What information seems outdated or in need of updating? Are there aspects of the subject that seem incomplete? How well does the information represent current consensus on the subject?

- Look again at the selection of topics and subtopics and how these are organized. Which aspects of the subject are emphasized by this organization? Which aspects are de-emphasized? Are any aspects of the subject not adequately reflected in this organization?

- To what extent do the images selected either complement or undercut the text? Which aspects of the subject are emphasized by the images? Which aspects are de-emphasized? Discuss at least one specific image you're familiar with that is not included in the entry but could be. What effect would including this image have on the impression this article makes on the viewer?

- How does the selection of experts affect the credibility of the article? Do the experts cited represent a balanced view of the subject? If the text does not cite any experts, discuss the effect of this lack. Cite at least one expert you're familiar with (from other sources) who is not cited in the Wikipedia entry. What would the addition of commentary from this expert add to the entry?

- Which of the subtopics is most likely to be considered controversial by readers? How does the article treat this subtopic? What elements make the article appear to be biased toward one side or the other of any controversy? What aspects of the article contribute to a neutral point of view?

- What conclusions can you draw from your efforts to fact-check the entry? How thoroughly sourced is the entry? Are there comments that really need to be documented but are not? Which aspects of the article contribute to its general credibility? Which aspects make the article seem less credible?

Evaluation

- How useful is this article? To whom would it be most useful? For what purpose(s) would it be most useful?
- Where might this article fall short? Where would someone need to turn if he or she needed more information?
- How successfully does this article maintain the neutral point of view, which is one of the pillars of Wikipedia culture? (See Jonathan Dee's discussion in his *New York Times Magazine* article "All the News That's Fit to Print Out" of the NPOV pillar.)

Students provide evidence that they have completed the process of description, analysis, and evaluation through a research journal. An informal presentation to the class would work well if the students were working in groups, but independent reports would be difficult to listen to.

Assessment

By the end of this process, students will have a hard copy of the original article, which has been thoroughly annotated, as well as a journal documenting their research as they complete the preceding steps. The final step in the process is to take action to improve the article. Students choose one aspect of the article that, in their judgment, needs to be expanded or improved. (They should clearly mark this section on their hard copy.) On a separate sheet of paper, they should write up a plan for how they will improve the article:

- What about this section needs to be improved? Is there incorrect information that needs to be corrected? Ambiguous information that needs to be clarified? Correct but unverified information that needs to have sources cited? Has a subtopic been omitted for which a new section needs to be written?
- List specific sources you will use in compiling information to expand the entry. For each source, list specific bibliographic information (URL or publishing info) as well as specific facts.

In some classes, you may simply wish to assess the students' plans for improving the article. However, students will learn even more from the process if they carry out their changes by actually editing the Wikipedia article. This requires students to create an account and will take considerably more time than simply planning revisions, so you may not want to require this step. But the experience is one students will not soon forget. You can direct students to Wikipedia's tutorial for editing pages ("Wikipedia: How to Edit a Page"), or you may wish to custom-design a tutorial for the class.

I also expect my students to complete a reflection (see Handout 1.3), answering the following questions:

- What was the hardest part of doing this project?
- If you had it to do over again, what would you do differently? Why? (If you don't think you'd do anything differently, instead consider what advice you would give someone about to start the project.)
- How did knowing you were going to contribute changes to the Wikipedia entry alter the way you looked at it? Were you more or less critical?
- How has this experience affected your view of Wikipedia? Will you have more or less confidence when you use Wikipedia in the future? What advice would you give someone who was beginning a research project about whether and how to use Wikipedia as part of that process?
- For students of Media Analysis: In making changes to your entry, which of the gatekeeper's four functions (to relay, expand, limit, and interpret information) did you serve? Be specific about each. What responsibilities do gatekeepers have in our society? Why is their role so crucial? What factors can get in the way of gatekeepers fulfilling these responsibilities?

A grading rubric for this project is available as Handout 1.4 on the website.

Connections and Adaptations

I developed this lesson as an introduction to media analysis and an exploration into the use of media in our lives. However, it could be adapted for any course that conducts research, and could be particularly effective as an introduction to the research process. Rather than simply banning students from using Wikipedia or warning them against overreliance on the website, you could build this lesson early in the research process, just after students have chosen their topics. In that context, this sequence would give students training in finding and evaluating sources, as well as help them to refine their topic and point them toward more substantial sources for their research. If I were using the lesson this way, I would assign the final step—improving the Wikipedia page—to be completed after they finished writing their research paper.

Works Cited

Dee, Jonathan. "All the News That's Fit to Print Out." *New York Times Magazine*. New York Times, 1 July 2007. Web. 17 Feb. 2010.

"Five Pillars of Wikipedia." *Wikipedia*. Wikimedia Foundation, n.d. Web. 17 Feb. 2010.

Olanoff, Lynn. "School Officials Unite in Banning Wikipedia." *Seattle Times*. Seattle Times Company, 21 Nov. 2007. Web. 17 Feb. 2010.

"Wikipedia: How to Edit a Page." *Wikipedia*. Wikimedia Foundation, n.d. Web. 17 Feb. 2010.

"Wikipedia: Neutral Point of View." *Wikipedia*. Wikimedia Foundation, n.d. Web. 17 Feb. 2010.

Supplemental Resources

Campbell, Richard, Christopher R. Martin, and Bettina Fabos. *Media and Culture: An Introduction to Mass Communication.* 7th ed. New York: Bedford/St. Martin's, 2009. Print.

"Wikipedia: Tutorial." *Wikipedia*. Wikimedia Foundation, n.d. Web. 22 July 2010.

Wilson, Chris. "Masters of the Wikiverse." *Slate*. Washington Post Co., 2 Sept. 2009. Web. 22 July 2010.

2   How Did That Get on My Facebook Page? Understanding Voice, Audience, and Purpose on Social Networking Sites

Mindy Hawley and John Golden
Portland Public Schools, Portland, Oregon

Context

We are curriculum specialists for Portland Public Schools, an urban district with more than 40,000 students, who represent seventy-two different languages. The demographics of the district are 54 percent White, 14 percent African American, 15 percent Latino, and 10 percent Asian, with 45 percent of our students eligible for free or reduced meals. This lesson has been developed for students in grades 9–12, though most of the discussion questions and activities could be modified to be appropriate for middle school students.

Rationale

Just as fish probably never look around and comment on the water, most of our students never really look around and think about the cyber sea in which they swim. And they do a lot of swimming. According to a study by the Kaiser Family Foundation, "8–18 year-olds devote an average of 7 hours and 38 minutes to using entertainment media across a typical day," and according to a study released by Cox Communications, "the vast majority of teens (72%) have a social networking profile" ("Teen Online"). Through this lesson, students will critically examine their own and other students' Facebook pages (though the activities are easily applicable to MySpace pages as well). They will look at the role, audience, and purpose of key elements on their page by asking essential questions, such as:

- Why is this picture, link, or comment on my page? How did it get here?
- What are these elements saying about me as the author of my page?
- What are the marketing and advertising forces that are driving specific elements on my page?
- What do my privacy settings allow me to share and to protect?
- What are the ethical implications of the elements of my page?

This lesson is not intended to scare students or to discourage them from their online writing and communicating; only through this type of critical reflection on the medium itself and its integrated parts will students become responsible and aware consumers of the new technologies. Just because we teachers are often considered digital immigrants and may be uncomfortable with these new literacies, it would be irresponsible of us not to prepare our students with and for these technologies. This lesson tries to ensure that students are asking the right questions about the ways they communicate and to encourage them to be active, aware, and ethical participants in this environment.

Objectives

Students will be able to:

- Understand how voice changes depending on audience, purpose, and medium
- Recognize the multiple modes of communication within social networking sites
- Analyze the effects of their word and image choices on their known and potential audiences
- Evaluate the commercial and marketing elements of social networking sites
- Identify and assess the role of security settings on social networking sites

NCTE/IRA standards addressed: 3, 4, 6

Materials/Preactivity Preparation

If you are not a regular Facebook user, you may want to set up an account (it's free, though not without costs, as you'll see below) to familiarize yourself with the functionality and types of communication available on social networking sites. Additionally, to prepare, you may want to preview a few videos available on YouTube about Facebook, some of which may not be appropriate for classroom viewing, but they will give you some insights into the similarities and differences between online and offline communication. Because the links will have changed or expired by the time this book goes to press, search on YouTube for "Facebook in Real Life," and you will have a number of short (and funny) videos from which to choose.

Ideally, the activities in this lesson would be completed in a fully functioning computer lab with all students at their own computers working on their own Facebook or MySpace pages. There are, however, several potential difficulties in achieving this ideal situation, including limited computer access, district policy that blocks access to social networking sites, and students who do not have their own Facebook accounts. Some possible solutions are to contact your district administrators to receive temporary proxies that allow for limited, teacher-supervised access to the site; have students work in pairs or small groups with a single computer and/or Facebook account; or have students complete these activities at home or at a public library. While the steps in the lesson describe students working with their own Facebook pages, all the activities can be completed by working with a partner or small group with one account.

Time Frame

This lesson consists of three parts, designed to fit into approximately three 50-minute class periods, with an additional class period devoted to assessment. As you will see, however, most of the sections are discrete activities and can be completed or eliminated to fit your specific scheduling needs.

Description of Activity

Introduction

Before students begin to look closely at their Facebook pages on the computer, take a few minutes to have them do a personal self-inventory on their Facebook usage. It is not necessary to have students write their answers, but you may wish to have them share with one another so that they get an idea of how their Facebook usage compares to that of their peers. Some questions you might want to ask are:

- How long have you had your Facebook account?
- Did you change from a different social networking site? If so, why?
- Why did you set up your Facebook account?
- How often do you check your Facebook account (for example, once a day, once an hour, a few times a week)?
- What is the average amount of time you spend once you have logged in?
- What are the first three things you check when you log in?
- What is your favorite form of communicating while on Facebook (e.g., status updates, wall-to-wall posts, poking, inbox, live chat)?

If students do not have a Facebook account—or a similar social networking site—you can ask them to respond to the following:

- Why do you not have an account?
- Do you find that many of your friends do or do not have accounts? What are their reasons for having or not having one?
- Describe your main methods of communicating with friends: phone, texting, email, etc.?
- Do you ever feel pressure from others to join Facebook or similar sites?

Part 1: What's on My Page?

There are many ways to design or set up a Facebook account. For the purpose of this portion of the lesson, we look specifically at the Info and Photos pages. Begin by having students log into their Facebook account and open their Info page. Give students a few minutes to reread the information they have included. Some people choose to spend a considerable amount of time including many facts and details; others complete their profiles with minimal information. Where do your students fall? Ask students to think about how they decided what information they would include by answering the following:

- Are there certain categories that you purposefully did not include? Why?
- At the bottom of the Info page is a list of the groups or pages the Facebook user has joined. How do you decide which groups or pages to join?

Have students choose one of their groups and discuss with a partner why they joined this group and what their membership in the group might say about them.

An essential topic to consider is the idea of online privacy. Facebook continually updates its privacy policies, so students have to read and understand the implications of the new policies quite often. Questions to consider are:

- Do you understand that when you agree to Facebook's privacy policy, you agree that some information will be viewable by everyone? For example, as of December 2009, a user's name, profile photo, and the names of work and school networks are all available to everyone.

- What other information is available to everyone? What information is available only to friends?

- What does *privacy* mean to you? Do you think this term means something different to people in your parents' generation?

Much has been made of employers or university admissions offices searching social networking sites to learn more about potential employees or students. Have students discuss with a partner who they think might have looked at their profile, and whether they are comfortable with the information they have shared being viewed by people they don't know well as well as by those they do. A couple of interesting questions to ask regarding this that never fail to generate lively discussion are:

- If your grandmother asked to be your friend on Facebook, would you accept her? Why or why not?

- Who is the intended audience for your Facebook page and how is that reflected in what information you share and do not share?

Honestly, the latter is a very difficult question because Facebook, by definition, has so many different audiences, and Facebook users typically have multiple purposes for their communications.

Next, have students open their Photos page. Give them a few minutes to glance through both the photos that have been added by others and a few of the albums they have chosen to create. Once they've had a few minutes to review, ask them to think about the following:

- How do you filter the pictures you add to your Facebook photo album before you post them?

- How do you determine which picture you will use for your profile photo? How often do you change your profile picture?

- Who has permission to see the pictures in your album?

In addition to students being able to post their own pictures, anyone on Facebook can post pictures and place a "tag" on the photo that identifies the people in it. Any photo in Facebook with your tag will also be posted to your Facebook page. Ask students to consider:

- Have you had pictures appear on Facebook that you were not happy with? Did you remove the tag(s)?
- Did you contact the person who tagged the photo to let him or her know you were not happy about being tagged?

Ask students to discuss with a partner the ethical conflicts or concerns that might arise about posting and tagging pictures on Facebook.

Another section of their page that students should consider is the listing of their friends. Direct them to scan through their list of friends (for some this may take a while). As they scan, ask them to consider the following:

- How many friends do you have? What percentage of these friends are also friends offline?
- Who do you most often communicate with when on Facebook (e.g., close friends, friends, acquaintances)?
- Are these people you normally communicate with when not on Facebook? Explain.

Other topics you might want students to discuss with a partner concern the ethics involving friends on Facebook, such as:

- How do you decide who to friend or not to friend?
- Have you ever "unfriended" someone? Why? Were there any online or offline effects? Have you ever been "unfriended" or not been added as a friend? Again, what were the online or offline effects?

Now that students have had some time to review the specifics of their Info and Photos pages, wrap up this part of the lesson by asking them to think back on the parts of their pages they examined and explain whether their Facebook page is an accurate reflection of who they are. What would they change, add, or delete to present themselves more accurately to their intended audience?

Part 2: How Do I Communicate?

Ask students to look through their sites and list the various methods of communication within the Facebook environment. They should come up with many of the following, though they may need some prompting to see each of these as distinct modes of communication:

- Inbox
- Status updates

- Wall postings
- Live chats
- Poking

After students have generated their lists, they should read a few of their postings in each of these categories and then explain, in writing or in a discussion with a partner, the similarities and differences between these modes of communication. For example:

- Do you use more formal language in your inbox than in wall postings?
- Do you tend to use one mode of communication for some friends and a different one for other friends? Why?
- Do you have different purposes for using the different modes of communication?
- How do you compare the ways you communicate on Facebook with the other ways you communicate with friends: phone, email, texting, Twitter, etc.?

Next, ask students to find messages they wrote to two very different people. Maybe the people are different by age, by gender, by profession, or some other factor. What's different and similar about the messages? Why? What specific language choices did they use? Why?

Finally, ask students to reread two postings they made to two different friends. One should be a friend they see offline regularly and the other should be a friend they communicate with mostly online. Again, students should compare their language choices and purposes for writing to these two friends. Some people like to use the terms *bridging* and *bonding* to describe different communication purposes. We "bridge" with people we are getting to know and would like to make more connections with, and we "bond" with people we already know and would like to deepen our connection with. Ask students to consider which of their friends they bridge with and and which they bond with on Facebook. How do they bridge and bond with people in offline communication?

Two highly effective tools for helping students think about their communication purposes are the following reading strategies:

Strategy 1: RAFT

Role (Who is the speaker of the message?)

Audience (To whom is the message delivered?)

Format (What is the mode of communication: email, letter, video, etc.?)

Topic (What is the purpose of the message?)

Strategy 2: SOAPSTone

Speaker

Occasion

Audience

Purpose

Subject

Tone

Ask students to analyze at least one of their written pieces from Face-book using one of these reading strategies. RAFT tends to be a little easier than SOAPSTone for younger students. As an extension activity, you might have students compare one of their Facebook pieces with one of their offline pieces.

Part 3: Who's Paying?

Facebook, like most social networking sites, does not charge to use its service, but in 2009, it was able to earn $550 million, according to Nicolas Carlson of *Business Insider*. How does it do this? This portion of the lesson examines the commercial side of Facebook. It is impor-tant to begin with an opportunity for students to define and discuss the following terms: *advertising*, *marketing*, and *commercialism*. For older students, you may also want to ask about terms such as *stealth marketing* and *consumerism*.

The first step, after discussing the terms, is to have students look at the ads that surround their Facebook page. You may need to inform them that the ads on their page are not the exact ads that appear on other people's pages; they are somewhat individual to each user based on pref-erences they have identified. Students should make a list of all the prod-ucts advertised there, refreshing their page a few times to see new ads appear. Ask them to write down what they think these advertisements have in common. Are most of them, for example, ads for clothing or food or music? Students should then pair up with another student to compare the ads on each other's pages. What do they have in common? Which are unique? Do ads for certain topics—e.g., shoes, fast food, music— seem to appear more often than others? Why? Wrap up this focus on advertising by having students do some detective work. Have them try to figure out what elements on their page (recalling their work in Part 1 of the lesson) might have triggered certain ads to appear there. They should look over their profile, groups they have joined, and pages they have visited. Ask them to make some inferences about why specific ads appear on their page but do not appear on their partner's page.

Ads are only the most obvious form of marketing found on Facebook. Marketers use many other methods in an attempt to influence Facebook users' purchasing choices. Ask students to look through their group pages. Questions for them to consider are:

- How many of your pages are linked to consumer products?

- How and why did you join that group?

- How many unsolicited requests or messages for commercial products do you have in your inbox or on your wall? What about games, surveys, and other activities? Do they have commercial connections? Examples might be surveys of favorite restaurants, a quiz about Harry Potter characters, or free song download offers.

- How do you think these marketing features came to be on your page, and do you think these elements might influence your purchasing decisions?

An interesting extension activity would be to ask students to research the business aspects of Facebook and other social networking sites. Questions to consider are:

- Who owns them?

- How do they make their money? How much money do they make?

- Which sites are most successful, and why?

Also, students should consider the similarities and differences between the advertising and marketing that appears on Facebook and that appearing on or in other, more traditional forms of media, such as television, magazines, and radio.

Assessment

Throughout this lesson, students have explored their Facebook pages by identifying the elements on their pages, by analyzing how they tend to communicate online, and by trying to understand the commerical aspects of the social network. Students have had a chance to respond to many of the bulleted questions and have discussed their responses with a partner or a small group. These activities have led up to two different types of assessment: a personal reflection and an argumentative essay.

A prompt for the personal reflection (see Handout 2.1 on the companion website) could be: How does your online self (as represented on Facebook or a similar site) compare to your offline self? If students are not regular users of an online social networking site, they could compare a friend's Facebook page to that person's offline persona. Questions they should consider as they write their reflection are:

- How does your online representation compare to your offline persona?
- How is your online communication with others similar to or different from your offline communication?
- What advertising and marketing forces affect your online activities, and how does the commercialism compare to your offline activities?

Another effective culminating assessment is to ask students to demonstrate what they have learned by writing an argumentative essay in the form of an op-ed piece or letter to the editor. Students might also enjoy using their pieces in a class debate afterward. Topics that work well for this include:

- Does online communication on social networking sites enhance or diminish offline communication skills?
- What are the benefits or drawbacks to having Facebook access blocked at school?
- Is it ethical or appropriate to post a picture of someone without his or her express written consent?
- Are offline friendships more satisfying and real than online friendships?
- Does Facebook create "drama" for adolescent relationships and communication?
- Should advertisers have access to the profiles and preferences that Facebook users have created so that they can generate specific advertisements for each user?
- What levels of privacy—if any—should exist on Facebook and other social networking sites?

Connections and Adaptations

We have found that because the topic of this lesson is so engaging for students, it is difficult to stay within the identified three classroom sessions. You'll note that we have already described several extensions to the lesson, including the investigation of Facebook's revenue and the ethics of friending and unfriending. Students may also enjoy examining the issues around online privacy, especially regarding how they relate to commercial and marketing forces. A final extension might be to ask students to research the ways that communication technologies have changed over time, from the Gutenberg press to telegraphs to the

Internet, and how they have impacted society. Because these technologies change so rapidly, it's possible that by the time this book goes to press your students will be saying, "What's Facebook?" Nevertheless, these activities, regardless of the actual medium, will help give students the skills and the awareness they need to communicate effectively both on- and offline.

Works Cited

Carlson, Nicolas. "Everything You Wanted to Know about Facebook's Revenue but Didn't Know Who to Ask." *Business Insider*. Business Insider, 2 July 2009. Web. 18 Dec. 2009.

Henry J. Kaiser Family Foundation. "Daily Media Use among Children and Teens Up Dramatically from Five Years Ago." *Kaiser Family Foundation*. 20 Jan. 2010. Web. 15 Sept. 2010.

"Teen Online & Wireless Safety Survey: Cyberbullying, Sexting, and Parental Controls." *Cox Communications*. Cox Communications, May 2009. Web. 4 Jan. 2010. http://www.cox.com/takecharge/safe_teens_2009/ media/2009_teen_survey_internet_and_wireless_safety.pdf.

3 Stop. Shoot. Send: Using Phone Cameras to Find Meaning and to Engage Students

Louis Mazza
The Arts Academy at Benjamin Rush,
Philadelphia, Pennsylvania

Context

The Arts Academy at Benjamin Rush is a small, public high school in a large, urban school district located in northeast Philadelphia. We have a rigorous college preparatory curriculum with a focus on the visual and performing arts. The demographics of our school reflect the city in general and the specific neighborhood we are located in: 52.0 percent White, 26.4 percent African American, 15.8 percent Latino, and 4.4 percent Asian.

Our mission is to provide a student-centered educational program that focuses on creativity and develops critical thinking skills. We believe the arts provide an unparalleled opportunity to develop the whole student as a contributing member of a caring community of learners. Through the visual and performing arts, our students actively engage their creative interests to develop multidisciplinary projects that reveal the connections between academic content areas that are usually isolated and separated in other, more traditional public schools. We believe it is through these connections that students can develop a true picture of the twenty-first-century world and their place in it.

Rationale

If a snapshot freezes a moment in time, can we ever really know anything about that moment? Who would know best how to describe that moment? The photographer? The subject? A bystander? Would each person in the photograph describe the moment in the same way? What is the significance of sharing? How do students understand themselves better by understanding the experience of others? Many digital tools allow us to bridge vast spaces and connect in a shared moment. Does this sharing enhance our understanding of ourselves and of our place in the world? Shared experiences create opportunities for deeper understanding of the world beyond our small routines. Meaningful and significant learning comes about through the connecting of previously unrelated topics, ideas, disciplines. The realization of this connection is a moment of true understanding.

This project is about the economy of a few words juxtaposed with the abundance of possible stories embedded in a photograph. It is also an attempt to extend learning beyond the classroom and provide a context for sharing multiple life experiences taking place simultaneously: to co-create a multidimensional picture of one moment in time, shared by all.

Objectives

Students will be able to:

- Describe and analyze the formal elements of a photographic composition
- Compare and contrast various types of photography (e.g., landscape, portrait, abstract, documentary)
- Analyze and identify the elements of a "micro" story (the six-word story) and describe the differences between *story* and *description*

By participating in a community project that is outside the realm of the traditional school day, students engage in an endeavor that is larger than school and that provides a broader context for learning.

NCTE/IRA standards addressed: 1, 3, 6, 12

Materials/Preactivity Preparation

- You will need a cell phone equipped with a camera and the capability to send picture mail.
- Students will also need a cell phone equipped with a camera and the capability to send picture mail. A form could be sent home that outlines the project and asks for a parent signature.
- You should have an account at flickr.com and configure the account to accept cell phone images via an assigned email address.

- Familiarize yourself with the Smithteens website (http://www.smithteens.com/) and the Six Word Stories site (http://www.sixwordstories.net/).
- Also for background information, read the article "Shawn Rocco's 'Cellular Obscura'" on photographic experiments with a cell phone by the North Carolina *News & Observer* staff photographer: http://www.pdnonline.com/pdn/content_display/esearch/e3i6229a90fa9a407c331281c730455c9bd

Time Frame

Be prepared to spend at least three 50-minute class periods addressing the topic before setting the assignment.

Day 1   Class analysis of the micro-narrative (six-word story)

Day 2   Class examination of photographs and visual culture

Day 3   Class discussion on the phenomenon of social networking and instant communication

Description of Activity

1. Story

Give a presentation to the class that illustrates the significance of story in human development. Examples of the use of stories in history include:

- Cave paintings at Lascaux
- Egyptian hieroglyphs
- Greek mythology
- Native American vision quests
- Campfire stories/ghost stories
- Family stories passed between generations, commonly transmitted through snapshots
- Blockbuster movies we pay to see in theaters

Stories are the primary vehicle for transmitting information between the human species. Our brains absorb stories because they give our lives context and purpose. Stories give us a way to relate to one another.

Here, students analyze the six-word story and the websites referred to earlier (Smithteens and Six Word Stories) following the steps below:

- Create a two-column table on a sheet of paper.
- Browse the site for about 15 minutes and write down the stories you feel a particular affinity to on one side of the table;

on the other side, write down the stories you did *not* find interesting.

- Share those stories you listed as interesting. Be specific about the elements you found particularly vivid.

- Share those stories you thought *didn't* work.

- Discuss, as a class, why one story worked and the other didn't.

- Discuss the idea of contrast and contradiction, highlighting a couple of stories that illustrate these elements. Why might contrast and contradiction add elements of tension and drama to a story? Here are some six-word story examples: "Love to sing, but tone deaf." "'I do', lied bride and groom." "Blind knife thrower seeking new assistant."

- As a class, discuss the qualities or characteristics of "good" stories.

Students will eventually realize that good stories work against expectation. They present a "gap" that the reader must fill with speculation. Help students work through to this insight if they don't immediately recognize it on their own.

2. Photography

Present some of the snapshots to the class found on the webpage for *click! photography changes everything*: http://click.si.edu/Story.aspx?story=100. As you view each photograph as a class, ask the following questions:

1. What is going on in this picture?

2. What do you see that makes you say that?

3. What else do you notice?

These three questions force the viewer to notice (perhaps subconsciously) several things:

1. They make assumptions about the image.

2. When they are asked to provide evidence for their assumptions, someone else (you or another student) will challenge with another assumption.

3. Their assumptions are not facts, but instead interpretations, which are not necessarily accurate. No one in the room can really know the truth of what's going on in that image (unless he or she took the photograph).

This line of questioning about photographs undermines what most people typically assume, which is that a photograph is evidence of a factual event. Here, you are helping students understand that a photograph is not necessarily a fact. They should not automatically believe what they *think* they see.

To help students distinguish between "truth" and "speculation," you might implement an activity that focuses on description. Show them a photograph and have them describe what they see. Emphasize that *description* constitutes only what one *sees*: they should list just the facts—only what is viewable in the photograph, without attaching any meaning to the items. This helps to clarify the distinction between facts and assumptions.

The Community Photoworks website, a joint project of the J. Paul Getty Museum and the Kennedy Center for the Performing Arts' ARTSEDGE program (http://artsedge.kennedy-center.org/content/3903/community_photoworks.html), is a great resource for breaking down the act of looking at photographs into distinct parts. You can use this resource to prepare for the photography discussion. It's also useful for students to explore the site and understand the formal elements and principles of photographic composition.

3. Social Networking

By now, social networking will not be a new concept to the students in your class. But because students already take this relatively new phenomenon for granted, pose the following question: *Can you share an experience with someone who is not in the same physical space with you? If so, describe how.*

Students must be deliberately prepared to participate in this lesson because, according to most kids, if you're not in the school building, you're not "in school." Therefore, what's outside of the building is "optional." Frame this activity as an experiment for which you, as a class, are gathering data. This experiment requires you and the students to exchange cell phone numbers; students do not need to exchange phone numbers with one another. Write up an agreement, which you and your students all sign, stating that the phone numbers shared will remain private and are to be used only for the purposes of this experimental project. The participating parties should also agree that they may be contacted via text message at times when they are not at school (e.g., evenings, weekends).

4. Procedure for Project Execution

Phase I: Send a text message to all students simultaneously containing the following instructions:

> STOP what you are doing. SHOOT a picture with your camera phone. SEND your picture with a six-word story to yourflickraccount@photos.flickr.com.

Phase II: When the class meets again in school, have everyone access your flickr.com page where the photographs and stories have been sent. Students will click on each classmate's picture and in the Comment section, interpret the photograph by writing their own six-word story.

Phase III: Students reflect on the experiment by looking at their own photographs and the six-word stories that classmates have attached to them and answering the following questions:

- How have others interpreted your photograph?
- Which interpretations were most unlike your own?
- What might someone have been thinking to lead them to write this story?

Assessment

A rubric is available in the online supplemental materials (Handout 3.1) that you can use as a guide when reviewing each student's photographs and stories. You can also have students fill out a self-evaluation (Handout 3.2).

Connections and Adaptations

This lesson could be accomplished using digital cameras for students who do not have cell phones equipped with camera functions. Create an assignment that asks students to take a photograph at a time when they are not in school. Immediately after taking the photo, they should craft a six-word story to accompany it. When they have access to a computer, they can upload the photo from the camera and email it to the flickr.com address you provide.

4   It's a Comic Life: Creating Information-Based Comics

Michele Luchs
Ministry of Education, Montreal, Québec, Canada

Andrew D. Adams
Lauren Hill Academy, Montreal, Québec, Canada

Context

Lauren Hill Academy (LHA) is an inner-city high school (grades 7–11) of 1,700 kids, located in Montreal, Québec, Canada. It is a lead school in an educational reform currently being implemented in the province of Québec from kindergarten through the end of high school. In English language arts, the new curriculum emphasizes developing critical literacy skills, opening up the kinds of texts being analyzed and produced in ELA to include more media and nonfiction texts, and focusing on the importance of talk in the classroom. Students at LHA are from a wide range of socioeconomic and cultural backgrounds. The school is also known as an arts magnet school and offers specializations in dance and visual arts. Clubs at LHA range from hip-hop dance to outdoor adventure education to the spelling bee team. The following unit was developed for use in a grade 8 English class and relied on students' natural curiosity and desire to bring to light social and environmental issues that were important to them and to other teens at the school.

Rationale

As English teachers, we are required to work with a variety of texts in our classrooms. When working with nonfiction texts, we most often have students write essays. The writing is usually very dry, and students struggle to synthesize information and make it their own. And because these texts don't often have an audience beyond the teacher, they remain "school" writing for the students.

How do we get students to both be aware of how to synthesize research and create a text that is relevant to them and to their target audience? By allowing students to choose their own subjects and research them, they will be invested in their topics. And by fusing texts in two media, essay writing and comic book writing, students can create a hybrid form of information-based text that is relevant to other students and teachers, as well as to a wider audience.

Comics and graphic novels are great at creating an appreciation for reading in general. Students retain information at a much higher rate when they read it in comic book format rather than in article format. For example, when Andrew's students were shown a comic about the conflict in Darfur, they retained much more information than they had after reading an article about the same subject. The article offered important examples and details about the conflict in Darfur but did a poor job of giving an overall picture or showing how the events were sequenced. The comic, which included words and images, simplified the topic to key information and made connections between key details that students remembered.

When students understand what goes into the creation of a comic book, they better understand how comics and graphic novels are created and why that format is so successful. When creating an "info comic," students will need to apply the principles of comic-book-making and learn how to pull the most important information out of their essays and research and present it in a visual form.

Objectives

Students will be able to:

- Brainstorm topics and collaborate with peers
- Synthesize information from nonfiction texts
- Adapt research into short informative comics
- Learn how comics work through an analysis of graphic novels and comic books
- Understand the foundations of portrait and landscape photography
- Communicate information through a visual text when creating their storyboards and comics
- Create texts for an audience of peers
- Explain their production decisions in terms of choice, framing and placement of images, and consideration of audience

NCTE/IRA standards addressed: 6, 7, 8, 12

Materials/Preactivity Preparation

- PC or Mac computers loaded with Comic Life software
- LCD projector
- Digital cameras
- Blank storyboard forms

Time Frame

The creation of information-based comics can be completed in ten 75-minute periods. In the first session, students explore how comics work. In the next two periods, students learn the elements of landscape photography and portrait photography and practice taking photos themselves. The following two periods focus on brainstorming and storyboarding. Two periods are needed for students to shoot their comics with digital still cameras. The editing of the info-comics can be completed in three periods. This project can also be spread out to allow other language arts activities to continue at the same time.

- Understanding comics (75 minutes)
- Understanding and practicing photography (150 minutes)
- Brainstorming (75 minutes)
- Storyboarding (75 minutes)
- Taking photos for the comics (150 minutes class time plus lunch time and after school if needed)
- Editing the comics with Comic Life (225 minutes)

Before this unit began in Andrew's class, students brainstormed topics of interest to them (three students for each topic) and then individually researched and wrote short essays on those topics. The subjects ranged from the perils of fast food to homeless youth to Internet dangers. If you do not plan to have students go through the entire process of writing short research essays, you will need to give them time to brainstorm subjects and research them before beginning this unit. Because of limited resources (three computers and three cameras), students in Andrew's classroom were working on other language arts activities during the same time period.

Description of Activity

Understanding Comics

Many students come into school having had a lot of experience reading comics, but they're not often aware of the key elements that go into creating them. Scott McCloud's *Understanding Comics* focuses on exactly that, as well as offering key information for creating quality comics. McCloud describes these five elements as essential, the choice of:

- moment (which to include in the comic and which to leave out)
- frame (the right distance and angle to view these moments)
- image (rendering the characters, objects, and environments in those frames clearly)
- word (picking words that add valuable information and that work well with the images around them)
- flow (guiding readers through and between panels on a page or screen)

The first day of the project, begin by helping students understand these essential elements to making comics. Then have them find these elements in comics and graphic novels they bring to class with them. Discuss how the elements are used, why they are successful, or how they could be better used.

Understanding Photography

Have students look at a variety of strong photographs. Introduce information about photography composition, such as camera angles and frames, color and lighting, and the rule of thirds. Then have students practice taking photos and trying out some of the composition techniques discussed in class. Ask them to share their photos with the class and explain their production. Students' final projects will be stronger if they first have the chance to study and experiment with photo techniques.

Andrew used information from a Kodak site (http://www .kodak.com/) as the main source for this section of the unit, but you'll find abundant resources in the library and on the Web that you can adapt to your specific circumstances and students.

Brainstorming

Brainstorming helps students figure out the focus for their project. They also see and hear ideas from their classmates and come into contact with new ways of thinking. Ask students to bring in the information they found on their topic through their research. Have them share the most important information with their groupmates. Then have groups brainstorm how they might share this information with their peers in a three-page comic. Which information would draw their readers in? What kind of scene could they create? What sorts of settings and characters can they imagine? Be sure to ask students to think about what could realistically be shot in a school setting.

Storyboarding

Storyboards are outlines for visual texts, templates that allow students to start thinking about what their audience will see and developing strategies for how to do accomplish this. Students need to figure out how to visually represent their subject by considering important moments and how they might frame them, conceptualizing images they would show in each frame, considering what dialogue the characters would use, and sketching out narration that would help the reader move from scene to scene. Storyboards are simply plans and can be drawn using stick figures.

Before students were allowed out with the cameras, each group had to walk Andrew through their finished storyboards. Groups took along their storyboards when they shot their photos. This helped students to move quickly from shot to shot and have a clear idea of the camera angles and framing they would use for each shot.

Taking Photos for the Comics

Once the storyboards have been approved and groups have brought in any necessary props and costumes, students are ready to shoot the photos for their comics. Some groups may be able to shoot their photo essays in the classroom. Others will need to shoot in locations around the school. With the storyboards as guides, photo shoots should go quickly. Ask students to shoot each frame a few times to avoid having to retake photos later.

This might be the most challenging activity of this project, depending on available equipment and school rules about students in the halls. Some teachers might choose to have students shoot their photos outside of class time. Andrew allowed students to shoot during class time if they were shooting in locations around the school. To do this, he gave groups hall passes, notified the administration that his students would be in the halls, and talked to the librarian and support staff. Generally, students in small groups behave well. Andrew reminded students to be mindful of other classes and to keep their voices low. He knew the location for each part of every group's shoot, and if the students had to move to a second location, one group member had to come and tell Andrew. He also checked on each group's progress during this period. Because they were working from their storyboards, it took most groups only 30 minutes or so to shoot the photos for the project.

Editing Comics with Comic Life

As soon as students finish their photo shoot, have them download their photos onto the computer, where they will create an album with the name of the group and transfer all of their photos. This way, when students open Comic Life, they easily will be able to find their folder of photos.

This project could be done with a number of different programs, including Word and PowerPoint, but Comic Life is the most flexible. It allows students to work with a variety of page layouts and to add narration boxes, titles, and speech bubbles. Students can also choose different lenses that will make their photos look like paintings or comics. Before they begin to work on their individual layouts, give students a brief introduction to the program. Students will find Comic Life easy to work with and will use it in very creative ways.

As mentioned earlier, Andrew had only three computers in his classroom. He rotated groups through, giving each one half the period to use a computer. Students worked efficiently because they knew other groups were waiting. When groups were not on the computers, they were working in literature circles.

Sharing Projects

When students have finished their work, ask each group to present their comic to the class. They can talk about how their comic translated from idea to finished product, the production choices they made, and what they would do differently next time. During this sharing, you will learn a lot about each group's process and the problems they had to overcome to create a finished project.

The students' comics can be displayed in the library or around the school. Alternatively, they can be assembled into an anthology and printed. See the companion website for a sample student comic (Handouts 4.1–4.3) and Andrew's Quick Reference Guide to implementing this lesson (Handout 4.4).

Assessment

Students can be assessed in many ways. Class discussion and brainstorming allow them to explore ideas in more depth and get feedback from classmates. At different points in the project, rubrics could be created to cover:

- Individual research on the topic
- Presentation of photos/description of photo composition
- Storyboard and presentation of the storyboard
- Group log detailing decisions made and steps in the production process
- Finished comic
- Presentation of the comic, including production choices and attention to audience
- Participation in different steps of the process

Connections and Adaptations

The skills acquired through this unit can easily be applied to a number of different projects. Here, students are following a production process that includes learning about the genre, brainstorming, storyboarding, and creating and editing a media text in a group for an audience of peers. These steps are essentially the same as those that students will follow when producing different sorts of media texts. Following the same research and production processes, students could produce public service announcements (print, radio, or video) or write newspaper articles. Comic Life could be used to create photo essays, photo stories, mini-memoirs, and other types of comics or short graphic stories.

Work Cited

McCloud, Scott. *Understanding Comics: The Invisible Art*. New York: Harper Perennial, 1993. Print.

5 Glogster: A Poster-Sized Look at Student Movie Stars

Belinha De Abreu
Drexel University

Context

This lesson has been used with a seventh-grade media and technology class at the Walsh Intermediate School in Connecticut. Since 1999, students at this school have been receiving media literacy education either within content area curricula or, since 2006, as part of their applied arts program. Walsh Intermediate School is a coastal, suburban middle school of 1,200 students encompassing grades 5–8. The students were shown how to use Glogster as a new Web 2.0 tool that could also be applied within different subject areas, but specifically within the unit on visual literacy, film, and advertising. The lesson is adaptable to both younger and older students.

Rationale

Glogster (http://www.glogster.com/) is a Web 2.0 program that takes the idea of posters to a new level. Instead of having students cut and paste items to a cardboard paper, they can now cut and paste items digitally. The poster becomes active as live images and voice recordings are incorporated into the whole presentation.

Attracting the teenager in today's very digital and multimedia society has become an issue amongst educators. The discussion of what will encourage adolescents to work and learn within the classroom must acknowledge that our students are already involved in and drawn to environments that are 3D, social, and more detailed than those that rely only on paper and pen. Glogster brings to the classroom an opportunity for students and teachers to realize all of these changes in a user-friendly format. Within the program, students can incorporate audio or video components along with text and images. Glogs can be added to the front page of websites, incorporated into wikis, or even added to various social networking sites. More important, they can be easily shared among students and their teacher (Dyck).

For this project, students were asked to create a movie poster of themselves using the same scenarios and introductions common to movie posters. Note, however, that the Glogster program transcends this particular lesson and can be used in a variety of ways within different disciplines.

Glogster was used in conjunction with a lesson on advertising and film, topics of great interest to students who were born in a consumer culture that reaches out to them continually in myriad ways. Each day we are the targets of thousands of media messages. The Kaiser Family Foundation claims that children view 20,000 television commercials every year. This is an astronomical figure that doesn't even come close to incorporating the full spectrum of media messages. Ask students where else they encounter advertisements, and they will tell you they can be found on buses, billboards, subways, taxis, fliers, church bulletins, and many other places. Ask students if they can think of a place where there is no advertising, and the answer is much more difficult to come by. A study of advertising also provides many opportunities for teaching students how to deconstruct the messages sent to them about the world they live in and the assumptions made about them as consumers.

This particular lesson also explored how filmmakers have found a way to pay for their films through a variety of means other than ticket sales. Product placement can be found throughout almost all of today's films, unless they are period pieces. While it may seem that these products are a natural part of the movie, companies pay for their products to be displayed throughout a film.

As a follow-up to the discussion on product placement, the class evaluated movie posters and trailers. The objective was to help students understand and analyze how images are used in these formats to attract an audience of moviegoers. The trailers helped students to see how images were cut and edited so that some of the best scenes enticed a person to see the movie. Movie posters are found at the entrances of movie theaters and in newspaper and magazine advertising for upcoming films. The images on these posters are designed to gain the most eye attention, again to attract patronage to the film. Students discussed the role and importance of such advertising and what elements they found most captivating.

At the end of the discussion and evaluation, students were given the assignment of creating a movie poster starring themselves (see Handout 5.1 on the companion website for the assignment details).

After selecting any genre of film—mystery, horror, romance, action, etc.—they were to create their posters using the Glogster program. Instructions included deciding on an overall theme for their film, taking a picture of themselves, and then selecting other images and text that would support that picture and work with their theme for the final film. They were also charged with creating a 30-second audio advertisement for the film.

The class discussed Glogster after reading the NeverEnding-Search blog (Valenza), which is written by a very reputable school library media specialist. Most educators today are looking for materials that are interesting, cost effective, and applicable to the classroom, especially with all the Web 2.0 tools and activities available. Glogs, like most other Web 2.0 programs, were originally intended for the general public, so those produced by the earliest users were at times not appropriate for teachers to use in the classroom. Glogster, wanting to attract more educators, created a secondary location, which is suitable for educators all across the K–12 spectrum ("Glogster Launches"). This secondary site—http://edu.glogster.com/—is housed at the main site, but provides private access for educators and students. Private access does require you to take a few extra steps before presenting the program to your students.

Objectives

Students will be able to

- Evaluate the composition of a digital poster
- Analyze current and past movie posters
- Design a Glog that is appropriate for a specific topic or genre
- Select images and text that support a specific topic or genre
- Choose or create audio and video clips that are suitable for a particular topic or genre
- Demonstrate knowledge through an alternative method of learning

NCTE/IRA standards addressed: 1, 3, 7

Materials/Preactivity Preparation

Before you implement this lesson:

- Gather examples of movie posters and movie trailers. You can use the following websites to help you:

Movieposter.com: http://www.movieposter.com/

FilmPosters.com: http://www.filmposters.com/

Internet Movie Database: http://www.imdb.com/features/video/browse/trailer/

- Create a teacher manager account for Glogster.
- Provide passwords and logins for each student on index cards.
- Arrange to have a computer lab available for the duration of this assignment.
- Provide microphones for each student so they can record their movie advertisements.

- Create and give students a worksheet that lays out your expectations for the assignment and that outlines the steps for creating a Glog (again, see Handout 5.1 on the companion website for a sample worksheet).

Time Frame

The entire lesson should take no more than seven 40- to 50-minute class periods.

- Classes 1–3: Introduce and explore advertising techniques relating to film trailers and posters.
- Class 4: Introduce the Glogster platform and register each student in it.
- Classes 5 and 6: Allow students to create their posters.
- Class 7: Have students present their posters to the class.

Description of Activity

As the instructor, you'll need to log in to Glogster to create your account. Once you have established the account, you will be asked for the number of accounts needed for your class. Each teacher can have up to 200 student accounts. For elementary teachers, this is excessive, but for high school teachers, with anywhere from five to seven classes, this is exactly what you need. Create the login name that your class will use by selecting something easy to remember that also represents the nature of the activity, such as "mediatech."

Once you have registered, Glogster provides you with the name and password for each student account. They will all begin with the assigned login, a number, and then a specific password. As the teacher manager for this program, you'll need to come up with a method of keeping track of who has which login. One simple way of doing this is to use index cards and labels. Type the logins and passwords onto a label template and print them out. Place one label on each index card, along with the name of a student. When students first enter the computer lab, hand each one an index card; when they leave the lab, collect them for safekeeping.

As students get ready to work, remind them that they are on a private area of Glogster. They can share their work with other students in the class, but it will not be available to anyone else. Hand out your worksheet assignment and a microphone for recording. Have students check items off the list as they complete each aspect of the assignment.

Because Glogster is a visual medium, it's important to discuss with students how people perceive images—how images evoke emotions such as fear, happiness, love; how people respond to color in general and to specific colors in particular, and how color will draw the viewer's attention; how a sense of space or clutter will affect the viewer's response. Students will need to experiment with these concepts in Glogster to achieve the desired effects of their posters.

Review with students the procedures for printing in Glogster. To print their completed Glogs, they need to right-click on the Glog and then print. Printing from the file manager will result in Glogs that are spaced out over several pages. Printing from the screen ensures that Glogs will print out on one page.

As students finish up the project, have them complete a brief reflection on using Glogs for advertising purposes and for this method of creating posters. They should consider the following:

- What did you like about the application?
- What did you not like about the application?
- Was the program easy to use? Why or why not?
- How did the audio or video components work with the design element of the application?
- What would you like to do more of with this application?
- How does an animated poster compare with other forms of advertising?

Also, have students suggest other reasons to use this tool. They might give you some ideas for future lessons.

Finally, Glogster allows you to rate students' work on a five-star scale, and you can determine what each combination of stars on the scale represents. In the "Assessment" section below, youll find a suggested rubric and example of how it can be used. You can also use the star scale on the worksheet assignment to provide students with their final grade.

Note: For those of you who have used Glogster in the past, the Glogster folks have been working hard to accommodate educators. Some of the major program changes have had to do with safety, such as eliminating some troublesome photo sources like TinyPic, a photo and video-sharing service much like Flickr, and discontinuing their connection to YouTube. Here are some of the newer features under Teacher Controls announced by Jim Dachos of Glogster.edu:

> Teachers will have complete control of all student activities within their account. This includes adding/deleting students, changing/lost passwords, student profile information, student settings, and all messaging and comments. Students will no longer be able to message one another except to offer teacher monitored comments on other students' Glogs. Teachers and students will now be able to regulate the progress status of Glogs with the following settings: Unfinished—student still working on the Glog (only teacher and Glog owner will be able to see this Glog), Finished—Glog is ready for teacher review and for other students to see it, Public for All—Teacher has the option to release the finished Glog to their profile and to all Glogster EDU visitors whether logged in or not. (Valenza)

As with all of their improvements, Glogster has made the program much more teacher- and student-friendly.

Assessment

Students deconstruct and review advertising techniques as part of this lesson, so they need to be able to show through their posters their comprehension of how advertisers use this visual medium to attract our attention. Assessment should be done through class discussion, observation of students' creative efforts in developing their posters, their reflection on the project, their use of advertising techniques in their posters and recordings, and the final product—the Glogster poster.

Glogs can be assessed on the five-star scale that is part of the Glogster tool. The student worksheet should also include a similar star scale. The scale might be represented as follows:

*****	Excellent
****	Good
***	Fair
**	Poor
*	Failed to meet standards

Excellent	Student has completed all the components required. Student has also achieved a well-designed and thought-out poster that demonstrates understanding of advertising techniques for the appropriate audience and genre of film.
Good	Student completed many of the components required. The design and poster are clean and appropriate, but it needed more planning and attention to how to visually capture the intended audience.
Fair	Student completed the bare minimum requirements to complete the project. The poster displayed some evidence of design and thought given to advertising techniques.
Poor	Student completed one or two of the required components. The poster displayed a lack of attention and limited thought given to design, planning, and advertising techniques.
Failed	Student did not complete the project to any visible degree. Requirements were not met, and the poster was given no thought or design consideration. The presentation revealed limited or no understanding of advertising techniques.

Connections and Adaptations

The practice of having students create posters has been part of many K–12 curricula for a long time. As more technology has been introduced into the classroom, the capability to make posters come virtually alive has increased. This Web 2.0 program offers teachers and students a way to use some of the more advanced audio and video design techniques to create advertising and explore the elements of persuasive texts.

This lesson is adaptable both to younger students in grades 4 through 6 and to high school students. When implemented in the high school classroom, it might be worthwhile showing specific clips and scenes from the movie *Minority Report* because it vividly demonstrates the audio/video technology of animated posters. Glogster also has the potential for being tailored to any lesson that has students create some form of poster, brochure, or flier that demonstrates what the students have learned from a specific lesson or unit.

Works Cited

Dyck, Brenda. "Hooked on Glogster: Poster 2.0." *Brenda's Blog.* Education
    World, 27 Feb. 2009. Web. 22 July 2010.

"Glogster Launches Education Development Program." *redOrbit.* redOrbit,
    23 Sept. 2008. Web. 22 July 2010.

Kaiser Family Foundation. "Generation M: Media in the Lives of 8–18 Year-
    Olds." *Kaiser Family Foundation,* March 2005. Web. 22 July 2010.

Valenza, Joyce. "New@Glogster.edu." *NeverEndingSearch* [Blog]. School
    Library Journal, 7 Oct. 2009. Web.

6 Survey Says! Using Google Forms to Evaluate Media Trends and Habits

Brian Turnbaugh
Community High School District 94, West Chicago, Illinois

Context

Community High School is a suburban school of 2,000 students in the western suburbs of Chicago. Our school is socioeconomically and ethnically diverse, with 48.5 percent White students and 44 percent Latino students. Media Literacy and Composition is a semester-long elective for college-prep seniors. The goals of the class are to cultivate a critical media eye through the careful examination of the core principles of media literacy. Through the inquiry of these principles, we uncover an interdisciplinary cross section of media studies, making connections between our collective understandings of economics, psychology, sociology, technology, and rhetoric. The students are expected to be active online, whether participating in the class social network on Ning (http://www.ning.com/) or creating presentations on Voice-Thread. This particular activity was developed to capture the habits of media consumption over a two-week span. While this activity fits in a media literacy course, Google Forms (found in Google Docs) can be adapted for any research that might require data culled from student peer groups.

Rationale

Since I've been teaching media literacy, I have witnessed the mass migration of students as they flocked to new communications websites and entertainment technologies. Within a few months, student allegiances dropped from social networks like Xanga to MySpace and now Facebook. These mercurial exits occur so fast that studies tracking these behaviors become obsolete within a year. In the absence of current and dependable data, perhaps we can use the features of Google Forms to create an immediate snapshot of media consumption among our students. I realize this will be a hard sell for some, as spreadsheets and English instruction go together like fish and bicycles. However, this Google Docs feature allows for a unique opportunity to generate authentic data with our students and provides meaningful connections to media literacy principles. What makes this tool so useful is its simplicity in generating and sharing the survey, as well as its slick presentation of data. From these results, students will be able to recognize trends and make informed projections about the future media consumption habits of their peers. For many students, this will be their first experience of articulating meaning about the ubiquitous presence of media in their lives in a mature academic forum. In *The Ad and the Ego*, Richard Pollay recalls that media theorist Marshall McLuhan once observed, "we don't know who discovered water, but it certainly wasn't a fish." The process of developing survey questions with students and analyzing the data generated from the survey is a first step to getting our students to see the water.

Objectives

Students will be able to:

- Contribute to survey design
- Evaluate data
- Anticipate media trends
- Critique the social significance of media consumption habits

NCTE/IRA standards addressed: 3, 6, 8, 11

Material/Preactivity Preparation

- You will need to register an account with Google. While the forms to create a survey are quite intuitive, allow yourself some time to catch the learning curve. Several useful tutorials can be found via a YouTube search using the keywords "Google Form Tutorial," or visit the brief tutorial videos I made: (1) Google Survey Set-up: http://screencast.com/t/NGFiZmI3, (2) How to Share Access to the Survey with Students: http://screencast.com/t/MDA1YzJhN, and (3) How to Share the Survey Results: http://screencast.com/t/NWFmZmUzND. You'll find links to these videos on the companion website as well.
- You will need to post the form link through Edline/Infinite Campus, TinyURL, a school webpage, Ning, or a blog because the form link is too large to type.

- Students will need Internet access to participate in the survey.
- The class should have access to a computer lab with Internet access for the survey data debrief.

Time Frame

The first phase of the activity will require an initial 50-minute period for you to introduce the purpose of the survey, brainstorm additional survey prompts with the class, and inform students about your expectations for their participation in the survey. The culminating debrief may require one to two 50-minute class periods to unpack the findings of the survey.

Description of Activity

I titled the survey "Media Diet" so as to create a metaphor consistent with the idea of media consumption (see Handout 6.1 in the supplementary materials). Just as we eat broccoli and chips, so do we digest various forms of media. The placement of this activity should fit in where you want a thoughtful reflection of our media habits. This activity could kick-start the course or be used as a culminating survey.

Before familiarizing yourself with the features of Google Forms, consider the following questions as you design the survey:

What do you want to measure with this survey?

The goal of the survey I created was to cast the widest net to measure the media consumption behaviors of my students. Here is a sample of the survey questions:

- How much time did you spend watching TV today?
- What genre of TV did you watch most?
- How much time did you spend surfing the Internet? (not social networking, as on Facebook)
- How much time did you spend on a social networking site? (e.g., Facebook)
- How many text messages did you send today?
- How many text messages did you receive today?
- How much time did you spend reading today?
- How much time did you spend playing video games today?
- How much money did you spend on a media product today?

How do you want the data quantified?

As you draft your survey, you will need to consider how the information is collected. Google Forms offers a selection of the following response options: text, paragraph text, multiple-choice, checkboxes, choose from list, scale, and grid. While text and paragraph text offer more space for the respondents to discuss, those features will not create the bar graphs or pie charts the other options provide. I would recommend using the checkbox and multiple-choice options exclusively because they provide the most manageable data and have the most aesthetic appeal for our students. The other options might provide an opportunity for more detailed responses, but they may not net more useful information for the purposes of this survey. These data will be the foundation activity and give a visual understanding of our media habits.

How will students be able to access this survey?

It is not realistic to have students input this Web address— https://spreadsheets.google.com/a/d94.org/gform?key=0Aq6T jrV4AkRMdEJITGlfV3VLcG9XNldvSmRfcDE0SEE&hl=en&gr idId=0#chart—into their browser for each survey entry. There are several ways to create a link to your survey so that your students can quickly access it. Make use of your school's webpage or course posting options like Edline/Infinite Campus to post the link to the survey. If you do not have such Internet publishing options, here is an easy accommodation for accessing the form more quickly: The Tiny website (http://tiny.cc/) can turn lengthy Web addresses into manageable links. Once you enter the Tiny webpage, you simply paste the Web address of your survey into the "Tiny your long URL" box and click it. This will create a much shorter link for your students to type into the browser. For example, the preceding long URL can now be accessed by typing http://tiny.cc/SyKoT.

When you have nearly completed the survey, it is time to introduce the activity to your class. You'll need to frame this survey in a way that does not cast judgment on student habits. There will be time later to debrief the survey results and comment on their implications. The best way to disarm any negative perception is to model your own media consumption. Share your typical media diet, be it the approximate daily use of a smartphone, Facebook updates, or hours spent lamenting your favorite sports team.

After sharing my typical media diet, we review the list of survey questions. I ask students to predict trends by answering the following questions:

- With which form of media do you think your peers spend most of their time?
- With which form of media do you think your peers spend the most money?
- What form of media do you see growing the fastest?

- What form of media appears to be on the decline?
- Which media product has the most positive effect on your peers?
- Which media product has the most negative effect on your peers?
- What question(s) would you add to this survey?

After students have had time to respond, have them share their ideas with a partner. In a few minutes, I survey the class for their predictions. Whether in a handout or in their notes, the students must save their predictions so they have a point of reference when the survey is complete.

For us to draw from a significant sample, obviously the students must participate in the survey. One of the features of Google Forms is that each student submission is time-stamped, so you can verify timely participation. While a majority of students have home Internet access, there are always a handful of students on the other side of the digital divide. Anticipate this reality and be flexible and creative in finding other ways for these students to include their daily data in the sample.

I recommend that the survey encompass a nine-day span starting on Friday and concluding on the following Sunday; including two weekends allows you to sample students' leisure time outside of school. Also, by limiting the survey to just over a week, you have a better chance of keeping student interest high.

Once the survey ends, it's time to review the results. Here is a quick review of how to access the data. This is featured in my video tutorial posted at http://www.d94.org/english/TurnbaughWeb/nctesurveysays.htm:

1. Before publishing the survey, you must make a quick edit while in the Edit Form page. Click on the box "More Actions" and then select the option "Edit Confirmation" from the drop-down menu.

2. Check the box "Let everyone see response summary." Click "Save." This action will allow you to review the results of the survey once you fill out the form. Be patient, as clicking away before it saves will not give you access to the results. (I learned from experience that after pressing "Save," the form sticks longer than a normal save feature does.) Click on the link "See Previous Responses" and you will be directed toward the graphical summary of the data and can begin your analysis of bar graphs and pie charts. (See Figures 6.1 and 6.2.)

3. You might run into bugs in viewing the survey results. The first time through this activity, I had no issues with students clicking through to view results. More recently, however,

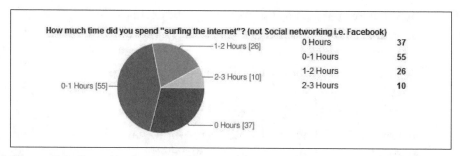

Figure 6.1. Sample pie chart.

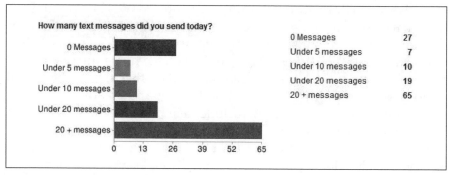

Figure 6.2. Sample bar graph.

the form redirected them to the Google homepage. To overcome this problem, I quickly created a PowerPoint using screen shots of the "Print Screen" button on the keyboard and pasting the image into the presentation. I created the video tutorials and cropped screen shots using Jing, a useful program that is available for free download at http://jingproject.com/. I was able to share the survey data with students on a shared file on the school server and post it online.

In a computer lab or using a hard copy of the data, I next ask students to interpret the results. We return to the handout or notes we created before participating in the survey so that we can compare our initial ideas with the survey results. You can use the following questions as a guide:

- Which predictions were correct?
- What trends do you see?
- What do these trends reveal about what your peers value?
- Did anything surprise you? Why?
- Do you have any reason to suspect the data might be a flawed sample?

- How might this behavior have been different four years ago?
- How might this behavior be different four years from now?
- Does this trend correlate to a core principle of media literacy?
- How does consumption of these media products impact school, relationships, personal budgets, and time obligations to other pursuits (music, art, sports, etc.)?

Assessment

The findings of this survey and subsequent debrief of its findings with students will no doubt provide them with much to consider. My department chair, Chris Covino, shared with me an effective writing exercise called a QHQ (Question–Hypothesis–Question) that helps unpack rich topics. This writing strategy is a brief written discussion that helps students arrive at a better understanding of a complex idea by pulling on the thread of the topic that is most interesting to them. Each student begins the reflection with a thoughtful question related to the issues raised in our survey debrief. For example, "Has our habit of texting made us less social?" The student writes a response to the question or hypothesis, answering the question by talking it through with him- or herself. This portion of the writing should be roughly one page so that it reflects a patient explanation. The last question should not be considered a conclusion but rather the key to opening up new possible doors, showing how their initial question leads to more ideas. This reflective writing is a great opportunity for students to uncover a deeper connection to their media habits as they draw from personal experience, survey data, and their own theories. From one QHQ response, a student sought out her sister's mobile phone bill and found that the sister had sent more than 20,000 text messages the previous month. This appears excessive in 2010, but the student arrived at the possibility that this number of texts could be the average for the next wave of media-savvy teens, and that this could have profound consequences for personal relationships and even language. This type of reflection is common through the QHQ because it creates space in writing for inquiry and synthesis.

Connections and Adaptations

While I originally designed this activity for a media literacy course, the skills and topic could be applied to any of our texts, such as *Fahrenheit 451*, *1984*, or *Brave New World*, that question our media indulgences. One could imagine returning to the survey results in a class discussion of *Fahrenheit 451* after reading that Professor Faber asks of Montag,

"Can you dance faster than the White Clown?" Or consider the great synthesis among these texts anchored by a classic quote from Neil Postman's *Amusing Ourselves to Death*: "In short, Orwell feared that what we fear will ruin us. Huxley feared that what we desire will ruin us" (viii). The results of the survey amplify the themes of these works because they provide an immediate connection to the lives of our students. For further available resources, I highly recommend the PBS *Frontline* documentaries *Digital Nation* and *Growing Up Online*, both available for viewing online at http://www.pbs.org/wgbh/pages/frontline/. However, returning to the power of Google Forms, our students could initiate their own demographic research as well. Next semester, I intend to have students design a survey using Google Forms as a means of determining how particular product brands found market dominance among their peers within our school. I can think of three immediate benefits to student-created Google Form surveys. The first is that the tool is very intuitive and therefore the learning curve short, so you don't need to spend much class time on tutoring. If students can fill in the fields for a Facebook account, they can create a survey on Google Forms. The second benefit is that students exercise critical thinking at the inception of the survey design and in the interpretation of the generated data at the end. Each part requires careful interpretation of the demographic meanings of the data. The third benefit is that students can disseminate their surveys through their own social networks such as Facebook, email, and their own blogs. The results will be more thorough and results will come back in ready-made graphics that students can use in a presentation or as a visual attachment for an essay.

Works Cited

The Ad and the Ego. Dir. Harold Boihem. California Newsreel, 1996. Video.

Postman, Neil. *Amusing Ourselves to Death: Public Discourse in the Age of Show Business.* New York: Penguin, 1985. Print.

7 Bringing the Year Together: The Digital Process Portfolio

Susanne Lee Nobles
Fredericksburg Academy, Fredericksburg, Virginia

Context

All students in grades 6 through 12 at Fredericksburg Academy, an independent day school in Fredericksburg, Virginia, a small city located halfway between our nation's capital and Virginia's capital of Richmond, create year-end portfolios. As an English department, we believe the reflection at the heart of portfolios is the most powerful way for students to end their year truly knowing how they have grown as writers and what goals they have for their writing in the future. Once students enter our 1:1 laptop program in the Upper School (grades 9 to 12), the portfolio becomes digital to encompass the many Web 2.0 writings students do. Since our courses fully integrate the technology available, with each of our students having laptops, our students complete very few, if any, writings on paper. Instead, they create webpages and wikis, they blog and email, and they delve into discussion boards and explore visual argumentation. The digital portfolio is therefore the perfect vehicle for capturing students' 21st century literacies.

In addition to becoming digital, Upper School portfolios shift from presentation (which students do in Middle School) to process. Upper School students include pieces "as is" to show the process of their learning throughout the year. The culminating aspects of the process portfolio are (1) a single in-depth rewritten piece with self-reflection traced throughout in Word comments, (2) a reflective letter focused on the student's thoughts on the year as a whole, and (3) fourteen additional pieces in process chosen to reflect the student's year of learning, for better and for worse. The portfolios are the final projects students complete each year, and while they do take considerable time to create and grade, they are a favorite of both students and teachers. Ending the year with a creative, reflective, and personal wrap-up is a positive and powerful finale.

Rationale

Reflection creates true learning, and process portfolios help students reflect on their writing skills and development. A digital portfolio takes the tried-and-true hard copy portfolio of the twentieth century into a format that embraces the ways twenty-first-century students write, communicate, and reflect using all of the media our technological world allows (NCTE/IRA standard 8; see also "The NCTE Definition of 21st Century Literacies" on the inside back cover). The digital portfolio can actually be a paradigm shift for us as teachers. When we know we are going to ask our students to collect their work on a CD or in an online drop box, we then have to be sure we offer as many opportunities for digital work as possible so students have many choices for what to include in their portfolios. While digital portfolios can and should also include work done on paper, "The NCTE Definition of 21st Century Literacies" makes it clear that we must help our students become literate members of their world: "Because technology has increased the intensity and complexity of literate environments, the twenty-first century demands that a literate person possess a wide range of abilities and competencies, many literacies." Digital portfolios can be the impetus we need to explore the digital world of our students.

So what does this digital world offer our students? My ninth graders communicate with the author of a short story they read via her blog, and she visits their blogs in return. The knowledge that writers are human and blog just like students do brings more writing energy to my classroom than I ever could instill on my own. My seniors explore William Shakespeare's *Othello* in a Ning along with college students training to be teachers. The challenges offered by their college partners push my students past the comfort of the four walls of our classroom, taking their understanding of Shakespeare and therefore their intellectual growth right out into the world with them. A traditional portfolio does not allow my students to truly capture these powerful learning moments. Printing out blog posts in an effort to re-create the back-and-forth nature of comments, or trying to capture the intricacies of an online Ning discussion on paper, just does not work. In their digital portfolios, students can link me right to the spot where their learning occurred. They still include work they did on paper in my classroom—we will not abandon this method of learning. But now they can truly collect their entire year of learning.

When the end of the year arrives, students begin their digital portfolios by sifting through their work to pick what best represents the highs and lows of their year. I offer overall guidelines for what to include, allowing choice in the fifteen total pieces while also requiring a broad representation of types and purposes of the writing students completed (NCTE/IRA standards 4, 5, 6, and 7). Students choose one piece to fully revise as an example of the best work they can now do after a year of learning. Finally, students write letters to me in which they reflect on each piece, hyperlinking to the piece so I can see the reflection and work simultaneously (NCTE/IRA standard 11). Students burn their portfolios onto a CD and create imaginative "containers" to visually represent themselves, or save the portfolios to an online drop box service.

Objectives

Students will be able to:

- Revise a single piece to illustrate the best writing they can do after a year of writing practice and instruction
- Reflect on themselves as writers and learners
- Using this reflection, compile a body of work they feel best illustrates their year of learning
- Use the following technology skills: create hyperlinks, save to a CD, upload to a website

NCTE/IRA standards addressed: 4, 5, 6, 7, 11

Materials/Preactivity Preparation

Materials

- Before the first day of portfolio work, students will need to collect all of their work on paper from the entire year.
- Before the first day of portfolio work, students will need to save to flash drives or their individual laptops all of their digital work and links to their online work from the entire year.
- Students will need access to computers with Microsoft Word and Internet access: individual laptops in a 1:1 program or a computer lab with enough machines for each student. (Note: This lesson plan is written using instructions for MS Word but can also be readily done with Apple computers.)
- You will need access to an LCD projector with a computer or your own laptop connected to it.
- Each student will need a CD if you choose to have them create the digital portfolios on CDs. Students can be asked to buy these, or the school can provide them relatively inexpensively.

Technology and Web 2.0 Training Experience

- Scanning: Students might want to scan papers to include on their CDs. They might also choose to create a portfolio container that has places for paperwork to be included so that scanning isn't necessary. I have found that if students have more than five pages of paper they wish to include in the portfolio, it is best to have a portfolio with a paper section. Because scanning each individual piece takes too much time and the images are not easily manipulated, students find it cumbersome to handle a lot of scans. Therefore, if you have a technology support person at your school who knows how to scan, you could ask that person to be on call during students' portfolio workdays to help those students who have five pages or less they want to scan. I have found this a better use of class time because then I am free to help students work on other aspects of the portfolio. If you do not have this option, learning how to scan is simple; you will need only about one half-hour with a scanner and computer to practice before you'll feel confident about showing students how to do it themselves. Every scanner is different, so your technology support personnel are the best resource for learning how to use your school's scanner.

- Hyperlinking: Learning how to hyperlink is also a simple process, so you will need again just about a half-hour to feel confident about showing your students how to hyperlink. You need to know two types of hyperlinking: hyperlinking to a website and hyperlinking to a different Word document. A great resource for learning how to hyperlink and practicing this skill is Microsoft Word's Internet4Classrooms tutorial at http://www.internet4classrooms.com/msword_hyperlink.htm. A video tutorial about hyperlinking is also available on YouTube at http://www.youtube.com/watch?v=TlHMZlD-8vw.

- Using Microsoft Word Comments: This About.com site, http://wordprocessing.about.com/od/wordprocessingsoftware/a/comments.htm, offers a simple guide to using this feature of MS Word. You will need only about 15 minutes to figure out and practice how to use these comments, as they are very easy to insert, modify, and delete.

- Saving to a CD: If you decide to have your students create their digital portfolios on CDs, there are more variations with this skill than with the previous skills, so you will want to play with a few different types of CDs and be sure to test your saved CDs on computers different from the one you saved with. You will need up to an hour to experiment with CDs. Practice saving an entire folder to a CD at one time using both the drag-and-drop method and the "Save as" method. This site, http://kb.iu.edu/data/akvi.html, has clear instructions for saving to a CD in all recent versions of Windows;

a helpful video can be found at http://www.youtube.com/watch?v=EXn3ha6X3Vg.

- Uploading to a website: If you decide to have your students create their digital portfolios using an online drop box website (such as Dropbox), you will want to practice this process yourself first. The online sites have their own instructions, so you'll need about a half-hour to follow the instructions once you have chosen the site you wish to use.

Time Frame

Students create their digital process portfolios mostly out of class, as they often have writing assignments they need to find at home or they want more quiet reflection time than a class period allows for. When a class is completing its first portfolios, you should allow for one 45-minute class to introduce the portfolio, a second 45-minute class a few days later to discuss the rewritten piece, a third 45-minute period for introducing the reflective letter and allowing for work time during which you float and informally check students' progress, and a final half of a 45-minute class to turn in the portfolios (to test the CDs to be sure they work or to do the actual uploading to the drop box site). It is helpful as well to assign students specific homework tasks each night to be sure they are moving methodically through all of the steps of portfolio production. For the first two nights, homework could entail, for example, choosing the pieces they want to include, and then choosing the piece they will rewrite. As students become more familiar with the portfolio-creation process—that is, if they are doing a portfolio at the end of every year—they become more aware of the work involved and can be more independent outside of class, thus requiring less class time.

Description of Activity

A few days before I introduce the digital process portfolios, I tell students to start gathering everything they have done all year for our class. "Yes, everything! And the more you can find, the better!" I reply to their inevitable questions. I tell them at the start of the year and remind them periodically throughout the year to never throw away anything they have done in my class, and as much as I hope they heed my words, I also know that as long as they have a large selection of their work, they will have choices for their portfolio, and that is what matters most.

On our first in-class portfolio day, the students and I look through the overall guidelines (see Handout 7.1 on the companion website). I emphasize the key aspects of a portfolio: its personal, individual nature and its reflective power. It is very important that students see from this first day that a portfolio is not just another English paper. Instead, it is their chance to create a representation of themselves. Every portfolio will be different, and that is the beauty of the process. It is helpful on this first day to show students a sample digital portfolio too—obviously, something you can only do once you have had a class complete portfolios. I made sure after my first year to keep a copy of the most unique portfolios; seeing these examples helps students really understand that there is no one "right" portfolio.

What is also important for students to understand is the concept of a *process* portfolio. Students should be choosing work they loved as a way to showcase their strengths, as well as work they maybe did not do so well on to show their struggles. The work should also be from all areas of writing they did during the year: in-class tests, formal papers, creative projects, notes, webpages, emails, Ning discussions, blog posts, and so on. These ups and downs and different examples ultimately show the learning process most vividly, and reflecting on them is a powerful experience for students. Students should also be including the work as is— it should have whatever teacher comments were put on it or individual notes or other marks. Only the rewritten piece needs to be finalized and fully brought to the presentation stage. At this time, I also talk to students about what they want to do with work that was done only on paper (a test, for example). I will have arranged before this class some periods during which students can use the school's scanner, and I explain to my students the scanning procedures. As mentioned earlier, I discourage scanning more than five pages, as the resulting scanned images are challenging to manipulate. If a student has a significant amount of paperwork he or she wishes to include, I talk to them about how to create a section of their portfolio container made to hold this work.

On this first day, I spend only about 15 minutes discussing the guidelines. I then turn the class period over to students so they can start sorting through their work. I have found that this time to ponder allows students to really think about the portfolio and ask questions. I walk around and help them identify work done for lessons or units they cannot quite fully remember and answer questions along the way. Often, this period becomes a great walk down memory lane as students rediscover work and have fun remembering assignments together. This period can also be a good time to work with the inevitable student who cannot find much of what he or she did during the year. A definite benefit to digital work is that students cannot truly lose it; you can sit with students and help them find again the websites where they did their work. But for the work done on paper, if a student has lost it, it is gone. That's why my maximum number of pieces (fifteen) is low compared to all that we did during the year. I can work with students to help them see that they still have some choice even when they cannot find very much.

Another key to this first day is that I do not actually do anything with the technology skills needed for compiling the portfolio. I tell students they just need to find the work they want to include and start saving it in one place. You will need to be in a computer lab or make sure your students have their laptops this day so they can search through the online and other technological work they have done, but you do not need to go any further with the technology.

Students' homework is to finish deciding on and actually finding each piece they wish to include in their portfolios. They also choose which piece they want to rewrite. I tell them they should be thinking about why they are choosing this particular piece, as it will help them on a future step. I allow a few nights for this selection process.

We spend the next class period (either the next day or a day or two later—you can begin the portfolio process while finishing up another unit) looking specifically at how to complete the rewritten piece. Each student needs to come to class with the piece he or she has chosen to rewrite, and the class should bring their laptops or meet in a computer lab. The goal of the rewritten piece is to have students show how they have worked on and mastered their writing goals for the course. Therefore, guidelines for the rewritten piece will be specific to the goals of your class. For example, in my ninth-grade Introduction to Genres course, students spend all year writing examples of each genre we read together as well as practicing developing and supporting strong written arguments. Guidelines for the rewritten piece are therefore to choose an excerpt from their favorite creative piece and an excerpt from their favorite expository piece and rewrite both using specifically the style and grammatical techniques we discussed. The students then trace, using Word comments, their revisions as well as examples of each of the techniques and how they have used them. This digital tool is far better than any reflection method I have had my students do on paper. The Word comments attach right to the specific spot students wish to discuss, and the expanding nature of the comment bubble encourages them to write more than they ever did on paper for me. As for pure practicality, the comments are legible, versus handwritten notes squeezed into margins of papers.

The key to setting up your guidelines is in what you require in the comments. To evaluate the rewritten pieces without having to reread the original piece plus the new one (a time-consuming process in what, as you will discover, is already a very time-consuming grading process), I use these comments as windows into what the student knows is or is not strong writing. So ask them to identify whatever you hope to see in the rewritten piece, and you will achieve a double benefit. Your grading time will be focused and well spent because you will be reading only what is in the comments, and, more important, you will truly know what your students have learned because they will have told you.

Homework for the next few nights is then to complete the rewritten piece, both the actual rewriting and the commenting. On the next portfolio day in class, when students again need computer access, I introduce the reflective letter (see Handout 7.2 in the supplementary materials). I emphasize that these are genuinely letters from the students to me—informal and personal. While I grade the rewritten pieces for both content and mechanics, I grade the letters only for content. I also take about five minutes to show students how to hyperlink. Their letters must, as the guidelines state, discuss every piece included in their portfolio, so what they do is hyperlink each piece to the correct spot in their letters. This means that as I read each letter, I can click on the hyperlink and see right away the piece the student is referring to: a perfect use of technology to closely link the reflection and the product. Students then use the rest of class to start on these letters or work on other aspects of their portfolios while I circulate and check on how things are going.

Before I move on to the final day when the portfolios are due, let me explain the different options for compiling the portfolios. As my guideline sheet shows, I use CDs for my students' digital portfolios. Our department has considered using online sites to which students can upload their work, but we are also keenly aware of how these sites come and go. We do not want students to end up losing their portfolios because a website no longer exists. We also do not want to use some of the sites available because of their public nature. Portfolios are private between the teacher and student and anyone the student feels comfortable sharing with. As you read students' reflective letters, you will see this very clearly too. The reflection a student will write in a safe, private environment with you is amazing. Finally, when I have students burn their work to a CD, they also create an imaginative container for the CD and any papers they wish to include, a holdover from traditional hard copy portfolios. Students really enjoy this chance to express themselves in a different, tangible way, and they would lose this with a completely online portfolio.

Still, some schools may want to do a fully online portfolio, and as time passes, new websites with more refined options for this will inevitably be created. Two that fit the bill right now are Box (http://www .box.net/) and Google Docs (http://www.google.com/google-d-s/intl/ en/tour1.html). Both of these can work well for this project because students can upload an entire folder of work rather than having to upload one document at a time. They can then invite you to share the folder, so it remains private. If you decide to go with the fully online option, it is important that most of the work students do in your class be digital. Otherwise, they will be spending an inordinate amount of time scanning paper documents to be able to upload them. Scanning always takes longer than we think it will, so it is important to consider how much time you want your students spending on this purely organizational step versus the more reflective steps.

Now comes portfolio due day! Using the CD method, I have the homework leading up to this day encompass three things. First, students need to have everything they want to include in their portfolio complete and saved in one folder on their laptops or on flash drives. Second, they need to have a CD. Third, they need to have their creative container. We meet once again, either in the computer lab or in class with laptops. We then burn the CDs together so I can show students how and so they can test their CDs on someone else's computer to be sure the saving process worked. I have found that many unanticipated glitches can occur in the CD-burning process, so by performing this step in class with the students, I can help them through it and be sure everyone has done it correctly. I don't want to make it sound as though this process is fraught with errors. CDs are oddly not uniform in how they work, so it just takes some patience and reassuring of students that everything will work out. I also have found it very helpful to ask the technology support person at my school to be in class with me this day to be the expert problem solver. Once you have every student's portfolio CD and begin reading them, you will see how the time it takes to compile them is absolutely worth it.

Once the CDs are burned and tested, students put them in their creative containers and turn them in. Voila—portfolios complete! If I were doing the online portfolio option, I would follow a similar process by having students come to class with everything they want to include in their portfolios complete and saved in one folder on their laptops or on flash drives. We would then perform the upload together, and I would be sure they had all correctly invited me to share their folder online. And again, voila—portfolios complete! Now you have hours of engaging and powerful reading in front of you.

Assessment

At Fredericksburg Academy, final portfolios are the last major grade of the fourth quarter. All parts of the portfolio are assessed, from the requirements to the level of reflection shown. Here are questions we ask as we read each portfolio:

- What do we learn about the student from the personal, creative container?
- Does the array of work the student has included show a broad view of his or her year of learning?
- Is the reflective letter honest about the student's setbacks and growth? Does the student link each piece of the portfolio to this letter to show his or her overall year of growth? Does the student recognize skills and knowledge he or she has obtained, and does the student have goals for future skills and knowledge he or she wants to continue to polish or learn?
- Does the student, through the rewritten piece itself and the comments about the rewritten piece, show mastery of the identified writing skills?
- Did the student successfully use the technology skills of hyperlinking all included pieces, annotating the rewritten piece with Word comments, and burning the CD?

Connections and Adaptations

At Fredericksburg Academy, we have students from grades 6 through 12 complete portfolios. Portfolios are truly adaptable to any level of student. I have found that students of all ages can be reflective and gain from this reflective practice. We adjust how many pieces a student must include, with fewer for younger students, and we give more deliberate instruction in the process of creating the portfolio to younger students.

The process portfolio can also be as cross-curricular as you want it to be. I allow my students to include writings from any of their other courses, and I love to see the works they are proud of from history or science or journalism. I learn even more about them as writers, and I also gain insight into what my colleagues are doing with writing. I have used this knowledge to begin conversations about cross-curricular writing.

Only with the rewritten piece do I do not allow my students to choose work from another course. My rationale is that I want to see their writing growth in skills we practiced in the forms we practiced them in. Since the portfolio is a major grade for my class, and the rewritten piece is a major part of the portfolio grade, I feel the rewritten piece needs to be from my classroom. I could see including writing from another course working well if teachers from different subject areas worked together on a joint final portfolio. In this way, the portfolio would be a grade for both of their courses, and the writing could be fully cross-curricular.

Supplemental Resources

Digital portfolios are being developed and adopted nearly every day by schools, colleges and universities, businesses, and employment counselors. You could spend a worthwhile hour just typing "digital portfolio" into your Internet search engine and seeing what results come up. Clicking through the different sites you find will give you a wonderful overview of the different ways such portfolios are being designed and used. You will find new ideas that will help you best tailor your portfolios to your students' needs.

To supplement this online reading, a book published in 1992 but still offering powerful insight into why portfolios are such beneficial tools in the writing classroom is *Portfolios in the Writing Classroom: An Introduction* edited by Kathleen Blake Yancey. Here is the full citation:

Yancey, Kathleen Blake, ed. *Portfolios in the Writing Classroom: An Introduction.*
   Urbana, IL: National Council of Teachers of English, 1992. Print.

II   A Classroom without Walls: Collaborating with Web-Based Applications

It's in the Margins: Social Media and Implications for Learning

William Kist
Kent State University

I should be blogging now. I should also be tweeting this and posting on Facebook (especially if I want to reach younger readers). Instead I'm writing this text for the book you are holding. I'm torn. Am I wasting my time writing this? I mean, if I were blogging this, I would get comments from people around the world, and if I were tweeting, these responses would be almost instantaneous. In fact, while I've been writing this, I tweeted a request to my followers on another matter and got three immediate answers. It will be months before this text gets to a reader (and potentially years). And I'll never have any idea what any reaction is to what I'm writing.

Ah, but there is a permanency with books. Presumably, this book will be purchased by libraries across the country and even the world and be deposited in the Library of Congress. These words may be read decades from now by someone stumbling through the stacks of a musty back shelf or picking through the piles of pages accumulated over the years. There's some comfort in that, right?

What do you think I should do? (I've seen many people query their Facebook friends about what they should have for dinner, so I might as well ask you about this.) Oh, I'm forgetting—you can't answer. I'm the only one who can talk in this "conversation."

Wait a minute! Louise Rosenblatt would argue with that last sentence. (Give a "thumbs up" if you saw one of Louise Rosenblatt's last public appearances at the NCTE Annual Convention in Indianapolis in 2004. Oh, wait, you can't do that either.) Anyway, Rosenblatt would have said that reading is mostly about the conversation the reader has with a text. In fact, if you take a postmodern perspective, you might ask whether the text can exist apart from the reader—it's certainly not stationary.

So, according to Rosenblatt's reader-response theory, you are having a conversation with this page-based text right now. You are constructing a meaning for yourself. To help you with this, you might even be writing marginalia such as "WTH?" or "Duh!" But face it—no one will ever read your comments. Unless perhaps you become famous someday and someone purchases the books you leave behind, records your musings, and publishes a book about them. This is what Zoltán Haraszti did with the marginalia of John Adams. If that happens, *then* maybe someone other than you will read your thoughts.

The main thing to keep in mind is that you're interacting with the text and constructing your own meaning of it. But it's still a nagging fact in this Web 2.0 world that no one else can "hear" you as the reader of a page-based book. The only person who can be "heard" in this conversation right now is me. And only if someone is reading this page. Reading page-based texts is kind of like a bad dream, then—a conversation in which only one of the speakers' words can be heard by anyone other than him- or herself.

I do have one solution—you could write your comments to me in an email (wkist@kent.edu). That's about the only solution I can think of, so I guess you're stuck listening to me, with no recourse other than to keep reading (which I hope you will), move on to some other part of the book, or simply close it. You probably are reading this book for the lesson plans, anyway. Who ever reads the interstitial essays? (I want to make *interstitial* into a link to a definition online of the word for those of you who have never heard of it. Now I'm trying to decide whether to take up precious space in print to define the word or just put the burden on you to look it up. Okay, I've decided. I'm going to put the burden on you. If this were a hyperlinked environment, I could just embed a link, and you could click on it if you wished and have it right there. Now you have to go find a dictionary.)

The lesson plans in this section of the book are written by teachers who are not bound by the page-based conventions I've been poking fun at. They are making the most of social media's opportunities for fostering a genuine real-time reader–text–reader interaction (or reader–reader interaction). If I were in Katherine Higgs-Coulthard's classroom, for example, I could be writing this chapter in the form of a story tree, in a collaborative manner, with readers contributing to my story tree, helping me to write the end. If I were in the classrooms of Heather A. Ingraham or Anna Meyers Caccitolo or Vicki Luthi Sherbert, I could set up an online discussion board or a document at Google Docs so that you could comment on this text as you read it. And I also could have set up questions along the way to help guide your reading (so you don't drift off!). If I were in Neil Rigler's or Abigail J. Kennedy's classroom, I could have recorded this text as a podcast, posted it to my website, and asked you to comment. I also could have set up a Ning, as Abigail J. Kennedy describes, adding a complete interactive allowance.

All of these things went through my mind as I read the lesson plans in this chapter—how can I write a text in this noninteractive medium that introduces everything these lesson plans allow a teacher to do, including a variety of ways for readers and writers to engage one another, meaningfully and instantly? Perhaps at the very least I can point out just what these lesson plans can do that this introductory text can't.

These lesson plans allow us to make student marginalia visible. The projects described in this section allow us to see the dialogue that our students have with the texts they "read," making their marginalia visible to all. Teachers of reading for years have categorized lessons as being "prereading," "during reading," or "after reading." Now teachers have a way to make transparent all the things that we know good readers do during reading: preview, question, and make connections to other texts and to themselves, to name a few. The teacher no longer has to rely on performing an oral think-aloud in front of the class, demonstrating how he or she previews or questions or makes connections. Both teacher and students can demonstrate this for each other. Using discussion boards, for example, allows students to perform ongoing think-alouds around the clock, recording their thinking for all to see. In classrooms that use these forms of communication, we get to see what has previously been hidden in the marginalia, or not expressed at all.

These lesson plans make explicit that literacy is social. Our communication forms have finally caught up with what many literacy scholars have been trying to tell us for a century, moving us out of a primarily cognitive-based model of literacy to a more social model. These new platforms reveal what was obvious to these thinkers long ago—that literacy is social, actually built on a series of activities that bind us to others, even as we learn about ourselves. It's not only that these new forms allow students to write collaboratively; they also allow for a kind of collaborative reading, because students can read one another's marginalia, and by reading that marginalia, they co-construct the text they are reading with their classmates, both in their own classroom and, potentially, in classrooms all over the world. We now have a way to demonstrate explicitly just how much we co-construct texts. Using wikis, Nings, and online discussion boards, as described in the lesson plans in this book, students can have virtual book clubs for everything they "read," discussing and reflecting on the texts twenty-four hours a day, seven days a week.

These lessons can allow for intervention. Seeing students collaborate in real time means that teachers have greater opportunities for intervention. If the thinking of students is visible, teachers may be able to spot potential for remediation. For the first time, teachers have the opportunity to see how their students are working through problems, assignments, and challenges. By following the patterns of thought a student took, the teacher has the chance to truly inform instructional practice, both in terms of teaching a lesson differently the next time and also on an individual intervention level. Following a student's chain of thought could help the teacher realize that a simple misunderstanding has gotten in the way of learning. (Of course, there are dangers to this: these new media could be used to overmonitor students. Doctorow describes the potential for a kind of mind control in schools in the chilling *Little Brother*; the futuristic plot includes a portrait of schools' turning into repressive thought-police states in the name of protecting against terrorism. I was reminded of this recently when I interviewed an educator who seemed to view Nings and wikis as great tools for keeping track of every step of her students' thought processes, sort of like an electronic monitoring ankle bracelet.) In the best uses of new media, these new forms allow teachers more than a glimpse inside the during-reading activities of students. The more we know about the way our students interact with texts, the more we can intervene in hopes of challenging them to be the best readers and writers they can be.

These lessons allow for co-construction of the curriculum. These fluid communication platforms make it more difficult and fundamentally anachronistic to create static, never-changing script-like curricula and instruction. As students question texts, compare and contrast what they are reading in class and in the outside world, and make predictions about the future, teachers are challenged to become true co-learners, with classrooms genuinely becoming virtual "communities of learning." Paradoxically, these new forms have come about during the twenty-five-year period in which policymakers have seen standardized curricula and assessment as the primary answers for school reform. As we are on the brink of what may be a national standardized curriculum (although some may argue that we have always had a national curriculum), the pioneers of new literacies (who are represented in this book) should make policymakers pause. These visionary teachers and students are making it clear that sometimes even constructing a standardized rubric is a fruitless task, as students transform the "end" product even as they are co-creating it. In fact, as important as it is to have rubrics for fairness in grading, these new forms of learning tend to make a mockery of the grading system that was firmly in place for most of the twentieth century. When a class assignment is focused on an ongoing, transformative dialogue, how can individual students be "graded" apart from their classmates and even apart from the teacher, who presumably was a participant in the group's work? And why should they be? These new ways of reading and writing make the "raising the bar" metaphor irrelevant, as classrooms become less about "personal bests" (to continue the track meet metaphor) and more about working through challenges together.

These lessons allow for archiving memories. The lessons described in this section allow for an archiving of students' work over time, preserving these times in our students' lives. I often assign a multigenre autobiography project (Kist) that asks students to assemble digital stories of their lives, making a kind of virtual collage of all the texts that have been important to them over a lifetime. As they present their projects to the class, students reminisce about small bits of information they still remember from watching a Saturday morning cartoon show, for example. One student said,

> The first TV show I remember connecting with is *Teenage Mutant Ninja Turtles*. . . . Michaelangelo was my favorite. He was the orange one who was the "cool" one. . . . At the end of every episode, the cartoon turtles would give an animated PSA about the environment. To this day, I still snip up the plastic can/bottle six pack holders because the turtles told me that a duck could get stuck and die.

Students also remember how desperately they craved a certain consumer item that they began to covet after seeing it in the media. One student stated, "I remember desperately wanting 'flare leg' jeans in the 7th grade. I was such an awkward duck at that age, and I wasn't into fashion or buying clothes other than hoodies. . . ." One student remembered wanting a Starter jacket. "It's the first time I ever really remember wanting a specific brand so bad," he said, "and I think it's because my older brothers had them, as well as everyone else. They were a big, popular trend." These memories become poignant monologues as students share these bolts of flashbacks related to old media texts.

As I've listened to these kinds of stories over the years, I've wondered what it will be like for those who came of age in these digital times and perhaps had a parent who blogged about every significant (and perhaps some insignificant) event of their young lives. Taking it one step further, students who go to schools in which the lessons portrayed in this book are implemented will have a very clear memory stream that can be called up at any time, one that demonstrates their various inquiry paths and their growth over the years through virtual transcripts of their learning. While my students seem to have their Proustian "madeleine" moments while working on their multigenre autobiographies, as these various texts trigger deep memories from their pasts, I wonder what it will be like years from now when students may be able to call up a minute-by-minute-by-minute record of their interactions with texts. Will memories become stronger when students have such a direct link to the past? Or will memories atrophy from lack of exercise?

Of course, as we learn more about the ways teens use new media, it appears that most of their uses outside of school (texting and Facebook/MySpace, for example) are so ephemeral that their thoughts and activities won't be archived at all and will be gone within a day or two. The Pew Internet report "Social Media and Young Adults" suggests that young people don't blog, and they don't even participate in the microblogging that is Twitter. The forms they tend to use (texting and social networking platforms such as Facebook) are less easily archived. So the school projects described in this book may serve as the only real method of preserving this important time in their lives. Schools have always had the primary function of preparing students for their futures, but as educators begin to use forms that lend themselves to archiving, they may also become keepers of our pasts.

As I've been writing this, I've been sending out some tweets myself and receiving some on Twitter. I haven't texted, but I've been confirming two friend requests on Facebook and conducting a synchronous chat with a high school friend. So my virtual marginalia would disintegrate just like the kids' were it not, in a way, included in this text I'm writing. The upper right corner margin of my laptop screen contains an irregular brief flash of a picture and some words from my use of Tweetdeck, providing a constant stream of tweets and status updates that appear for about three seconds and then fade away. If I want, I can even have a little "tweet" sound go off whenever an update appears, although I have it muted now because I'm also watching a film—*The Hills Have Eyes*—to prepare to review a book about the horror genre. But you really didn't need to know that, did you? I'm beginning to feel like the main character in Eco's *The Mysterious Flame of Queen Loana*, who is reduced to remembering only the text associations in his life and can't remember his human connections. Even the "old" media of Turner Classic Movies is connecting every movie being shown during these "31 Days of Oscar" as I write this, with the first and last movies of the month starring Kevin Bacon, and each film in between is linked by one actor appearing in the previous film to an actor in the following film.

Eventually all our texts may be connected in a kind of huge unfiltered stream of marginalia. Of course, perhaps all the marginalia I've written in my books over the years could be thought of in this way, too. Having just gone through a move, it was very hard to give away any of my books, as they all seemed to be connected, whether they had marginalia or not, to my life experiences. I think I got rid of only a couple, and they were connected to parts of my life that I wanted to forget.

It is stating the obvious that the kinds of lessons described in this section of this book have the potential to completely transform the way we do school. But are we really interested in doing that? As more and more schools block more and more sites, it appears that the pendulum is not swinging. We are now in our third decade of putting all of our eggs in the basket of standardized curriculum and assessment. And yet the more we know about this new media and the more we know about the way humans learn, the more we may realize that this emphasis has been badly mistaken. As our students are busy texting away their lives, many of us in schools are not fully taking advantage of these new forms of communication. The teachers in this book are. If they had written these lesson plans in Facebook, I would give them a thumbs-up, showing that I "like this." I know you will do that, too, as you mark up this book (if you own it) and make your own marginalia.

References

Doctorow, Cory. *Little Brother*. New York: Tor, 2008. Print.

Eco, Umberto. *The Mysterious Flame of Queen Loana*. Orlando: Harcourt, 2005. Print.

Haraszti, Zoltán. *John Adams and the Prophets of Progress*. 1952. New York: Grosset & Dunlap, 1964. Print.

The Hills Have Eyes. Screenplay by Wes Craven. Dir. Wes Craven. Anchor Bay Entertainment, 1997. Film.

Kist, William. *The Socially Networked Classroom: Teaching in the New Media Age.* Thousand Oaks, CA: Corwin, 2010. Print.

Pew Internet & American Life Project."Social Media and Young Adults." *Pew Internet & American Life Project,* 3 Feb. 2010. Web. 4 Feb. 2010.

Rosenblatt, Louise M. *Literature as Exploration.* New York: Appleton-Century, 1938. Print.

8 Creating a Classroom Ning: Developing an Environment for Social Networking

Abigail J. Kennedy
Pasco High School, Dade City, Florida

Context

Pasco High School consists of more than 1,200 students in a fairly rural, small-townish community. The student body encompasses numerous ethnicities, with a fairly large migrant/ESOL population. I've used Ning, a networking website, with regular and honors students, as well as Advanced Placement students in both English classes and elective courses such as journalism and multimedia productions, both as a communication tool and for class assignments. I also use Ning as a way for alumni students to keep in touch.

Rationale

Students communicate differently today and, as their teachers, we need to be in tune with how to best reach them. In an era of instant connection and real-time learning, our brick-and-mortar classrooms are becoming outdated. By embracing the social networking world, we allow students to be more successful in and outside of our individual classrooms. Creating a social networking space for your classes allows students to feel more involved with you, your class, and their peers (Kist). Since many of the popular social networking sites such as Facebook and MySpace are blocked within our school systems, how do we utilize such a site in the classroom? I've tried using blogs and discussion boards but found them limiting and not as user-friendly as Facebook or MySpace. Therefore, I suggest looking into creating a Ning. When the National Council of Teachers of English (NCTE) started a Ning for their Annual Convention in 2008, I discovered how easy it was to create my own "network," and decided it would be a great arena for my students in the online environment. You can start your own Ning by going to http://www.ning.com/.

A Ning is essentially your own personal social network site where you can have "friends," create and tweak your own profile, and post blogs, comments, pictures, and video. Not only do you have your own page, but if you create a Ning network, you can also open up a platform for whatever purpose you choose. NCTE used its Ning as a way to let Annual Convention attendees and presenters prepare for and then share during and after the meeting, so I decided to have my own Ning, "Kennedy's Krib," which would be home to all of my students, current and past. As the creator of "Kennedy's Krib," I have control over who joins and can limit access and allow for all sorts of privacy settings—perfect personalization capabilities for a teacher (see Handout 8.1 on the companion website).

Previously, I had been using a free online discussion board with my students. I immediately found the Ning to be much more user-friendly than the online discussion board and, as a teacher with five different preps, found it easier to allow for separate class assignments while at the same time providing opportunities through various forums and areas for students to collaborate across classes. I find that expanding my classroom to a virtual space allows me to "know" my students better, which ultimately allows me to be a better teacher because I can better address their specific needs.

Objectives

Students will be able to:

- Communicate with peers in their own class, as well as across classes and subjects, to develop a larger understanding of their assignment's purpose and find a wider audience for their work
- Express their individuality and customize their own "page" within the network
- Instantly chat with peers online, blogging, commenting, and discussing various topics posed by the teacher and other students
- Reflect on their own time regarding in-class reading and discussions
- Access instant information regarding classwork and obtain help from both teacher and peers

NCTE/IRA standards addressed: 1, 6, 11, and 12

Materials/Preactivity Preparation

- Internet access
- Email address

You will need to set up the Ning and customize it for your own purposes before explaining it to your students. Privacy settings can be changed or altered depending on what you want to do with the site, so you need to establish the environment you want. My Ning is open to anyone surfing the Internet, and I monitor membership. As the creator of your Ning, you have master control. Under the "Manage" tab, set privacy preferences. Since I have mine set to "Public," I have to physically delete any person who is an "outsider" if I feel they don't belong, but I would rather keep our Ning available to anybody to view, so this is my preference. Your options under the privacy settings are Public—people can see everything *or* just the main page—and Private—anyone can sign up *or* only those invited can sign up. This setting will affect your entire Ning site.

You can also set specific privacy settings for various features within the Ning, such as groups. I keep the groups private, so members have to request membership, and this is where we do the bulk of our class-by-class work. You can design the Ning so that you have to invite people to join by sending them an email. As a teacher, I find this route time-consuming and troublesome because students sometimes get confused about how to log in or join and might forget to check their email for the invite. You would also have to remember to send invitations to any new student you get throughout the school year.

A good question here is how to deal with district or school guidelines. My district and school are much like others—they do not encourage public display of student work or information. I keep my students' Internet use forms on hand, as well as their video/photo release forms. I also discuss Internet safety with my students and explore the ways to stay "anonymous" on the World Wide Web, such as making up nonspecific screen names and not posting personal pictures or information. I do not require that their screen names be identifying at all, nor require them to include a picture on their login.

Time Frame

Teacher Prep: 1–2 Hours

This time will vary depending on your technological capabilities. For those adept in social networking websites such as Facebook, MySpace, and Twitter, setting up and personalizing your own Ning could take as little as 5 to 10 minutes, depending on how personalized you wish to make it. For those new to Web 2.0 technologies, it could take up to an hour to get it all set up the way you'd like or to figure out where various buttons and settings are located. As you set it up, the site will pretty much walk you through all functions; however, you may wish to make further changes after seeing what the final site looks like. Once you're launched, you will be given a URL that includes your designated name for the page, so now you will always log in to your specific page. Mine is http://turtlesteach.ning.com/. To make adjustments from here, look for the "Manage" tab, which is normally located at the far right top of the page. This will allow you to make any changes to appearance or privacy settings.

Student Instruction: 1–2 Hours

The best way to introduce your class Ning to your students is to do a little direct instruction with a computer and/or projector. One class period should be sufficient to show the students the website, how to create an account, ways to customize it, and the various features available.

If you plan to use a specific area for a required assignment or task, as I use mine as an integral part of our sustained silent reading (SSR) unit, explain this particular aspect in another class period, after students have had a chance to create their own accounts and log in. Then you can focus on the requirements or guidelines for the assignment after they're comfortable with navigating the site (see Figure 8.1).

Maintenance Time: 1 Hour a Week

Site maintenance time is variable. I have my Ning account set up to send me emails whenever a user posts or responds to something in the discussion or group areas, so I'm aware of the activity occurring at anytime, but this can be adjusted. I also have to approve any photos or videos posted by members, so the time it takes to accomplish some of these tasks is much greater when students are first getting signed up.

As the year progresses, maintenance time depends on how I'm using the site with my students. For online postings, it takes less than 5 minutes to post the new week's topic and maybe 30 minutes each week to assess students' work based on the rubric (see Handout 8.2 in the supplemental materials).

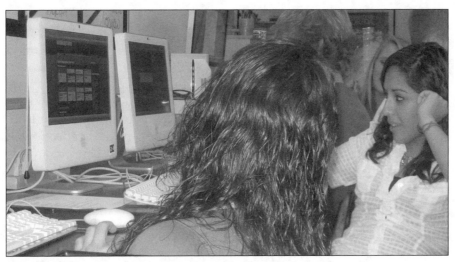

Figure 8.1. Students are getting logged into and personalizing their Ning pages and accounts for the first time.

Description of Activity

I set up my classroom Ning with students at the very beginning of the school year. I create a "group" for each subject I focus on. Once the Ning is initially set up, it just needs to be adjusted each new school year. All this requires is going to http://www.ning.com/ and creating a username and password login. Your username is part of the Ning address, such as www.turtlesteach.ning.com. Once you've created an account, you can walk through the various preferences to change the theme, colors, and privacy settings—all very similar to a Facebook or MySpace page.

I set the tone for the Ning at the start of the school year by telling students that this is their online forum for getting help and discussing topics and ideas with one another, and that we will use it in various ways throughout the school year. I normally give them a week after showing them the Ning to get their accounts set up. For some classes, I give students one period to get on, get set up, and play around a bit (the time depends on the class environment and students). I find that some students will need to create an email address first because they don't already have one. For some classes, I just show them the login process and ask them to have an account by the following class period or week. I often give little prizes and incentives (they *love* candy!) for the first posters and most creative uses of their pages to make it all a little more interesting.

Then when I set up the SSR format (or ISP—independent study project—for AP students), I revisit the Ning as their arena for posting their weekly reading reflections. We review the rubric guidelines and I explain how and where they need to post their work. I use the "group" function on the Ning because these are closed areas. Only those who have requested membership into that group are allowed to see or post in the area. I feel this is necessary to provide a comfortable environment in which students can be open and honest in their reflections. I encourage them to respond openly and honestly with their classmates in this forum (making this a part of their grade helps as well).

Assessment

Since my students are required to post weekly on the Ning based on their in-class SSR reading, I created a specific rubric that focuses on what I'm looking for (see Handout 8.2 in the supplemental materials). Most of the items are worth five points each, such as formatting correctly, posting correctly by the deadline, including the title (underlined), including author names, listing pages read with range, quoting with explanation, summarizing, using proper grammar and spelling (there is a spellcheck feature on the Ning), as well as the overall look. Two categories are worth more points because that's where I want students to focus: response to the book (their reaction/reflection) is worth twenty points, and their response with others is worth ten points. These online postings occur in the discussion forum, and I post a new thread (with the due date) each week on Thursday morning. I call them "reading reflections," so students have a week to create their posts before the deadline on Wednesday night at midnight.

Connections and Adaptations

Blogging

When members create an account on your Ning, they have their own page with their own preferences and themes. They also have an individual blog. From an assessment perspective, these are challenging because you physically have to navigate to every student's page. However, this tool is useful for an in-class culminating activity geared toward a specific book, such as posting an overall, theme-based question and having the students blog about it, or posting their essay responses. This is especially useful if you're trying to go paperless in your classroom.

Picture/Video Uploads

Students are able to upload pictures and videos to the Ning. This is a great avenue for assessing photography assignments or video projects. For example, my multimedia production students can upload their work directly to the website, which saves space and deals with the transfer issues. This feature requires Internet access in the classroom.

Adapting to Fee-Based Use of Ning

As of July 2010, the Ning network decided to move to paid services. As of this writing, they provide three pricing plans, the Ning Mini ($19.95/year, $2.95/month), Ning Plus ($199.95/year, $19.95/month), and Ning Pro ($499.95/year, $49.95/month). The Ning Mini is limited to up to 150 members but does not include groups. For teachers, 150 members should be enough in most cases. However, the ability to use groups is an option now available only in the Ning Plus package. A number of different features available through Ning Plus and other limitations with Ning Mini are all described at http://about.ning.com/plans/. The Ning Pro doesn't seem worth the investment from an educational standpoint, as the only difference between the Ning Plus and Pro is storage and bandwidth size, and the Plus package size would be sufficient.

One privacy feature that will soon be available is the ability to create a quiz or enable email verification for new members. This way you can avoid spammers by "testing" registrants to verify that they are eligible.

Work Cited

Kist, William. *The Socially Networked Classroom: Teaching in the New Media Age.* Thousand Oaks, CA: Corwin, 2010. Print.

9 Keep Them Talking about *The Fifth Child*: Reclaiming Instructional Time with Discussion Boards

Heather A. Ingraham
Niles North High School, Skokie, Illinois

Context

Located just beyond the northern edge of Chicago, Niles North High School features a remarkably diverse student population. Among our enrollment of approximately 2,100, the accents of more than forty different languages enhance classroom conversations, almost half of our population registers as students of color, and special educational inclusion can reach as high as 10 percent of mainstream classes (Niles North High School). We enjoy a vibrant atmosphere and work hard to meet our population's divergent needs.

Our district, like many others, must balance instructional time with the demands of standardized testing, professional development, and enrichment opportunities that take students out of the classroom. For this reason, online discussion boards hold strong appeal: they allow me to invite students, whatever their backgrounds, to join a shared and meaningful conversation that transcends interruptions. My students and I prize these conversations because they allow us to keep talking until we have asked questions and explored answers to a satisfying conclusion—not just to the end of the period. I first turned to discussion boards to reclaim instructional time during Advanced Placement exams, and now I regularly use them whenever classroom conversations run longer than the bell. This particular lesson plan uses discussion boards and a high-interest novel, Doris Lessing's *The Fifth Child*, to keep seniors talking—and learning—well into May.

Rationale

There are two parts to this rationale: why I value discussion boards as a Web 2.0 application, and why *The Fifth Child* kindles a good online discussion. The educational value of discussion boards has overcome my initial skepticism because, in contrast to some aspects of technology, they offer substance rather than sizzle. Time-intensive and requiring careful thought, discussion boards—in keeping with key tenets of NCTE's "Definition of 21st Century Literacies"—challenge students to work together to make meaning, a process my students generally enjoy and which alumni praise as having prepared them well for college. A discussion board's round-the-clock availability and generous "think time" allow students to participate at their own pace after sports, work, or activities, and to converse without the verbal anxiety sometimes caused by accents or autism. Egalitarian in form as well as spirit, a discussion board threads every student's voice equally, in contrast to a blog's dominant entry followed by subordinate comments. Because they work so well to foster meaningful exploration, I especially rely on discussion boards to bring closure to the open-ended questions that guide our curriculum's thematic units, and I offer the boards as a collaborative workspace for students to prepare for more traditional individual assessments. Therefore, online discussions provide the best of both worlds: I can monitor and reward individual participation while students direct their own learning and create meaning through shared inquiry, mutual feedback, and ongoing revision of ideas.

To fuel the online discussion, I choose a high-interest text that casts new light on the questions my students have been exploring in other readings. Doris Lessing's brief, powerful *The Fifth Child* concludes a unit exploring literary responses to violence, and it offers vivid connections to texts as varied as Shakespeare's *Macbeth*, Voltaire's *Candide*, Dostoevsky's *Crime and Punishment*, Conrad's *Heart of Darkness*, and Camus's *The Stranger*. By challenging students to address important ethical as well as narrative considerations, *The Fifth Child* typically elicits mature thought and nuanced writing, lets students work out real-world applications of issues we have discussed in more canonical texts, and keeps seniors engaged even at the end of the second semester.

Objectives

Students will be able to:

- Read individually and work collaboratively to analyze a challenging noncanonical text as part of a larger literary unit

- Identify and analyze the author's thesis on violence and argue the implications of that thesis for real-world experience
- Write with care and precision about sensitive subject matter for an audience of peers and adults
- Continue learning even when not in class

NCTE/IRA standards addressed: 2, 3, 5, 11

Materials/Preactivity Preparation

- Doris Lessing's *The Fifth Child*
- Opening questions for *The Fifth Child*
- Discussion board contract for *The Fifth Child*
- Discussion board evaluation form for *The Fifth Child*
- An online discussion board (available through Akiva, Blackboard, Microsoft, phpBB, or other providers)

Preparation for Teachers

Before beginning an online discussion with students, it is a good idea to participate in one yourself; a continuing education course with an online component can provide helpful experience. You might also find that an informal discussion, though nonacademic, offers an introduction to social netiquette, the appropriate length and tone of posts, the art of surviving technological glitches, and the joy of connecting through ideas. By doing so, you will learn what it feels like to write a heartfelt post only to have users ignore it for being lengthy or off-topic, how flammable jokes can become in the absence of face-to-face social cues, and how rewarding it feels to see your ideas become part of an extended conversation. Choose a discussion with which you feel comfortable and where the focus remains professional rather than personal, and then join in until you get the hang of it.

Preparation for Students

Tech-savvy individuals can post immediately to almost any format, but each new group of students will benefit from the chance to learn software-specific skills and to develop a sense of community. My classes spend a full day in the school's computer lab to learn login procedures, review the school's Acceptable Use Policy, discuss the grading contract (see Handout 9.1 in the supplemental materials), and practice responding to conversational questions. Specifically, I want each student to know how to reply to an existing thread, how to begin a new topic, how to log in from a remote location, and how to sort posts by subject, by username, and by oldest-to-newest (conversational order) or newest-to-oldest (useful for seeing what's new). These technological skills vary by software, which often changes over the summer, so I learn as much as my students do from this investment of time. Once the technological elements are attended to, our class can focus on analyzing literary content and developing the respectful give-and-take that characterizes the most successful online learning communities. By the time my students begin *The Fifth Child* discussion board in May, they are well-versed in online etiquette, have strengthened their voices as writers, can successfully collaborate with and challenge one another to present insightful readings, and can discuss sensitive subjects with both directness and diplomacy.

Especially if this is your first time hosting an online discussion, I recommend following the initial evening of posting with a full class period to review what worked and what could have been better. Frequently, a commendable desire to support their peers will lead classmates to post "I agree!" statements, but these fail to advance the conversation. Shallow or repetitive entries will kill a discussion board, so I take class time to review the initial posts and tease out subtle details; differing interpretations create more interesting dialogue. Be explicit about what you hope to see. For instance, I advise students to blend affirmation ("I like what you said about . . .") with constructive challenge ("but the author also suggests . . .") and exploration ("so I wonder if we could accurately say . . ."). This kind of follow-up instruction takes time, but it reinforces good writing practices and creates a far more rewarding learning environment.

To cultivate that environment, I invite students to respond to one another by name, build community by connecting ideas from more than one person's posting, and alert me by email to any problems. Students who respond only with emotion must be prompted to include evidence; students who quote only the assigned texts need to acknowledge classmates' ideas. It may also be worthwhile to differentiate a discussion board from a study guide. Whereas study guides ask students to provide concrete answers, discussion boards lead beyond the literal to the possible: authorial intent, social implications, and long-term relevance make great subjects for developing inferences. When my students become confident about asking thoughtful and open-ended questions, I know they are creating real meaning.

Finally, be prepared to adapt: as the Internet evolves and students' needs change, so do my responsibilities as teacher. Five years ago, I spent a fair amount of time helping students resolve how-to problems with uncooperative software, whereas now I find myself prompting students to write in greater depth, as appropriate for academic discourse rather than Facebook, and asking them to wait patiently for responses to develop. One particularly strong exchange (see Handout 9.2 in the supplemental materials) evolved over a period of several nights, but I have to work with some groups not to demand instant gratification. For the habitually impatient, I recommend checking the discussion board only once in any 24-hour period. I also remind students that this is not a standardized test with only one correct answer: when encouraged to revisit their own posts, my seniors often discover how much their thinking has changed over the time the discussion board has been active.

Time Frame

For beginning users, I schedule at least two 40-minute class periods (one in the computer lab, one in the classroom) to familiarize students with online discussion. For experienced users, I need only about 10 minutes of direct classroom instruction—a review of online policies and procedures, an introduction to *The Fifth Child*, and a reminder of my expectations and the grading contract—before beginning the following lesson. The discussion board itself requires no in-class time and can run from three days to several more, depending on your needs. During AP testing, when my seniors miss a lot of class, I provide a full week to allow them time to read, think, and post between exams. When students return, I usually schedule a follow-up day to bring the discussion back into the classroom.

Description of Activity

A few days before Advanced Placement exams begin, I distribute Doris Lessing's *The Fifth Child*, the discussion board contract, opening questions, and sample grading sheets. I then encourage students to start reading. Especially during the first week of AP testing, when attendance is irregular, I use class time for individual writing conferences on the senior thesis. Students read and post from home, which fosters a nice sense of community during this stressful exam period.

To foster active and frequent participation, I set up a new question every twenty-five pages, which allows students to join the conversation immediately, even before they finish the book. Although I post opening prompts, students drive the discussion by developing their own questions as they read. As a bonus, the book reads so quickly and proves so gripping that many students finish it in one sitting and add *The Fifth Child* to their list of exam-worthy texts.

My opening questions are simple, highlighting textual specifics but worded broadly enough to allow students a wide range of possible responses. The goal is to have students propose and explore new questions with one another, not hand in "answers" to me.

- Pages 1–25: What are your thoughts on the characters, their courtship and marriage, the pace of the Lovatts' childbearing? What passages, about the house or anything else, stand out, and why?

- Pages 26–50: What reasons has Lessing provided, either directly or indirectly, for why the fifth child behaves the way he does? What passages stand out, and why?

- Pages 51–75: Discuss the effect Ben has on his family and the people around him. What actions, passages, or narrative techniques evoke your revulsion or sympathy for Ben, and why?

- Pages 76–100: Comment on the decision Harriet faces about whether to institutionalize Ben. Did she make the right decision(s)? Did David? How did Lessing's portrayal of the institution influence your feelings? In what ways might this scene be metaphorical for how we treat anyone who is "other"?

- Pages 100–133: What do you make of Ben's social interactions, first with John and his pals, and later with the second group of boys? Is this a positive or a negative development, and why? What might Lessing be prodding us to recognize, question, or do?

- Closing Questions: In many ways, this book takes us full circle in our curriculum and returns us to themes regarding the limits of ambition, the sources and control of violence, and having a socially responsible role to play, and it incorporates elements of tragedy, comedy, and satire. What answers does this book provide, and to what questions? What questions does it raise but leave unanswered? What thematic, genre, and/or philosophical conversations might this book create with previous texts?

As the discussion board dialogue develops, it is imperative to monitor tone as well as content. No matter how experienced my students are with online discussions, I log in to the board each night to supervise their work. Inappropriate posts or hurt feelings happen infrequently but must be dealt with immediately. I send a private email if an entry can be edited before others see it, but if a post has already received responses or if students are recycling a sustained misreading, I address this publicly. Otherwise, I let my students do the writing as they direct the discussion.

Eventually, when it comes time to bring our online discussion back into the classroom, I select a topic for a brief reflective writing assignment. Unresolved questions and heated exchanges provide good starting points. Once students finish writing, I select volunteers to begin the discussion and remind them to refer to classmates' online work; the conversation usually picks up right where it should. Even better, some of the quieter kids will have enjoyed chatting online and will now join the class discussion. I give students at least one class period to balance affective responses with continued exploration of the book's intellectual elements before moving on. Finally, I solicit student feedback on what worked well and what could be improved for future boards. I usually ask for this in writing so that I can refer to it later, but it works just as well in class discussion. You can ask for student feedback anonymously or face-to-face, depending on what you deem appropriate.

Assessment

One of the hardest things for me to figure out when I first started using discussion boards was how to grade them. An active weeklong board can easily generate a hundred printed pages, especially with large classes, and I struggled to manage the sheer volume of posts and the occasional irregularities of students' online writing. With experience, I have learned that establishing a grading contract not only lets me grade more efficiently but also helps students understand my expectations. Students may have been texting and social networking for years, but they are generally not accustomed to having their online writing evaluated, and some will struggle to shed "textspeak" for academic discourse. The grading contract (see Handout 9.1 in the supplemental materials) helps everyone understand what is expected, and our online conversations have exhibited consistently greater quality since I introduced these guidelines.

The grading contract specifies that I evaluate my students' work based on both quantitative (number and timing of posts) and qualitative (insight, evidence, editing, and argument) elements. Poorly written or inappropriate posts receive no credit. The discussion board uses these basic criteria:

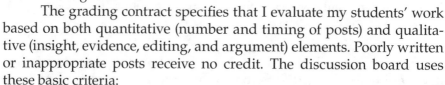

- **To Be Eligible for a "C":** Read the book; engage in adequate, textually based online conversation; and post a minimum of five times (on at least three separate days) before the deadline.

- **To Be Eligible for "B":** Read the book; engage in responsive, textually based online conversation; and post a minimum of seven times (on at least four separate days) before the deadline.

- **To Be Eligible for an "A":** Read the book; engage in insightful, responsive, textually based online conversation; and post a minimum of ten times (on at least five separate days) before the deadline.

- **Note:** Meeting minimum requirements does not guarantee full credit. Editing, insight, and timing also factor into the grade.

These minimum numbers may not sound especially taxing, but a good discussion board requires users to read and think about one another's posts—a significant investment of students' time. I find that asking for one or two thoughtful posts each day elicits better responses than demanding three or more; I want to emphasize careful reading, writing, and reconsideration rather than verbiage.

The process of evaluating student posts varies somewhat according to different discussions, but I always use tally sheets with boxes representing each day the board was active. I read and record each post with a check (adequate), check-plus (superior), or check-minus (inadequate or inadequately edited) for the day it was posted. This system makes it easy to review the posts and quickly summarize their quality by eyeballing the check-plus or check-minus marks. This combination of qualitative and quantitative elements can then be translated into a final grade. I assess timing (see Handout 9.3 in the supplemental materials) because twelve responses distributed over several days generally contribute more to the conversation than a flurry of twelve posts in the closing minutes of the final night. Such reading and tallying can be labor-intensive, but it is worth it to me to regain instructional time. Making the process easier is the fact that my seniors generally enjoy this assignment and produce high-quality work, a special treat when many classes are battling senioritis.

Connections and Adaptations

As noted earlier, other works in this unit might include *Macbeth*, *Crime and Punishment*, *Candide*, *Heart of Darkness*, or *The Stranger*, and I usually follow *The Fifth Child* with critical viewing and online discussion of a film, either Coppola's *Apocalypse Now* or Eastwood's *Unforgiven*. A non-AP class might use Lessing's novel as a capstone work accompanying a variety of stories and poems or another full-length text, and I have had good luck pairing it with Richard Matheson's "Born of Man and Woman" in lower-level classes. You can substitute any high-interest work that fits your curriculum. By varying the reading material, questions, and time frame to meet the needs of specific users, I feel that any instructor whose classes have online access can adapt the discussion board format to enhance student learning.

But *do* all students have online access? With nearly one-quarter of my school's students qualifying for free or reduced lunch (District 219), I must schedule lab time or provide study hall computer passes to make sure that every student has access to the online discussion. This might seem like a redundancy—if they're in school, why not converse face-to-face?—but experience suggests that writing out their thoughts creates greater confidence and, over time, greater ability. Developing readers and writers will need more structure, supervision, and daily feedback to foster success, but online discussions can work for them. The larger class sizes and less polished writing of non-AP students can create certain challenges, but illustrative samples and clear expectations provide helpful guidance. With appropriate adaptations, these very deserving students can enjoy the same benefits of online discussion as their more privileged peers.

Finally, other kinds of discussion boards provide other kinds of rewards. My regular-level seniors engage in collaborative research leading to the senior thesis, and they particularly benefit from two aspects of the discussion board: the chance for everyone to be heard (not always easy in large classes) and the opportunity to test their hypotheses among supportive peers before committing their ideas to paper. I have also used discussion boards to document individual contributions to group projects, help students plan oral poetry presentations, create shared audiences for independent reading, extend the critical discussions of films we view in class, build cultural literacies through the exploration of literary allusions, and review course materials for unit or semester exams.

Works Cited in Lesson

District 219 Niles Township High Schools. "2008 Illinois School Report Card: Niles North High School." *District 219 Niles North High Schools.* NTHS Website Documents, n.d. Web. 14 Dec. 2009. http://sharepoint.niles-hs .k12.il.us/webdocs/School%20Report%20Cards/Forms/AllItems.aspx.

Lessing, Doris. *The Fifth Child*. New York: Vintage International, 1988. Print.

Matheson, Richard. "Born of Man and Woman." *Duel: Terror Stories*. New York: Tor, 2003. 65–68. Print.

National Council of Teachers of English. "Position Statement: The NCTE Definition of 21st Century Literacies." *National Council of Teachers of English*, 15 Feb. 2008. Web. 24 Nov. 2009.

Niles North High School. "2008–09 Profile of District 219: Niles North High School." *Niles North High School*, n.d. Schools/College Resources/College Career Resource Center 16 May 2009.

Works Cited in Supplemental Materials

Fox, Clayton. Post to AP English Discussion Board on *The Fifth Child*. *Miss Heather Ingraham's Niles North Website*, 10 May 2007. Web.

Hakimi, Nathan. Post to AP English Discussion Board on *The Fifth Child*. *Miss Heather Ingraham's Niles North Website*, 8 May 2007. Web.

McGowan, Josh. Post to AP English Discussion Board on *The Fifth Child*. *Miss Heather Ingraham's Niles North Website*, 9 May 2007. Web.

Vernon, Marian. Post to AP English Discussion Board on *The Fifth Child*. *Miss Heather Ingraham's Niles North Website*, 8 May 2007. Web.

10 *Crash* into Prejudice: Cinema Studies in a Web 2.0 Environment

Anna Meyers Caccitolo
Lyons Township High School, LaGrange, Illinois

Context

Lyons Township High School is a public high school in the western suburbs of Chicago that hosts around 4,000 students. During sophomore year, most students (at varying ability levels) are required to take a course entitled Interpersonal Communications (IPC), which is a semester English course that focuses on what we communicate, why we communicate, and how we communicate. It was developed in early 2005 by a panel of speech-certified teachers to better prepare students for 21st century literacy and learning, focusing on the idea that all students need to be competent communicators. The units include Oral Literacy, Media Literacy, and Cultural Literacy. These units evolve every year as current communication styles dictate; the course changes as society changes. This specific lesson plan fits into the Cultural Literacy unit and challenges students to use a discussion board to debate issues surrounding racism and prejudice.

Rationale

Traditionally, students have a difficult time discussing issues concerning racism, prejudice, stereotyping, etc.—these are controversial topics for most adults. It is a huge risk to share an opinion on any of these subjects while surrounded by peers. The movie *Crash* is simply a vehicle to get students thinking about prejudice and how it plays into everyday life. To analyze the characters and the decisions they make, students draw from personal experiences and explore their own biases. They are forced to use critical thinking skills to analyze a complicated text while connecting it to both personal and societal prejudices. Given the subject matter, students might be hesitant to discuss these issues out loud. Therefore, the discussion board functions as a medium for the students' voices. Because students have grown up discussing personal issues through media (e.g., Facebook, MySpace, texting), they are more willing to share their opinions in this venue. They are comfortable with Internet communication and view it as less of a risk than face-to-face discussion. The questions asked on the discussion board force students to share beliefs about the characters' choices and make personal connections at the same time using a familiar medium.

Objectives

Students will be able to:

- Evaluate the movie *Crash* and analyze which biases and stereotypes cause the characters to make their choices
- Analyze the evolution of the characters in *Crash,* tracking changes in their belief systems as the movie progresses
- Synthesize the information from *Crash* through an online discussion board and apply it to current society

NCTE/IRA standards addressed: 1, 4, 5, 6

Materials/Preactivity Preparation

- A copy of the movie *Crash*
- A DVD player, VCR, or projector
- Access to an online discussion board
- Student access to computers, either in class or at home

Before the lesson begins, give students permission slips for viewing the movie *Crash* (see Handout 10.1, a sample permission slip that includes a viewing rationale). The film is rated R for strong language and a brief scene of sexuality, which I choose not to show in class. Then preview the movie—it is a fairly intense film with a multitude of overlapping storylines and characters—and set up the discussion board.

I use the Turnitin discussion board because it is already provided by our district, but other free discussion boards are available at Google Groups, Goodreads, and Blogger. Another option is Google Docs; although it is not an actual discussion board, Google Docs creates a document that all students can see and to which they can respond. Regardless of which discussion board you use, both you and the students need to create individual accounts. Once everyone has an account, you can log in and invite students to join the group/discussion board by entering the students' email addresses when prompted.

Once you have invited all your students, create a new post or discussion topic and let students reply.

Time Frame

This lesson plan will require three to four 50-minute class periods to show the film and have a meaningful discussion of the postings. *Crash* is 112 minutes long, which allows for approximately 40 minutes of class discussion on the third day. Before the third day, students will be posting to the discussion board each night for homework. Note that once you have all finished watching the movie, students may have questions about the plot. They might want to spend time clarifying how the characters fit together and what the ending means, and some will even want to replay parts of the film (they *love* this film). If you want to limit the lesson to a total of three days, keep this discussion to a minimum. If a four-day lesson fits your schedule, this discussion can continue for an extended time and the postings conversation can take place on the fourth day.

Description of Activity

Before we begin watching the movie, I display the discussion board through my computer, projector, and onto a screen. At this point, I model exactly how to post. I model a sample response so students can watch the entire process, and we discuss what makes a quality post. I show both strong and weak posts, and the class discusses what elements help strengthen a post: length, specific references to characters' thoughts and actions, real-life examples that connect to the film, and so forth. I also remind students that since this is an English class, they are to respond professionally to their peers and think of their writing as a paragraph in a published essay. Without this warning, students will sometimes compose one- or two-line posts written in shorthand language. I then explain that after they view the film in class each day, they will need to do one posting for homework. All postings are labeled separately (Crash Posting Night #1, Crash Posting Night #2, etc.) so students know where and when to respond. They post once each night of the movie and every night respond to a different topic. You can, of course, assign as many postings as you see fit. I also let students know that they have two choices when it comes to postings: they can respond directly to the questions asked, or they can reply to something another student has said. This is a great way to get them dialoguing on the discussion board. Examples of topics used in the past include the following:

1. Think about Sandra Bullock's (Jean's) reaction before the carjacking. When she sees the two African American men, she grabs her husband's arm. Do you feel her reaction is prejudiced? Why or why not? Should she have said something to her husband when she "got scared," or does that make her racist? How so?

2. Is the scene where Sandra Bullock (Jean) goes on a rant about the man changing her locks an example of racism? Why or why not? Considering that she was carjacked earlier that night and feels it was her fault because she "didn't say anything" when she "got scared," is she justified in her remarks? Is it more "okay" because of her earlier experience?

3. Do you feel that the first incident involving the police officer and the African American couple is an incident of racial profiling, or did Officer Ryan pull them over for another reason? Do you feel he would have pulled them over if they were Caucasian? Do you believe in racial profiling? Why or why not? Give an example to prove your point.

4. When the Persian man wanted to buy the gun, the store owner refused him. Do you think race played a role? Do you feel he should have refused him? Would you refuse him? If he was of another race, would your answer change? Explain. What if he spoke English? Would that change your answer or the reaction of the store owner?

5. If the Persian man were Arabic, would it be right to refuse to sell him a weapon after the 9/11 attacks? Why or why not? Let's say this was an in-class discussion and I called on you to answer this question; would your answer be different? Explain.

6. Is Officer Hansen guilty of a hate crime? A hate crime is defined in *Merriam-Webster*'s online dictionary as "any of various crimes (as assault or defacement of property) when motivated by hostility to the victim as a member of a group (as one based on color, creed, gender, or sexual orientation)." Did he shoot because he was prejudiced against the African American man, or did he feel threatened and respond purely in self-defense? Cite specific examples from the scene to support your answer.

7. *Crash* goes full circle as a movie. Do you think that any of the characters' actions negate what they did earlier? For example, does the fact that Officer Ryan saves the African American woman from the exploding car make the first incident of "searching" okay? Are they "even" now? In other words, are

these incidents of stereotyping and prejudice lessened now that they "made up" for them? Is it just human nature to make mistakes and then do what we can to fix them? Or were the first incidents so bad that they could never be forgiven? Can racism be forgiven? Can prejudice be changed?

Once the discussion board demonstration is over, I remind students of one last thing: pay close attention to even the smallest parts of the film, even what is omitted, because *it all matters*. For instance, the character's names are rarely stated, and with the multitude of characters, it is easy to miss them. Following any last-minute clarifying questions, I begin the film. At the end of class each day, I remind students that they need to do their postings for homework. My deadline requires that they post on the message board before class the next day.

The next step is to print out the postings and look for possible discussion starters and debatable statements. I highlight controversial statements and generate possible discussion questions. On the third day (once the film is over), we have a quick in-class conversation to set norms since the upcoming discussion revolves around sensitive topics. You can do this any way you like, but it's a good idea to preface the conversation with some kind of reminder. I focus on the fact that my classroom is a safe space and encourage everyone to share their opinions, keeping in mind that others may not agree. We discuss that it is *the way* they share their opinions that is most important. Then I tell students I am going to read some of the postings out loud and stress that the authors *should not* reveal themselves. (Sometimes the students want to, but this usually ends badly.) Then, one by one I read the statements aloud, asking the corresponding questions. I include here one sample posting response from my sophomore accelerated IPC class and the corresponding discussion questions. This post is in response to questions 1 and 2 above.

> I think her response of grabbing her husband's arm isn't out of racism. They are on an empty street, and are being approached by two shady looking men. I would admit I would be slightly uncomfortable, regardless of their race. Perhaps in her mind it was racism, because her comments later on make her seem a bit prejudiced. I don't think her remarks about the man changing her locks were at all justifiable. Just because earlier she was attacked by two black men doesn't give her the right to judge a completely unrelated Hispanic man changing her locks. I understand she was still frightened, but stereotyping is never justifiable.

Corresponding Discussion Questions

- What defines a "shady looking man"?
- What characteristics does he have?
- If I use the term *shady*, do you always think of a man? Do you think of a woman? Why?
- This person said "I would be slightly uncomfortable, regardless of race." Do you think that is the case? For example, if you are a white male and you see two white males approaching, would you be afraid?
- How does the situation change if you are a white male and two black males approach? How would this change if you are a female and see two males approaching?
- This student made the statement that "stereotyping is never justifiable." Is that a true statement? Why or why not? Can you think of a time when stereotyping is justifiable? Be specific.

As a side note, I usually keep all the postings until we're done watching the the movie, and we discuss them on the last day. However, you might want to have a short discussion to begin class each day before continuing the film. This could be a great way to get students refocused. Just be careful to limit the discussion, because students tend to get into heated debates about these topics, and it may be difficult to cut them off to finish the film.

Assessment

The great thing about this particular assignment is that there are a variety of ways to assess it. At the end of this cycle, you will have multiple days of postings at your disposal. Traditionally, I assess each individual posting according to these criteria:

- Did the student answer all the questions? Was the content of the posting substantial?
- Did the student provide examples from the film or personal experience to back up his or her opinion?
- Did the student synthesize the information from *Crash* and apply it to current society?

Another exercise is to take statements from the postings and hold a formal class debate. Take, for example, the statement "stereotyping is never justifiable." I would pair up students, one who feels stereotyping is justifiable with one who does not. They research examples of past stereotyping, compile information, and prove their points during a formal in-class debate. One student presents his or her side in a formal speech (possibly 3 minutes), and then the partner arguing the other side speaks. Once both sides have presented their case, open debating begins. Since students tend to enjoy this part of the activity, you might want to set a time limit (possibly 5 minutes) and keep a countdown. Once time is up, each student can make a short (30 seconds to 1 minute) closing argument. As a fun component, you could have students vote on who won the debate. As my class is about interpersonal communications, the debaters are graded on both the content of their manuscripts and the six speaking traits they develop during the course:

- Did the student write a coherent essay? Did the student use proper transitions to link ideas? Did the student employ research effectively to prove his or her point? Did the student choose valuable research sources?
- How did the student perform on each of the six speaking traits?
  - ◆ Eye contact
  - ◆ Physical expression
  - ◆ Pitch/Emphasis
  - ◆ Rate/Fluency
  - ◆ Volume
  - ◆ Articulation

If you aren't interested in including a speaking component, forget the debate and have students compile their information in a formal persuasive writing assignment instead. Of all the possible assessments, grading the individual postings has worked best for me because it forces students to create quality responses, preserves the integrity of the discussion board, and helps prompt a valuable in-class discussion.

Connections and Adaptations

In the past, I have also paired Reginald Rose's *Twelve Angry Men* with the viewing of *Crash* and the use of the discussion board. As the jurors in *Twelve Angry Men* also battle prejudices, it is a great comparison/contrast exercise to discuss it along with *Crash*. For example: "What does Juror 3 have in common with Officer Ryan? How do their prejudices influence their decision making?" Also, this lesson easily can be adapted across levels to fit any unit or text. When teaching *Romeo and Juliet*, for example, you can simply post the following statement: "The Beatles feel 'All you need is love.' Do people need only love? Can people survive on love alone? Respond to this question through the eyes of one of the characters in *Romeo and Juliet*. Choose a quotation to support your point." Students can also respond to this statement more than once; they can trace the character's feelings (and themes) throughout the play. For example, "Would Romeo respond differently at the beginning of the play versus at the end of the play? What about Juliet? How would the Friar feel?" This type of exercise can work with any piece of literature.

Works Cited

Heilbroner, Robert L. "Don't Let Stereotypes Warp Your Judgment." *We Are America: A Thematic Reader and Guide to Writing.* Anna Joy. 6th ed. Boston: Thomson Wadsworth, 2008. 372–75. Print.

Blogger. 1999–2009. Google. Web. 9 Nov. 2009.

Crash. Dir. Paul Haggis. Perf. Sandra Bullock, Don Cheadle, Matt Dillon, Terrence Howard, Chris "Ludacris" Bridges, Thandie Newton, Ryan Phillippe, and Larenz Tate. 2004. Lions Gate Entertainment, 2005. DVD.

Good Reads. 2009. Good Reads. Web. 9 Nov. 2009.

Google Docs. 2009. Google. Web. 9 Nov. 2009.

Google Groups. 2009. Google. Web. 9 Nov. 2009.

Rose, Reginald. *Twelve Angry Men.* Woodstock, IL: Dramatic, 1983. Print.

Shakespeare, William. *The Tragedy of Romeo and Juliet.* Ed. Barbara A. Mowat and Paul Werstine. New York: Simon & Schuster, 2009. Print.

Turnitin. 2008. iParadigms, LLC. Web. 9 Nov. 2009. http://www.turnitin.com.

Supplemental Reading

A great article is "Don't Let Stereotypes Warp Your Judgments" by Robert L. Heilbroner. This article explains why the human brain relies on stereotyping as a way to categorize the changing world. I use it in conjunction with the worksheet "Isms" (see Handout 10.2 in the supplemental materials). The class reads the article, fills in the worksheet, and holds a discussion before we watch *Crash.* It also works well to include this article while discussing the postings the day after viewing the movie.

11 Write Your Own Adventure: A Lesson in Collaborative Writing Using Webspiration

Katherine Higgs-Coulthard
Michiana Writers' Center, South Bend, Indiana

Context

Michiana Writers' Center is located in South Bend, the fourth largest city in Indiana. While South Bend itself has a population of just over 100,000, the city is a hub for other communities within the Michiana area and encompasses several college campuses, including Notre Dame, Indiana University at South Bend, Bethel College, and Saint Mary's. All told, the regional population is more than 800,000.

Our writers' center was formed by several teacher consultants of the National Writing Project's northern Indiana site, the Hoosier Writing Project. Designed to serve as a resource for local writers and teachers of writing, our center provides writing classes and workshops for individuals of all ages and abilities, is involved in summer youth writing camps, and works closely with several local school districts to provide teacher inservices, parent education, and classroom writing opportunities.

Our primary goal is to support writers, but as classroom teachers we can't resist the urge to hook children who may not yet consider themselves writers. To that end, we have designed several high-interest, low-ability workshops for use in local schools. One such workshop is the "Write Your Own Adventure." The lesson is flexible by nature and may be used with a variety of populations.

Rationale

It is nearly impossible to design a writing prompt that will appeal to every student in a deep and meaningful way. Often such attempts result in generic prompts, like "Think of a time when you've been scared. What frightened you? How did you cope with your fear? How did this situation impact the person you have become?" Some students may dig deep and respond on a personal level, but many others will write superficially, without investing much of themselves in the piece.

Much research has been done into the reluctance of students to engage in writing tasks, but Bruning and Horn believe that disengagement tends to be the result of lack of motivation: "Writers need to develop strong beliefs in the relevance and importance of writing and as they grapple with writing's complexities and frustrations" (26). Ralph Fletcher, citing the energy children will devote to instant messaging (IMing), suggests that students may begin to see writing tasks as relevant and important when writing is linked with social interaction:

> When boys send off an IM they get an almost immediate reaction from another person. It's like playing catch; one boy tosses a verbal ball to his friend, confident that his friend will throw it back. This social dynamic keeps the energy high, the conversation moving, and the writing flowing. (35)

Another component that affects student motivation is choice. As in the previous generic example, the teacher might think choice is built into the prompt; the students are not told to write about being scared of storms, but allowed to choose any situation in which they have experienced fear. Students, however, see only a directive: write about fear.

This lesson is designed to capitalize on the social dynamic of writing while allowing for maximum student choice. Students can create their story tree in any genre, addressing any topic. Further, they decide which stories to contribute to, based on their own preferences for certain genres, topics, and word limits. As classmates choose to extend one another's stories, they simultaneously reinforce the original writer's efforts while increasing the original author's motivation to add more to his or her own story, effectively re-creating Fletcher's game of verbal catch.

Like most classroom situations, this activity is deepened through teacher participation. When students see teachers take risks by writing within student-determined confines, students become more willing to take risks themselves.

Objectives

Students will be able to:

- Describe the features and possible uses of Webspiration tools
- Create their own story tree documents using Webspiration

- Create collaborative groups, invite users, and manage sharing within their Webspiration documents

- Import graphics into Webspiration documents

- Edit and expand on their own and other students' Webspiration documents

NCTE/IRA standards addressed: 5, 6, 11

Materials/Preactivity Preparation

- Teacher access to the Webspiration website and a basic knowledge of how to use it.

- One sample story tree from the One Million Monkeys Typing website (http://www.1000000monkeys.com/) for group analysis. It's best to access it live online and project it on a screen, although it can be printed and photocopied for the class.

- Student access to computers during class time.

Before beginning the lesson, visit the One Million Monkeys Typing website (Kreymerman and Zito) and select a story that will interest most students. The stories on the site are organic; they grow as writers contribute snippets. Contributing writers are encouraged to rate their snippets PG or R in content, but you may find the rating system does not adequately reflect the preferences of your school setting. As a result, I encourage you to read as much of the story as possible and use only what you have previewed as an example for the class. When I last checked, "Brendan Metcalf Saves the Universe" was a new story tree planted by one of the site's most prolific contributors. The story features a teenage boy who discovers that his job site is built upon an ancient burial ground. Ideally, you should display the actual website on a projector so your class can see how the site operates. If a projector is not available, print out the story snippets.

Time Frame

This lesson will require one 50-minute class period to acquaint students with the idea of story trees as collaborative writing and another one or two 50-minute sessions to introduce the Webspiration program, explain how it facilitates collaborative writing, and get students started on the project. The rest of the process can be completed outside of class over one to two weeks, depending on how long the students' motivation sustains the growth of story threads. At the conclusion of the project, devote another class period to analysis and reflection on the experience.

Description of Activity

A great entry point into this activity is through a discussion of movies and books with disappointing endings. It may be necessary to prod students' memories by invoking a recent movie that ended with a cliffhanger or has differed significantly from the novel version. Usually students have very strong opinions about how movies and books could have been better if only the author had [killed off the main character/ added in another car chase/made the hero fall in love with someone else/let the villain get away with it, . . .]. One example I have used is the ever-popular Twilight Saga. Many of the girls in my classes have been rooting for Bella to fall in love with Jacob Black, Edward's nemesis. A discussion of how they would rewrite the books or reshoot the movies to make that happen is always lively. The discussion might segue into times the students themselves have had to make choices in their writing and the rationale for such decisions.

To guide the discussion toward our upcoming project, I bring out old copies from the Choose Your Own Adventure series that was popular back in the 1980s. Students get in groups of three to four to read part of the book aloud and make decisions together on how to proceed within the book. We then come back together to discuss the basic premise of reader as decision maker, and I pose a few questions:

- What if the reader could do more than select from predetermined choices?
- What if the reader could create the choices and their consequences?

I then introduce the One Million Monkeys Typing website using a projector. We peruse several story seeds and eventually read a sample story, with students choosing which branches to take. Although One Million Monkeys Typing does not follow the Choose Your Own Adventure format (with the exception of one recent contribution), students are able to see how the choices made by each successive writer change the shape and underlying meaning of each story. As we read, I ask students to think about:

- Which story seeds have the most offshoots?
- Which characteristics contribute to the growth of the story tree?
- What unwritten rules do writers follow as they contribute to the story trees of others?
- What, if anything, happens to a story tree when a writer violates those rules?

If time allows, I invite the class to help me extend the story by "grafting on" a new snippet. Note: While the general public may access the stories on One Million Monkeys Typing, only those who have officially become members through the free registration process can contribute to stories.

For homework, I require students to create their own story seeds modeled after the One Million Monkeys Typing site. Each seed must set up the beginning scene of a story so that successive writers know the main character(s), genre, and student-determined word count of snippets, as well as some idea of the intended plot.

For the second class period, I introduce Webspiration as a vehicle for students to create their own story trees. Again, I use the projector to guide students in setting up their own Webspiration accounts and creating story tree documents. I have had the most success through requiring students to use a preexisting template, preferably the tree chart template, although that template needs modification—a few branches are dead ends, which can be deleted or left as an option for quick endings. The tree chart most resembles the branch-like structure found on the One Million Monkeys Typing website, which we have used as a guide. Other templates available from Webspiration are either too complex or too simplistic for creating a story tree.

On the screen, I demonstrate how to choose a template and begin a document, as well as how students can save their own story trees using their last names followed by the titles of their stories. Once each student has her or his own document, I demonstrate the procedure for laying out the story using the template:

- The story title and the creator's name go in the top box (referred to as a "symbol" in Webspiration).
- The opening scene is added as a "note" linked to that first symbol. To create a note, select the symbol, then click on the Note icon in the toolbar.
- As new snippets are added to the story tree, the contributing author will enter the title of her snippet, followed by her own name, in the symbol that builds on the last snippet. Her text will be linked in note form to the symbol containing her name and title.

For students to contribute to one another's story trees, you'll need to create contributor groups and have students invite one another as collaborators. Although the procedure for this is available on the Webspiration Help page, it is not explained well. Students should click on "Manage Documents" on the toolbar and select the Invite icon, inputting the email addresses of fellow students or selecting a preestablished collaboration group that you have set up. It is also vital that you be invited as a collaborator so that you can assess the project.

Once we have gone over how to work within the Webspiration program, I give students the actual assignment, which has four components. Each student must:

- Establish his own story tree
- Contribute to the story trees of at least ten classmates
- Complete a peer assessment
- Reflect on his participation in the story tree process and suggest improvements for future collaborative writing projects

Assessment

At the conclusion of the story tree project, students are required to hand in a reflection paper that includes the following components.

Document Trail

The Document Trail (see Handout 11.1 in the supplemental materials) allows me to easily trace the work students have completed. It includes

- A printout of the student's initial story tree seed, along with its corresponding Webspiration document name.
- A list of snippets the student has contributed to the story trees of at least ten classmates, along with those corresponding Webspiration document names. Note: I do allow students to contribute more than one snippet to a particular classmate's tree, but that is in addition to the work they do on the trees of ten different classmates.

Peer Assessment

Peer assessment requires students to examine the complete story tree of one classmate. The purpose of this activity is to examine the organic nature of collaborative writing, not necessarily to assess the writing of one's peer. Students use a response form (see Handout 11.2) that addresses:

- The effectiveness of the initial story seed:

    Did the writer include enough information for subsequent writers to build on the tree?

    Was the story's premise strong enough to attract contributors?

    Did the seed generate three separate branches?

    Were the branches different enough to create three separate story lines?

- The overall growth of the tree:

  How many writers contributed to this tree?

  How did their contributions shape the tree's growth?

  Which branches grew the most offshoots?

  What factors may have contributed to the growth of some branches and the failure of others?

Reflection

When assessing this project, I avoid linking the growth of students' trees directly to their grades. While I do expect them to realize that the quality of their initial seeds impacts the number of contributing writers they attract, other factors can influence tree growth. I look for students to address those factors in their reflection pieces. For guidance, I suggest students address at least three of the following questions in their reflection:

- Which story seeds grew the largest trees? What do those seeds have in common? Which ones withered? Why?

- Does a student's social standing impact the growth of her tree?

- What impact do genre, word limit, and title have on tree growth?

- What rules would you create for a group of writers wishing to collaborate?

- How did knowing you were going to contribute to stories change the way you read? Has this spilled over into other areas of reading?

- How has this experience affected your view of writing? Will you have more or less confidence in your own writing?

Connections and Adaptations

In my work with local school corporations, the recurring theme seems to be a need to increase student motivation. As I struggled to help teachers create dynamic lessons that addressed standards, I came upon Ralph Fletcher's comparison of instant messaging to high-interest, low-ability writing. With that in mind, this lesson was designed with the intention of hooking disengaged students by building in components that allowed for choice and authentic audience. While it is effective at that level, its appeal is universal. When students who already consider themselves to be good writers are introduced to the world of collaborative writing, they often go way beyond the minimum snippet requirements.

This lesson could also be adapted for any course that incorporates writing. In a creative writing course, we might discuss story arc and require snippets that establish character, build tension, and resolve the story problem. The story tree strategy also works well for writing across the curriculum. A social studies course might require students to create snippets as journal entries written during a certain historical period. Science teachers could require students to incorporate science-based facts into science fiction stories. In one school, we did just that: the class was studying planets within our solar system and used story trees to create science fiction populated by characters who had evolved to survive within the confines of an assigned planet.

Works Cited

Bruning, Roger, and Christy Horn. "Developing Motivation to Write." *Educational Psychologist* 35.1 (2000): 25–37. Web. 1 Dec. 2009.

Fletcher, Ralph. *Boy Writers: Reclaiming Their Voices.* Portland, ME: Stenhouse, 2006. Print.

Kreymerman, Ilya, and Nina Zito. "One Million Monkeys Typing: How It Works." *One Million Monkeys Typing,* n.d. Web. 27 Nov. 2009.

"Webspiration: Quick Start Guide." *Webspiration.* Inspiration Software, n.d. Web. 27 Nov. 2009.

Supplemental Reading

Nolen, Susan Bobbitt. "Young Children's Motivation to Read and Write: Development in Social Contexts." *Cognition and Instruction* 25.2-3 (2007): 219–270. Web. 4 Aug. 2010.

Rettberg, Scott. "All Together Now: Collective Knowledge, Collective Narratives, and Architectures of Participation." *Scott Rettberg Documents,* 1 Dec. 2005. Web. 4 Aug. 2010.

Zimmet, Nancy. "Engaging the Disaffected: Collaborative Writing Across the Curriculum Projects." *English Journal* 90.1 (2000): 102–106. Print.

12 Collaborating, Composing, and Communicating Using Google Docs: A Lesson Exploring Cyber Ethics in the Classroom

Vicki Luthi Sherbert
Wakefield School, Wakefield, Kansas

Context

Wakefield School is a K–12 public school located in a small, rural town in Kansas with an approximate enrollment of 300 students. Our student body includes students whose families have lived in the area for several generations, students whose families have moved to the area because of the nearby military post, as well as students whose families were attracted to the small town setting. Though we are a small, rural school, we are fortunate in that our school district has made technology a priority. Our students have many opportunities to use this technology independently and collaboratively to further their learning in all subject areas. As a reading and language arts teacher of sixth-, seventh-, and eighth-grade students, I strive to encourage a sense of community and collaboration among my students as they engage in the composing process. After using Google Docs to facilitate a book-writing project with a local published author, I realized that this tool could be used to further establish a sense of community and trust as students work together to explore appropriate uses of the technology available to them while investigating the concept of cyber ethics in education.

Rationale

When I began this series of lessons, I knew that I did not want my students simply to summarize a list of "rules for using the computers." I wanted them to embark on a collaborative journey of discovery resulting in an article persuading their classmates to engage in ethical practices when using technology in the classroom. Using Google Docs to facilitate this learning event has allowed my students to compile and share ideas, revise and edit collaboratively, and ultimately publish a composition that can be shared with their classmates as well as with a larger audience outside the classroom. Once students become proficient using the Google Docs application, they then have access to a tool that can be used for collaborative projects in all subject areas.

One of the requirements for this project is for students to invite me to be a collaborator on this document. This allows me to monitor group and individual contributions as well as offer suggestions and encouragement to each group. While Google is continually making improvements and upgrades to this tool, the basic principles of use remain constant. Components of this lesson involve gathering and reflecting on information about the concept of cyber ethics, exploring the Google Documents application, composing text, and inviting collaborators to edit or to view a document.

Objectives

Students will be able to:

- Create a document using Google Docs
- Invite group members to edit the document and to record their thoughts and responses regarding cyber ethics in schools
- Revise and edit the document to collaboratively compose an article that informs and persuades classmates to engage in ethical practices when using technology in the classroom
- Create a link to share the document with a wider audience on the Web

NCTE/IRA standards addressed: 1, 3, 4, 5, 6, 7, 11

Materials/Preactivity Preparation

- You will need to become familiar with the Google Docs application. Google offers information specifically for educators.

- Students will need access to computers in class. Computer access at home can provide extended opportunities for collaboration.
- Students will need access to information on cyber ethics.

Before beginning this lesson, you should become familiar with the Google Docs application. Google offers explanations and step-by-step instructions for using Google Docs as well as helpful suggestions for using this application in the classroom ("Docs Help"; "Forms: Creating Forms"; "Google Docs"; "Using Google Docs"). Because Google frequently updates information regarding all of its applications, performing a Web search for "Google Docs" will yield the most current information and helpful tips.

I have chosen to direct my students to two sites from which to launch their investigation of cyber ethics in the classroom (Starr; "The Cyber Citizen Partnership"). From there, I encourage them to expand their research to include other sites and sources. I anticipate that, as occurs in Internet explorations of all topics, more information regarding cyber ethics will become available at a rapid rate, and I want my students to explore several different, current sources of information.

Time Frame

This lesson series comprises three to four parts, which might include:

- Exploring the topic of cyber ethics in the classroom
- Creating Google accounts and exploring Google Docs
- Composing and publishing a composition
- Accessing the webpage articles published by students

One 50-minute class period can be devoted to student research of the topic of cyber ethics. This research could also be assigned as homework if students have computers and access to the Internet. The time frame for the second part will vary depending on whether students have previously generated their own Google accounts or whether they will be creating those accounts in class. Google's Terms of Service require that students be thirteen years of age or older to use Google Docs. If students create their Google accounts in class, one 50-minute class period will be required for students to create and explore their accounts. You should compile a list of all student email addresses to be used for Google accounts. Google recommends that teachers not ask for student passwords since those addresses will now be connected with the students' personal Google accounts. For the remainder of that class period, you might want to have students browse the various applications associated with a Google account. One 50-minute class period will then be needed for a brief teacher demonstration of the Google Docs application and to allow time for students to explore the possibilities. After students have explored the topic of cyber ethics in the classroom through their own independent research, they can begin collaborating with other students in their groups to compile their discoveries, information, and thoughts by creating a document in Google Docs. This collaborative process could be done over a span of three to four 50-minute class periods, depending on how much collaborating students do outside of class time. The final 50-minute period is spent accessing the articles the other groups published as webpages and discussing the concept of cyber ethics.

Description of Activity

A discussion of the concept of cyber ethics launches this activity. I do not want to impose my definitions of this concept on the students, so our initial class conversation begins with students sharing their knowledge of, or predictions about, the meaning of cyber ethics. I soon direct them to two websites from which they can begin their investigation of the topic. I give them the rest of the class period to visit these sites, as well as other sources of information they might discover through links on these websites or other searches. In our school, we have mobile carts containing thirty laptop computers. When I conduct this activity, each student has access to his or her own computer. In classrooms that do not have enough computers available at one time for students to work on their own, students can work in groups to explore the websites. Another option is for students to explore these sites outside of class time.

My reading and language arts students create Google accounts when they are in seventh grade. To access Google Docs for this project, my students and I need to have Google accounts. The accounts can be connected with any email address a student is currently using, an address distributed by the school, or an address created for the sole purpose of accessing Google Docs. Whichever email address a student chooses to use, a Google account will need to be created using this address. I encourage my students to create Gmail addresses because these addresses come with a built-in Google account. Establishing a Google account allows users to use the same email address and password for all Google services they choose to use, including Google Docs. If students are creating their Google accounts in class, I allow one 50-minute class period to accomplish this, and allow them to explore the different Google applications available to them. If students establish Google accounts outside of class time, we take a few minutes for them to share their email addresses associated with their Google accounts and then move on into the next part of the activity.

Once Google accounts have been created, we establish collaborative student groups. I then spend a few minutes modeling some features of the Google Docs application. I have found it helpful to project my computer on the screen so that students can look at my list of documents. I show them how to create a new document, and we talk about the similarities between Google Docs and other Word document programs they may have previously used. I demonstrate how to change fonts and text size, how to highlight text, and how to justify and align text. I also show them how to share their documents by inviting others to edit or to view the document. I point out that for this activity they will need to invite their group members to edit so that they can make comments, edit passages, or add texts during their collaborative composing. We also discuss adding others who can view, but not edit, their documents. This sharing feature allows users to invite others to read their document but not make changes to the document. At this point, I create a document, type a sentence on it, and then share the document with one of my students by inviting him or her to edit. I direct students' attention to the screen so they can observe the "Also viewing [student's name]" flag that appears at the top of the document window the moment the invited student opens my document on his or her computer. I ask the student to click on the document and type a sentence. The sentence will then appear on my document projected on the screen. The student and I then type, highlight, and delete text so that all students can view how this document has truly become a collaborative piece of writing. I casually mention that it is important to respect the writing of every group member and to be thoughtful in our comments and revisions. Usually, even though at this point we have not revisited the theme of this activity, a student will say, "Hey, isn't that what cyber ethics is really about?" I tell them they are on the right track! Students spend the rest of the class period creating and sharing documents with group members.

Once students have become familiar with Google Docs, we return to the topic of cyber ethics. During the next 50-minute class period, students revisit the sites they explored on the first day of the activity and begin to share their thoughts about cyber ethics with the members of their groups. I have found it is best to have one group member create a document titled "Cyber Ethics" and then share that document with other group members who are invited to edit. Group members then begin to record their ideas about cyber ethics on the group's Google Doc. We have found that having each member type using a different font or a different color allows them to distinguish one another's contributions. The first time we did this, I asked the students for their feedback on the process. At first glance, as I was walking around the groups and listening to their conversations, I wondered if it was somewhat confusing having three to four people typing on one document at a time. However, when I asked the class if they would perhaps prefer to each work on a separate document, or if they wanted to take turns dictating to one typist on the document, they unanimously wanted to continue individual composing on the same document. One student asked, "Isn't this the whole purpose of using Google Docs, so that all our writing is in the same place instantly?" The student was correct—the two alternatives I offered really negated the whole concept of the synchronous collaboration that Google Docs affords. The students were not the least bit daunted by the chaos of collaboration on one document. What a great example of how students are willing to experiment and struggle with technology!

Once students have recorded notes from and thoughts about the information they've gathered about cyber ethics, they begin to look critically at what they have written. They are now ready to move into the next phase of the composition process. They must come to a consensus about how to organize their information into an article, the purpose of which is to persuade other students to engage in ethical practices when using technology in the classroom. If students are completing the activity only in the classroom, verbal as well as digital conversations will ensue as group members focus their thoughts into a cohesive composition. I encourage groups to keep the articles to a length appropriate for inclusion in a school newspaper: four to five paragraphs that include a definition or explanation of cyber ethics, examples of ethical and unethical practices when using technology, and a conclusion persuading other students to practice cyber ethics. I usually allow two 50-minute class periods for students to complete this phase of the activity. I also remind them that they can access their document online at home and that they might need to find time outside of class to collaborate and edit their final product. Once group members feel satisfied that their article is ready for publication, I encourage them to have one member read the article aloud to the rest of the group to catch any last edits they might want to make.

The final step in the composing process is to publish the article to be read by an audience outside the group. Students accomplish this by creating a link through Google Docs that other people can access to read the document online. At this time, I again direct students' attention to the screen, where I project from my computer a quick demonstration of creating a link to share the document online. When students click on the "Share" button and select "Publish as a webpage," the document is assigned a unique URL. Students can share this URL for viewing the document online with anyone they choose, but the document will not appear in a Google search index. The student who initially created the document, rather than one of the collaborators, must be the one to publish the document as a webpage. This publishing feature also includes an option for updating the document online each time it is revised in Google Docs. To activate this feature, the student simply checks the box beside "Automatically re-publish when changes are made" when they first publish the document.

This series of lessons culminates with class time devoted to reading the published articles of other groups. The final 50-minute class period is spent having students share the links to their published articles with their classmates. I have found it works best to have each group email me the URL to their article, and then I email a compiled list of the links to each student. From there, each student can click on the link to read each article. Another option is to project the links on the screen or write them on the board so students can enter them on their own computers. Once everyone has read the articles, we have an informal class discussion about the similarities and differences in the concepts presented in each article. Possible points of discussion might include:

- Do all the articles demonstrate a basic agreement about what it means to engage in ethical practices when using technology in the classroom?
- What issues were mentioned most frequently in our articles about cyber ethics? What issues were mentioned in only a few articles?
- Do our articles offer information that will persuade other students to engage in ethical practices when they are using technology in the classroom?
- What pieces of information do you think will have the most influence in persuading other students to use technology appropriately in the classroom?

Assessment

There are various options for assessment of this activity. Since this is a collaborative learning activity, I have found that a collaborative assessment process extends the learning to include critical thinking and reflection. I create a brainstorming Google Doc and then ask the students to record on this document what they feel are the most important aspects of the activity and what they would like to be graded on. We think back to the class conversation we had when we finished recording our thoughts and information about cyber ethics on the document and before groups began to compose the actual articles. For some projects and activities, students receive a scoring rubric before they begin working. However, I have found this activity to be one primarily of discovery, so it has made the most sense for us to develop the scoring guidelines once the project has evolved. Comments such as "Our article had several good points about cyber ethics—we should be graded on that," "Our article was really organized. People said it was easy to read and made sense," and "We worked well together and didn't argue. We should get points for that!" appeared on the document. After further discussion, we came up with the following rubric for the article produced:

15 pts.	Article explained the concept of cyber ethics.
15 pts.	Article gave examples of students practicing cyber ethics in the classroom.
15 pts.	Article attempted to persuade other students to practice cyber ethics.
5 pts.	Article was organized and easy to read, with few errors that would hinder the reader's understanding.

I also think it's important for students to reflect on the collaborative nature of this activity. I asked my students to respond to the following questions:

- How did you feel about collaborating with your group members?

- What, if anything, did you like about using Google Docs? What, if anything, did you dislike?

- What do you think we could do to make this a better activity?

- Would you want to use Google Docs again when working in a group?

- If you had to give each member of your group, including yourself, a score between 1 and 5 for contributing to the activity, what would you give, with a 5 meaning "was very involved and contributed a lot to the activity" and a 1 meaning "was not very involved and contributed little to the activity." Please list each group member and give each a score.

While these reflections can be collected using a paper-and-pencil survey, the Forms feature of Google Docs allows me to create a survey document that can be shared with the students online (see Handout 12.1 in the supplemental materials). Students can type in their responses to each question. Their responses can then be viewed either in survey or spreadsheet form. I usually award students ten points for thoughtfully completing the reflection.

Connections and Adaptations

Although this lesson uses Google Docs as a collaborative tool for composing a document in a reading and language arts classroom, it could be adapted to any composition process in all curricular areas. Google Docs also allows users to create and share spreadsheets, forms, and presentations. Students can extend this activity of exploring cyber ethics beyond collaboratively writing an article to creating a presentation slide show and sharing it as a webpage with others. They might also use the Forms feature of the application to survey other students about their perceptions of ethical practices in the classroom. Teachers will also find Google Docs to be a valuable collaborative tool for planning and presenting. I have used the basic outline of this lesson to work with colleagues as we planned our presentations for the NCTE Annual Convention, the ALAN Workshop, and the Rural Sites Network conference. My colleagues and I used the Document feature in the same way my students did: we each recorded our ideas for the presentation and commented on one another's contributions, edited the text, and outlined our presentation all on one document without having to email changes back and forth.

The versatility of Google Docs offers endless possibilities for students and teachers in all curricular areas. As Google continually works to update and add to the features of their applications, they publish lesson ideas and updated support for educators interested in using Google applications. I've found that my students are often my best sources of ideas for using this adaptable tool.

Works Cited

"Docs Help." *Google Docs.* Google, n.d. Web. 9 Dec. 2009.

"Forms: Creating Forms." *Google Docs.* Docs Help. Google, n.d. Web. 12 Dec. 2009.

"Google Docs." *Google for Educators.* Google, n.d. Web. 9 Dec. 2009.

Starr, Linda. "Tools for Teaching Cyber Ethics." *Education World*, 2003. Web. 9 Dec. 2009.

"The Cyber Citizen Partnership." *cybercitizenship.org*, n.d. Web. 9 Dec. 2009.

"Using Google Docs in the Classroom: Simple as ABC." *Google Docs.* Google, 2008. Web. 9 Dec. 2009.

13 Blogging the Examined Life: Expressing, Testing, and Publishing Ideas to Deepen Understanding

Neil Rigler
Deerfield High School, Deerfield, Illinois

Context

Deerfield High School is in the northern suburbs of Chicago. Currently, it educates just over 1,600 students. This lesson has been used in a Senior English class and could work with students of all ability levels. While the initial creation of individual blogs took place at the start of the year, and exchanges of comments were included as a part of each unit, the focus of this lesson is on the "Personal Philosophy" unit at the end of the school year.

Rationale

The "NCTE Definition of 21st Century Literacies" is at the heart of this lesson, specifically the goals of using technology, building community, and considering the ethical dimensions of students' choices as writers. Furthermore, I wanted to incorporate my yearlong emphasis on writing in both reflective and dialogic modes. For the former, my students will become more aware of the power of their language, especially as they prepare to leave the high school environment and encounter a wider range of ideas and expressions. Then they will become comfortable using writing as a way to express ideas, open themselves to challenges, engage in meaningful conversation about them, and see their thinking grow as a result.

Objectives

Students will be able to:

- Create and maintain a blog open only to members of the class at first, and then to all

- Reflect on their language choices and determine the best way to express their analysis, opinions, and beliefs
- Read a range of texts based on a philosophical question they want to explore
- Engage in dialogue with other students and consider a range of different viewpoints
- Synthesize their findings in a collection of essays

NCTE/IRA standards addressed: 4, 7, 8, 11

Materials/Preactivity Preparation

- Internet access for students (to ensure access to the blog sites, you may need to work with your school's technology department to determine which sites might be blocked by filtering software)
- Teacher preparation—just an hour or so to get started and comfortable with the world of blogging!

  - Make a blog of your own. For me, this was an essential first step before taking my students on the journey through the world of blogging. The summer is the perfect time for this, not only to learn the ins and outs of creating and maintaining a blog, but also to have an active example to share with your students. For this lesson, I use Google's Blogger site, https://www.blogger.com/start, as well as their support site, http://www.google.com/support/blogger/. I also highly recommend using the tutorial videos on YouTube; just type "Blogger Set Up" into the search bar, play the video, and follow the steps. Finally, easy-to-follow instructions can be found on the NCTE/IRA http://www.readwritethink.org/ website.

  - Search for interesting blogs. The amount of information available on the Web is endless, so you need to develop ways to focus your attention and energy so you can help your students do the same. I have students use three different search engines, although there are many available: Technorati (http://technorati.com/), Google Blogs (http://blogsearch.google.com/), and Blogged (http://www.blogged.com/directory).

  - Once you have found a few blogs you like, either subscribe to their RSS feeds or add a link onto your blog. An RSS (most often expanded to mean Really Simple Syndication, but sometimes short for Rich Site Summary) feed is a simple way of having regularly updated information from websites delivered right to you instead of you having to visit the sites themselves; instead of having to click on links to the blogs you read, new posts are delivered directly to you. This happens through a program called a Reader rather than adding more messages to your email. Let's say I'm following a blog of a friend studying abroad for the semester. Instead of clicking on her blog to see if there is new content (post, pictures, videos, etc.), I subscribe to her blog (just like subscribing to a magazine) by adding her RSS feed to my Reader. Then, anytime she adds anything, it goes directly to my Reader. In Blogger this is easy to set up. A series of helper programs ("gadgets") is built in to the software. One of these will help you easily set up this subscription feed—just go to "add a gadget," scroll down to "Feed," and enter the address of the site you want to follow. Once you click "Save," the feed will appear on your blog.

Time Frame

Before the class convened in the computer lab, we had a conversation about blogs—what they are, who reads them, who writes them, and whether any students currently blog. A lot of our conversation included a talk about social networking sites, primarily Facebook, and the ways in which students use it. Next, I had each student brainstorm a list of personal interest topics they'd like to read and write about. We then spent one 57-minute period in the computer lab looking at different blogs before I had each student create his or her own blog, including naming it and adding basic elements. It was helpful to work with the technology staff ahead of time to make sure the sites I needed were all accessible. I also put the link to Google's Blogger Help page (http://www.google.com/support/blogger/), with its easy-to-access information about how to create a blog, search for blogs, add RSS feeds, etc., on my blog so students would not have to type it in each time they needed it.

Over the rest of the semester, we spent four or five periods in the lab on a variety of tasks: adding information to the blogs and then posting and responding to comments. This happened both in the context of specific texts we were reading in class and in terms of students' personal interests (blog topics).

The "Personal Philosophy" section of the lesson was the unit that closed the year for my classes. The unit itself lasted six weeks, of which six to eight class periods focused entirely on blogging, before students completed a final written assignment.

Description of Activity

The label "Internet Generation" is often used to describe today's students, so I wanted to embrace the changing sense of the ways we communicate and restructure the final unit for my Senior English class. For several years, the "Personal Philosophy" essay was the lone grade for fourth quarter. Students select a philosophical question from their writing over the course of the year, research the work of several major philosophers who addressed it in some way, link their question back into one of the books we read, and write a personal essay combining analysis of these texts with personal stories and reflection. Almost as an afterthought, we close the year with a "Socrates Café," which is basically an informal sharing of their discoveries and conclusions. Historically, the assignment has been quite popular, giving students a chance to "look inward as they prepare to look outward," while having their beliefs challenged. For years students have told me they want their time in school during those final months to be meaningful, and the chance to have in-depth conversations about their faith, the role of free will, or the shaping of their identity (among others) has been a highlight.

I recently started blogging, both to find out what all the excitement is about and to explore ways in which I might use it in my class. I knew I would need to change my approach to the teaching of English in the face of rapid transitions in the forms of daily communication, and connecting this change with something I already knew to be a valuable experience seemed to bring together the best of two worlds: the investment in dealing with a topic of personal significance and the appeal of using new forms of technology to express it. I knew I would have to start the year with it so that students created a blog that represented them over a long period of time, not just for one class assignment, and so I opened that door at the start of the year.

Our opening conversation about blogging and the uses of the Internet tried to track what already happens. Virtually all of my students reported using email and Facebook, as expected, but I was surprised to find that for the most part, Internet use stopped there, other than using online study guides and assigned research. Few of them even knew what a blog was, some of them knew sites to go to for free music downloads or sports information, and none of them maintained a blog. I brought my computer into the classroom on that first day and, using my wireless connection and a projector, had students call out suggestions. I was able to quickly show them how to find blogs and information using available search sites like Technorati (http://technorati.com/), Google Blogs (http://blogsearch.google.com/), and Blogged (http://www.blogged.com/directory). So many of them were busy writing down URLs as we surfed the Web together that it was only natural to show them a little bit of what a blog can do. I next took them to my blog and showed them the daily rundown of music news, poetry, college basketball standings, and headlines I typically refer to at the start of my day. With the help of a few RSS feeds and mouse clicks, I was able to show them how much information comes directly to me. Beyond that, I showed them how easy it is for me to engage in conversation about these topics with people from around the world.

Now it was time for students to create their own blogs. I spent time with our school's technology staff to make sure the main blogging sites were accessible through the school's filter. I chose to go with Google's Blogger site because I had found it the easiest to understand for those who had never used a blog before, as well as the one with the best support. Armed with ideas about topics to write about and research, each student spent the better part of an hour going through the simple steps of creating a blog by going to https://www.blogger.com/start and following the directions there. To provide support to students, I sent them each a link to the blog I had created for the class; on it they found links to YouTube video tutorials for creating a blog, as well as step-by-step directions in a traditional text form. Just about all of the students were able to get through these steps quickly and without my assistance, but I did have a projector connected to one computer and walked them through each step. They quickly raced ahead, stopping the longest to come up with creative names for their blogs. At first, I told them just to create—not to worry about anything other than making their blogs whatever they wanted them to be, since these early versions would not be available on the open Web.

The next step was a critical one, and it was the focus of our second day in the computer lab. I had students reread their blogs (everyone was easily able to create one and write at least one post on that first day) and write about the following issues: If this blog were going to be identifiably connected with you and not anonymous, how would that change what you want to write about? What would you do differently if you knew the blog could be read by anyone in the class at any time? What would you change if you knew it would also be accessible through my teacher website, where my identity would be connected to yours? How does all of this affect your writing for this blog? With the responses in their notebooks, I asked them if they needed to edit their blogs, and many of them did so even without my urging. Suddenly they had a new sense of their writing—it was not just something funny to show to the person sitting next to them, but language available to a much wider audience and traceable back to the writer. Many students talked about how this exercise caused them to slow down, to think carefully about their words, and to want their writing to "sound good." When we looked at a few websites describing proper "netiquette" and advice for effective blog posting, such as http://www.goodcomment.com/, students were happy to see they had already reached similar conclusions and written them down for one another. I had never before felt such a sense of genuine ownership on the part of my students, and it excited me for what would come next. (See Handout 13.1 on the companion website for an outline of this assignment.)

On a separate note, I should mention the role of RSS feeds in the creation of the students' blogs. Having a Rich Site Summary from websites they had recently discovered show up in their blogs was like giving them a new pile of toys. I had them select a few blogs (or other sites with RSS feeds) to subscribe to in addition to the other "gadgets" they added from the Blogger site. I also had each student send me a link to their blog, and I added links to all of these on my site, organized by class period. We spent some time at the end of that second day looking at one another's blogs, and even without my prompting many of them posted comments for one another. I couldn't help but smile when kids would look up from their computers to call out to a person across the room, often someone they didn't usually talk with, to acknowledge a common interest.

Over the course of the next few months, I took the class to the computer lab toward the end of each unit. I asked each student to create a new blog post with their thoughts about the essay or project they were working on, as well as some questions for their readers. These posts could range from collecting opinions to making connections beyond the text to asking about specific passages. Students then had to respond to at least three other students, and I structured this assignment in a way that ensured each person would receive multiple responses. Since this did not take the entire hour, I also asked each person to add a personal post to their own blog, as well as explore the other features available through the Blogger site, including the ability to add links, photos, and videos into each posting.

By the time fourth quarter and the philosophy essay rolled around, the students were comfortable with the software and the ways to express themselves on a blog. They started the process by generating a philosophical question to explore and answer. On their blogs, they wrote a post about their initial beliefs regarding the question, as well as a story (personal or otherwise) that led them to where they were in their thinking. When I assigned the students to read one another's posts and to ask questions, they found that they wanted to read what each person in the class said, and they readily continued the work at home, in many cases writing more than I assigned them to do. Over the weeks that followed, as each student read the work of a philosopher and explored the role of his or her question within one of the books we read, I hardly needed to give instructions once we got to the computer lab. By that point, students had learned how to respectfully disagree with a person's assertions or to push ahead someone else's thinking by suggesting a new possibility. Philosophical questions were the perfect vehicle for this type of interaction as students were able not only to post their own thoughts, but also to send links to news stories and postings on other blogs. For example, a student writing about capital punishment found more than twenty-five comments filled with suggested links from her fellow students after just one day in the lab. The Web 2.0 environment effectively opened the world to each student, not just with researched information but also with user-generated insights and a richer dialogue.

Part of the final essay is a reflection on the entire process, including naming the most effective steps. It wasn't the essays by major philosophers, or the chance to relook at books from the past year, or the chance to read one another's blog postings and questions that stuck out for them, but rather the interaction of all these activities, facilitated through the blogs. Each student still needed to write his or her own essay and reach his or her own conclusions, and it was leading what Plato called the "examined life" through their blogs that led them to be successful in multiple ways.

Assessment

Assessing students' blogging can be a challenge, but when they help to create the rubric, as they did here, it becomes a much easier job. Each post was evaluated for being on topic, adding to the conversation or moving it forward, and clarity of ideas. To help create the standards, I had the students look at some blog postings I randomly selected from our first sessions, and we rated them together, similar to the way people can rate Amazon reviews as helpful or not. When we saw postings that were effective, we identified why, and then made suggestions for the ones that needed to improve. In the real world of blogging, a successful entry is one that gets forwarded to others, or commented on more frequently. In the future, I'll be investigating ways to create classroom standards that align with those characteristics.

Connections and Adaptations

Writing in a Web 2.0 environment asks students to take a more active role in the ownership of their language. Instead of submitting essays for one reader (the teacher), students make their thoughts, questions, and responses available to a wider audience. Furthermore, this will not happen anonymously, since each comment is linked back to the personal site of each student. The transparency of these interactions makes it not only a safe environment but also one in which students grow as a result of more authentic dialogue. The creation of blogs, including the posting of responses and questions, is useful in just about any classroom that uses traditional modes of discussion. One additional advantage is that instead of teachers facing the usual challenges with facilitation, all students can be speaking and writing at once. Furthermore, the ability to incorporate images, audio, and Web links enables students to work with the material on a variety of levels, in accordance with the goal of having students "manage, analyze and synthesize multiple streams of simultaneous information" ("NCTE Definition"). This interactive and multimedia environment leads to increased student investment, engagement, and fun. While I've focused on the articulation of a personal philosophy for students ready to leave the world of high school, this lesson can easily be adapted for conversation about any topic. In the future, I'm hoping students will upload video interviews, photo essays, and podcasts, as well as update their sites from mobile devices or other out-of-school tools. Once they come to see their sites as their own, knowing their words are out there for anyone to read, they will come to care about their writing and thinking in an entirely new way, and that goes for students of all ability levels.

Work Cited

National Council of Teachers of English. "The NCTE Definition of 21st Century Literacy." *National Council of Teachers of English*. NCTE, 15 Feb. 2008. Web. 4 Aug. 2010.

Supplemental Reading and Viewing

"Blogger Help." *Blogger*. Google, n.d. Web. 4 Aug. 2010.

Electronic Frontier Foundation. "Bloggers' Legal Guide: Student Bloggers." *Electronic Frontier Foundation*. EFF, n.d. Web. 4 Aug. 2010.

"Good Comment." *Good Comment* [Advice for Writing a Great Blog Comment]. Back to God Ministries International, 2008. Web. 4 Aug. 2010.

Hillocks, Jr., George. *Teaching Writing as Reflective Practice*. New York: Teachers College P, 1995. Print.

III The 21st Century Essay: Researching, Collaborating, and Composing

20th Century Pedagogy + Today's Technology = The 21st Century Essay: A Familiar Equation

David P. Noskin
Adlai E. Stevenson High School, Lincolnshire, Illinois

About ten years ago, I wrote an article for *English Journal* titled "Teaching Writing in the High School: Fifteen Years in the Making." Ironically, the title of that September 2000 issue was *Teaching Writing in the Twenty-First Century*. Drafting my words in 1999, I was not as much guided by the new millennium as I was by the last several years of the twentieth century. In my article, I described my journey from idealism to cynicism to a renewed pragmatism and concluded that a sound essay-writing pedagogy needs to be based on the following tenets:

- Prewriting must begin with creating and end with organizing, two paradoxical behaviors that need to be modeled, nurtured, and balanced.

- Writing needs to be seen as drafting because, semantics aside, the latter captures the recursive nature of essay writing where the act is interrupted with pauses for revisiting purpose, changing focus, brainstorming additionally, talking through a "block," or clarifying one's understanding or knowledge base.

- Revising and editing need to be seen as two different acts with two different purposes; the former involves questions about purpose, audience, and content, whereas the latter addresses more surface-level concerns.

- Essay writing needs to be social: students need to talk to their peers and teacher as they generate ideas, draft, revise, and even edit—the extensive research from the 1980s on writing groups and creating a community of writers enlightened us to the dialogic nature of the act.

So, ten years later, how would my twenty-five-year journey inform others about teaching essay writing? Essentially, it would look very similar to the conclusions reached in 1999 with one exception: today we have the power of technological tools that allow the individual to participate in the creation of discourse that might be read by several audiences. In 1999, technology, for the most part, was a glorified typewriter. For those of us writing theses or dissertations in the 1990s, let's not underestimate our gratitude to that tool. However, it was not until the 2000s that technology enabled the teaching of essay writing to become truly a dialogic venture—a community of writers—due to the most recent phrase of Internet development: Web 2.0. And as I stated above, sound writing instruction needs to ensure that students have a wide social fabric of support during the process. Instead of writing in isolation or waiting for that writing conference that is never long enough, students need to be able to receive immediate, frequent feedback from peers and teachers along the way. Enter wikis, blogs, Nings, Wordles, digital sources, or the latest reincarnation of EBSCO, just to name a few. These tools are ways to connect with our students' digital lives that are often recorded on Facebook walls. This section showcases several useful lesson plans that patiently explain *how* to incorporate Web 2.0 technologies into the ELA classroom to help students become independent and critical writers of meaningful texts in the twenty-first century.

Some of us already embrace these tools and will confront these six chapters with enthusiasm and confidence. Others of us are on the opposite side of the "digital divide" but are willing to dip our toes in the pool to test how comfortable these tools might be to our apprehensive bodies and souls. Some of us became teachers years before we even heard of the Internet and hope we can remain unbothered, while others have a digital prowess but see Web 2.0 tools contributing to the demise of a literate society, a society we ELA teachers must protect.

A brief exploration of the few but significant articles and books on the topic of using Web 2.0 technology to teach and promote literacy in the twenty-first century might provide a helpful context for the various audiences who will devour enthusiastically, tread gingerly, or study suspiciously through this section's lesson plans teeming with useful ideas. A recent article that appeared in the online version of the *Chronicle of Higher Education* captures the controversial elements behind a seemingly benign venture into the teaching of writing and research (Keller). While many writing instructors at the collegiate level contend that social networks promote more frequent, purposeful, and relevant types of written communication and therefore need to be incorporated into the way we teach writing, others hold that these Web 2.0 technologies have done more harm than good to their students' syntax and cohesion of thought. True, many of us have been troubled by the Web 2.0 lingo that invades our students' essays: the ubiquitous "u" to replace a three-letter word, or the colloquialisms that rob the essay of its formality, or even the syntax that lacks grace or subtlety. But what is it that bothers us? Is it a fear that our students' immersion in a digital world is polluting their writing, or is it that we are not sure how the two worlds can coincide and co-mingle to promote an even greater literacy than ever before imagined?

Inherent in this question is the need to admit that the composing a student does outside of class is adaptable, meaningful, immediate, and purposeful, whereas the composing a student does inside of or for the classroom is often finite, a means to an end, intended for evaluation, and, sadly, irrelevant. When students write on Facebook, Twitter, MySpace, or whatever the next iteration is, they see writing as a fluid way to express themselves with immediate and relevant purpose. How many times in the past few years have we heard our most reticent participants or least prolific writers enthusiastically ask, "Didn't you read my wall?" while talking to their friends before entering classrooms? These students' Facebook screens are organic and dialogic. They open up a discourse community in which our students are prolific, passionate, and engaged creators and receivers of information. Conversely, most students view writing for the classroom—essay writing—as artificial and obligatory. Their essays, even when flashing on the computer screen, are written to capture their mastery of the discipline, which, at best, has a neutral connotation. Such traditional prose is sent to the teacher for evaluation, a one-way form of communication.

However, a more careful look at the two screens mentioned above—Facebook and the school essay—suggests some commonalities between the world of daily, practical discourse for a social purpose and essay writing as a discipline for a grade. Both contexts require students to conceive of their purpose and their audience. Both contexts require students to adhere to a form: Facebook, for example, does have a formula or template to follow, just as a literary analysis or persuasive essay follows a structure. Both contexts demand that students adhere to a code of language, thus addressing issues of diction and syntax. And both contexts rely on the writer's ability to arrange or synthesize information. Therefore, it is with this more careful look at the two "sides" or contexts (outside and inside the classroom) that I recommend we view the upcoming six lesson plans. As stated in a recent article on online writing instruction in NCTE's *Council Chronicle*, "Students might use message boards to critique one another's writing, a wiki in which they can collaborate on a single piece of writing, or video/digital writing that includes images, video, and music. While many of the tools are different, the goal . . . is to help students become analytical readers and writers and critical thinkers" (Aronson 18). Viewing the merge of Web 2.0 technologies with a tradition of best practices in the teaching of writing mitigates the need to view the cyber world as a force to be reckoned with or hotly debated. It's just an extension.

Similarly, when essay writing is combined with research, the use of Google or Wikipedia is fodder for debate among educators. How many of us have stood behind our classroom pulpits to denigrate the veracity or credibility of these tools but, privately, have relied on them for immediate access to information? Some ELA teachers scoff at the lack of agency or credibility these sources have when students use them for "research." Recently, my sophomores were engaged in a research project and, much to their surprise, the librarian and I included Google as a viable database from which to search in order to determine current approaches and solutions to their assigned societal problem. Whether using a webpage, a Wikipedia entry, or an article from a recognized database, it is incumbent upon us to help our students ask the important questions about source credibility, accessibility, accuracy, and the like. I embrace the use of the most recent generation of databases in our school library because they encourage the students to study the titles and abstracts—to really read and think about them—as they proceed to select sources that might help their research goals. Instead of focusing the majority of my time on overseeing my students' ability to write down all the important bibliographic information in the proper MLA citation—which, by the way, seems to change every few years—I can spend my time helping students to evaluate the appropriateness of a source, since many of today's databases provide the citation.

Whether our students are using the *Readers' Guide* (how many of you ever used this?) or EBSCO or Google to locate sources, we want them to be able to evaluate a source. And whether our students consult sources ranging from YouTube to an article from a database or from a newspaper that they cut out by hand, aren't we asking that they do the same things? Good research behaviors that enhance essay writing dependent on external sources should adhere to these principles:

- Sources that are accessed should support ideas, not *become* the ideas.

- Research ought to transform the process so that sources are not merely confirming one's hypothesis but adding to the complexity of a topic.

- Research consists of many skills that must be carefully scaffolded, including the following: define the task and generate relevant questions and ideas; locate and evaluate sources; read and extract the relevant information that will support ideas and open new doors; synthesize the various sources and integrate with initial, student-generated questions and ideas; and present in a coherent essay.

These principles apply to research for essay writing today just as they did when I was in high school thirty years ago. The goal for us today is to embrace the new tools that can help our students expedite the laborious task of locating useful sources so that we can focus on the preceding principles. The technologies of the twenty-first century will allow us to be coaches of critical thinking instead of surveyors of note cards and punctuation of a works cited entry.

Therefore, we ELA teachers have an obligation to find a way to see the crossover between worlds; to embrace or at least begin to incorporate Web 2.0 technologies that will support better writing through collaboration, accessibility, and immediacy; and to help students negotiate purposes for writing and realize the value of both out-of-class and in-class tasks. Web 2.0 tools are merely the next generation of technology, just like the typewriter once was. But this book teaches us an important lesson: for teachers to see gains in student writing, they will need to approach these tools with a different mindset. When we incorporated the computer into our classrooms so that students could use the word-processing function to write and revise more efficiently, we treated the computer as an extension of the typewriter. Today, we are faced with a new opportunity that we must handle differently. Today's technology has the capability to help our students become better at establishing voice and purpose and then executing a coherent, focused essay, and it does this by tapping into how our students are programmed. They often know how to blog, they know how to write on people's virtual walls, they know how to construct messages that have specific aims, they know how to access and locate information, and they know how to network. Blogs, wikis, Wordles, digital sources, and whatever will be the newest, latest tool once this book is published can help us coach students so that they can write with a clear purpose, back up well-conceived ideas with relevant support, and deliver prose with an effective voice and a mature style.

As I studied the various titles of the lessons that follow, all offering strategies to help us actually use the technology to help our students become better essay writers and thinkers, I found myself seeing many opportunities to cross over that "divide." For example, my students are just weeks away from their dreaded research paper requirement for Junior English. This year, in an effort to guide my students' inquiry away from topics that experience shows will not be kind to them, I am trying a collaborative approach to the unit. I have identified six issues that affect or could impact their lives as high school students, such as moving the starting time for high school to better align with their biological clocks or whether peer juries complement student discipline procedures. I want several students across my three sections to collaborate as they determine the issue, brainstorm questions, consider the opposition, consider alternative views, study the underlying issues as well as the causes and effects, and so forth. I want them to share sources, talk about the ideas in the sources, and find the pitfalls in the texts. I, too, want to help shape these conversations and provide guidance as every student creates his or her own "term paper" based on a truly dialogic experience.

While this plan will work, there are some obvious shortfalls. How will I be able to encourage communication between students working on the same topic but who are in different sections? How will students in the same section be able to record all the exchanges of ideas? And will these students be ready to be productive from 9:05 to 9:55 in the morning? What happens if their productivity is better at 9:00 that evening? Some of my colleagues who are avid users of Web 2.0 technologies have shared with me how they encourage collaboration amongst their students outside of the confines of the classroom, as an extension of what occurs within the walls of class. They argue that it is unrealistic to expect students to be able always to digest information and contemplate their responses to the information within the confines of the class period. Therefore, they have turned to blogs or wikis to set up discussion boards so that students can continue having conversations about their topics outside of class. I find myself nearing that proverbial moment of truth: will I seek out their support to set up a wiki site so my six topic groups can communicate as an extension of what occurs within the traditional classroom? Not as a replacement for but as an extension of.

One of my colleagues shared how he uses Ning to post a question about literature. For the next few days, students respond, first to his question and then to one another's responses. Two days later, the class has a product: a series of insightful comments about a particular question that will help everyone develop a deeper understanding of the task at hand, such as a particular extended metaphor in a novel that students are reading in class. Compare that discussion board and the way the comments are representative of most voices in the classroom to the traditional teacher-led discussion for a 40-minute period. Which venue will elicit more of a dialogic experience and a democratic construction of knowledge? Which venue will promote the written expression of ideas? Which venue will afford students the chance to study the "transcript" of the discourse in order to make meaning so that they can "answer the question"? *T.H.E. Journal* recently devoted a cover story to studying the pros and even some cons of blogging as a means to improving student writing (Ramaswami). The article cites studies that indicate that teen bloggers are better and more frequent writers than their counterparts who do not blog. Moreover, the article cites a study showing that students who engaged in an interactive writing component several times during the research paper unit attribute their success to blogging, stating that it helped increase the quality of their final drafts. The article warns us, however, that blogging just to incorporate twenty-first-century technologies is not what impacts writing instruction. Instead, blogs or wikis or whatever Web 2.0 tools are used are simply the vehicle we use to help our students build a writing community with their peers and their teachers.

Before turning to the six lesson plans in this section, I leave you with this thought: 20th Century Pedagogy + Today's Technology = The 21st Century Essay. Our purpose for teaching English is to help students write effectively, along with the cultivation of reading, speaking, and listening skills. We want to help our twenty-first-century learners craft essays that are coherent, focused, purposeful, and effective. We want them to have something important to say and to say it well. We agree that students can benefit from meaningful collaboration with peers and teachers. We agree that students can benefit from knowing that what they write matters and will be read by a real audience. And we agree that writing is a recursive process that is cultural and dialogic, reliant on a community of writers. To that end, let us turn to the lesson plans that will provide us with the missing piece of the equation.

Works Cited

Aronson, Deb. "Online Writing Instruction: No Longer a Novelty." *The Council Chronicle* 19.2 (2009): 18–21.

Keller, Josh. "Studies Explore Whether the Internet Makes Students Better Writers." *The Chronicle of Higher Education*. Chronicle of Higher Education, 11 June 2009. Web. 15 June 2009.

Noskin, David P. "Teaching Writing in the High School: Fifteen Years in the Making." *English Journal* 90.1 (2000): 34–38.

Ramaswami, Rama. "The Prose of Blogging (and a Few Cons, Too)." *T.H.E. Journal* 35.11 (2008): 21–25. *EBSCO Professional Development Collection*. Web. 18 Dec. 2009.

Recommended Resources

Beach, Richard, Chris Anson, Lee-Ann Kastman Breuch, and Thom Swiss. *Teaching Writing Using Blogs, Wikis, and Other Digital Tools*. Norwood, MA: Christopher-Gordon, 2009. Print.

Eisenberg, Michael B., and Robert E. Berkowitz. *Curriculum Initiative: An Agenda and Strategy for Library Media Programs*. Norwood, NJ: Ablex, 1988. Print.

Palfrey, John G., and Urs Gasser. *Born Digital: Understanding the First Generation of Digital Natives*. New York: Basic Books, 2008. Print.

Stross, Randall. *Planet Google: One Company's Audacious Plan to Organize Everything We Know*. New York: Free Press, 2008. Print.

Tapscott, Don, and Anthony D. Williams. *Wikinomics: How Mass Collaboration Changes Everything*. Exp. ed. New York: Portfolio, 2008. Print.

14 Nice Digg: Evaluating Student-Selected Digital Sources within a Social Context

Chris Judson
Concord High School, Elkhart, Indiana

Context

Concord High School is located in an urban fringe of a mid-sized city and has a student population of 1,425, with 37 percent students eligible for free or reduced lunch. Sixty-eight percent of the students are white. The school has been on a trimester schedule (five classes a day for twelve weeks) for ten years, and all students are required to take two trimesters of English for each grade. Students may choose to take Honors/AP English or what is referred to as "regular" English. This particular lesson was used in the second section of "regular" English 10 (sophomores) where the emphasis is on a variety of ways of reading and responding to a variety of texts. Students represent a wide range of socioeconomic and cognitive backgrounds. This lesson was part of a larger project-based learning (PBL) unit for which the driving question was: "How can a person win friends and influence people?" and our major text was the popular book by the same name penned by Dale Carnegie. Students had been working with parts of an online version of the book, and now we were moving toward updating the ideas that Carnegie wrote about. Using a Digg-like site, students were able to pull in current ideas about influence and motivation from websites and blogs into one place to discuss.

Rationale

With each new technology there are new cries for schools to implement those technologies into the school curriculum; some of those cries can turn into accusations that schools are teaching old ideas and skills that do the next generation a disservice. But those who watch these technologies evolve know the shelf life of radio or film or television or, more recently, Web-based ways of doing things, and also know that what is "hot" today on the Internet could be the next Netscape, Napster, or Compuserve. Instead of trying to "keep up" with all the newer ways of doing things, we as educators need to clear the new graphic interfaces and find the heart of how students ought to communicate in Standard English in such a way that a student's message is clear to the readers or listeners and that the message actually does something or prompts a (desired) reaction. This lesson represents what I believe is at the heart of communicating, whether on paper or on a blog comment: being able to paraphrase (understand) a text and then to evaluate that text by giving a reasonable opinion (adding to the conversation). This process becomes really interesting as students are given the chance to select the content that is being acted upon.

Objectives

Student will be able to:

- Summarize and categorize websites according to a unit of study
- Synthesize and comment on other student-generated content
- Evaluate the usefulness of student-generated content

NCTE/IRA standards addressed: 1, 7, 8, 11

Materials/Preactivity Preparation

- Computers with Internet access for students
- A familiarity of Digg.com
- A website running Digg-like software

Digg is a social networking site where its users generate the content by entering a URL for an article (or blog post, or video, or image) they find interesting, writing a short response on why that particular article is interesting, and then tagging that information so that others can find the story without having to rely solely on a traditional categorical organization for searching. When a Digg site references several different articles on a page, other users can read through the reviews, make comments, and even vote on which articles seem to be "good."

I chose to use an open source version of Digg called Pligg ("About Pligg"). Whereas Digg is a popular, commercially run social networking site (like Facebook), the Pligg software allows users to run their own Digg-like site wherever they choose. I already have personal server space, and by following the directions in the Install file, I was able to start posting in ten minutes. Some Web-hosting companies have "one-button" installs of Pligg for those teachers who want to host their own sites. If the thought of installing software on a website sounds daunting, ask your school or district technology department to do the tech work. Because many schools have their own websites, the software to run Pligg will be familiar to those in charge of maintaining the school or corporation sites. I use both Digg and Pligg; they are essentially interchangeable.

Aside from installation or setup of the site, teachers should be comfortable with general Web-based skills (e.g., copying and pasting URLs, following links, using tab features in browsers). In short, if you have spent time "social networking" on the Internet on any of the popular Web 2.0 sites (e.g., Facebook, Ning, Twitter, WordPress), then using a site like Pligg is a natural extension of those ideas.

Beyond the technology, this lesson embraces the ideas of reader response and of constructing responses that *say* something. Two texts that are helpful in exploring these ideas are *A Teacher's Introduction to Reader-Response Theories* (Beach), which gives an overview of the various reader-response applications and then provides practical ideas on how to implement those applications in a classroom, and *The Thinker's Guide to How to Read a Paragraph and Beyond* (Paul and Elder), which walks the learner through the "hows" of critically thinking through the reading of a paragraph. And finally, for the teacher trying to make sense of the shift toward a student-constructed curriculum through technology, *Teaching with Technology: Creating Student-Centered Classrooms* (Sandholtz, Ringstaff, and Dwyer) provides practical ways to transition from a traditional classroom format to one that infuses technology.

Time Frame

You'll need three days (30-minute learning segments) with this lesson to get students signed in and have them do a practice posting, find pertinent sites for the unit, and comment on other student posts.

On the first day, students sign up for an account (name, username, email, and password) and then read a description of Pligg. It's a good idea to model the directions for using a website. I use an LCD projector for this part of the lesson to model the process for students.

On the next day, students take the previous day's skills of copying and pasting URLs and writing comments and use them to find online content that relates to your topic of study: in my case, Dale Carnegie's *How to Win Friends and Influence People*. My students used the "Friends/Influence" category so we could have an easy reference to those sites. Students used various search engines to find these sites, and I encouraged them to work with many different keywords in their searches. The Pligg site doesn't accept duplicate URLs, so we didn't get repeated information.

On the third day, students comment on five to seven Pligg entries and select the sites they found most helpful.

 See Handout 14.1 in the supplemental materials for an outline of this activity and some student samples. Note: This lesson could continue throughout the grading period to produce student-generated content for a wide variety of units.

Description of Activity

I spent a few minutes every day in class reading the local paper and then talking about any item of interest. I asked students to read a wide variety of articles and to respond to those texts, beginning with a general "Read and then explain in two sentences" and then moving on to what Paul and Elder call an explication: a paragraph in which the student paraphrases, elaborates, gives examples, and creates a simile (10). As we moved into the main nonfiction text, *How to Win Friends and Influence People*, we used the same types of responses ("explain in two sentences" and explication paragraphs). Students also wrote two-sentence summary responses and two-sentence opinion responses.

By the time we approached the 108 Digg site (instead of naming the site something witty, I just used my classroom number), students were familiar with a few ways to respond to a text. We had also had some discussion about why it's a good idea to write these responses in Standard rather than colloquial English; one English is not better than the other, but Standard English will reach the widest audience of English speakers, whereas colloquial English will appeal to a much narrower audience.

All of this preparation in responding to a text helps students understand our Digg site and what we're trying to accomplish with it. Students have experience writing response paragraphs, and the idea of explaining something they have just read is a key idea in the course. If students can write a four-sentence paragraph that follows the sequence of paraphrase, elaboration, example, and comparative construction (simile), they are well prepared for Digg and Pligg.

Because my district has carts of laptops that teachers can use in the classroom, I use computers in my class every day. After writing the explication paragraph, we created a sample Pligg posting together on the LCD projector. In general, the site prompts users for the necessary information. In fact, the advice it provides on how and what to post is solid. Following a few simple guidelines makes this an even better site:

- *Assess quality of content:* Is your story relevant to the site?
- *Link directly to the source:* Save people time by linking directly to the original news story.
- *Search first:* Avoid duplicate submissions by searching to make sure someone else has not submitted the story already.
- *Be descriptive:* You are the story editor, so explain what it is and why it is cool.

As an example of how to use the site, here is a sample posting I created with students regarding an article about the U.S. dollar and Canadian hockey:

> Even though the US dollar isn't very strong, that doesn't mean that other countries are worse off. For instance, Canadian hockey is doing fairly well financially due to the strength of the Canadian dollar. It's interesting that even though our country's economy isn't doing that well, that our neighbors to the north can be enjoying a strong economy. I just wish I liked hockey more.

Students then found their own articles, completed a posting on the Digg site, and proceeded to make comments on other students' postings.

When students submit a post on the Pligg site, they are encouraged to include keywords or "tags." As the World Wide Web has grown and the information we have access to increases exponentially, various ways of organizing Internet information have followed older models, such as bookmarks and folders on a computer. Some use a predefined category much like a filing cabinet to organize information. Recently, however, the idea of tagging information has become a popular way to organize. To "tag" a site, for instance on the popular photo-sharing site Flickr, a user types in many separate words that describe that photo. For a text-information site such as a blog or Pligg, the user again would key in many separate words to describe the information found in the blog post. Using only a predefined category limits the ability to search for information; using tags or keywords allows users to find many more connections to a subject.

In our discussion about what their comments on other entries should look like, we decided on a familiar three-sentence model: a sentence or two of paraphrasing the student entry and a sentence or two of opinion regarding the topic and/or article. Some students followed these directions; others resorted to a typical chat/text message response.

108

Typically, I like to have students return the very next day of class to a website or tool that we worked with the day before, but because of our schedule we didn't return to the 108 Digg site until the following week. By then, we had finished reading the primary text of the unit (*How to Win Friends and Influence People*), and now students were making lists of things a person should possess to build healthy relationships and motivate others. Again we had laptops, and students followed the posted sequence of events.

Now it was time to take the skills developed during the training stage of finding, explaining, and commenting and use them to find and explore the content for the class. Instead of me providing websites that contain this information, students develop the list of available information on our topic of study. They used searches to find useful sites and worked their way through the process we had established in training. Again, don't allow students to submit the same article (URL); that forces them to add more variables to their searches and to scroll through the search results beyond the first page.

Most of the questions I received from students concerned why I had rejected their submission. I encouraged them to look a bit deeper in the site as it appeared that another student had already submitted that particular article or URL, and to think through exactly what we were looking for rather than merely copying and pasting my keywords from the assignment into a Google search. This is an area where most users of search engines are weak: we lack good search terms and don't use operators skillfully. It's a good idea, for students and teachers alike, to take 5 or 10 minutes to remind one another what a good search looks like and what we can do as Internet information miners to avoid scrolling through page after page and instead make searches work for us. A nice source I would use next time is the "Advanced Search Tools" option on Google and possibly the FAQ file for Using Advanced Search ("Google Help").

After a day of finding, posting, and explaining useful posts for our topic, we were ready to explore the information that would be helpful to the class as a whole. Students spent the third day looking through the posts and the accompanying websites and then commenting on what they found and how useful the information was.

This is a natural progression with Web 2.0 tools: users become creators and generators of information rather than passive recipients. Instead of teachers doing all the prep work, students find and post the information, and other users get a chance to read and evaluate that information's usefulness. Our particular purpose was to update the ideas that Carnegie shared in his 1936 text to a modern understanding (and opinion) of the twin ideas of relationships and motivation. Students had to search widely for information, visit quite a few posts on the 108 Digg site, and then comment on those sites they felt were useful. Although they had the opportunity to vote on which sites were the most useful, we didn't take much advantage of this feature.

So ended our use of Pligg for this unit. Students found useful sites on our class topic, wrote up a review of those sites, looked at other posts, and posted their own comments. When students generate information and then hold a conversation online regarding the usefulness of that information, they are developing communication skills for a Web 2.0 or 3.0 world. We will continue to read texts and try to make meaning of those texts, whether they be on paper or online, as long as true learning continues to take place.

Assessment

Most of the assessment for this unit was based on an error-branded approach: did the student fulfill the directions as noted? Instead of using rubrics, I tend to lean toward the idea that if a student follows the directions of a writing engagement and uses Standard English, then the student should be awarded almost all of the available points (for example, if a student follows the directions for writing the explication paragraph about an article/site and uses Standard English, but the writing isn't as clear as that of another student, I might award 19 points out of 20, giving me a point to award to those students whose writing is especially clear and insightful). When a student does not meet the expectations of the assignment, I simply give that student a holding grade of one point and ask the student to complete the assignment as directed.

Connections and Adaptations

Because this activity and Web 2.0 tool is based on selecting, explaining, and evaluating sources, the general outline of this lesson can be used for a variety of purposes. In another class, I used the 108 Digg site as a way for students to post, explain, and comment on the current events of the day or week. In this lesson, I used it to fill in the knowledge gap within a particular unit of study. For other content area classes, teachers could use a Digg site whenever they want to involve students in searching for current information on a given topic. It's important, of course, to have a context for using this site, but the magic of using a Digg site, or any Web 2.0 tool, lies in the ability for classes to work together to build understanding and knowledge and to make sense of a rapidly changing world.

Works Cited

"About Pligg." *Pligg.* Pligg CMS. Pligg, LLC, n.d. Web. 3 Jan 2010.

Beach, Richard. *A Teacher's Introduction to Reader-Response Theories.* Urbana, IL: National Council of Teachers of English, 1993. Print.

Carnegie, Dale. *How to Win Friends and Influence People.* 1936. New York: Simon & Schuster, 1981. Print.

"Google Search Basics: More Search Help." *Google Web Search Help.* Google, n.d. Web. 3 Jan 2010.

Paul, Richard, and Linda Elder. *The Thinker's Guide to How to Read a Paragraph and Beyond: The Art of Close Reading.* Dillion Beach, CA: Foundation for Critical Thinking, 2003. Print.

Sandholtz, Judith Haymore, Cathy Ringstaff, and David C. Dwyer. *Teaching with Technology: Creating Student-Centered Classrooms.* New York: Teachers College P, 1997. Print.

15 Using a Wiki to Collaborate during the Research Process

Sara Wilcher Zeek
Lord Botetourt High School, Daleville, Virginia

Context

As an eight-year veteran teacher of dual enrollment college composition (English 111/112) and AP English Literature and Composition, I have examined, considered, and evaluated multiple ways to teach the research paper. Until the 2008–09 school year, I had not found a plan or tool that would make the research process simpler and more enjoyable for students and myself. That year, eighty-three students enrolled in advanced English courses, and I felt a desperate need to make the process more focused just so I could manage the paper load.

Lord Botetourt High School is a suburban school with nearly 1,100 students, most of whom are middle class and white. Our division, Botetourt County Public Schools, employs instructional technology resource teachers (ITRTs) to assist classroom teachers with new technology. I collaborated with our ITRT to discover how we could make the research process more focused by blending Web 2.0 skills with traditional college research skills. As a result, I developed and facilitated this lesson plan that uses a wiki to build a database of resources for student use in writing the research paper.

Rationale

Over the last eight years, I have seen students become discouraged with the research process as they toiled independently to master research skills. While I have always believed that writing is recursive, the research process seemed to bend that belief into a straight road that students traveled in isolation. The wiki changed all of that for my students and for me because the process is more student centered and reduced the grading required in the traditional research process.

Given the focus of the Internet and social networking in the lives of young writers today, the following lesson offers a plan that encourages students to use the plethora of electronic sources available to them today while teaching responsibility and accountability during the research process. The use of a wiki in the research process also provides students with opportunities to use higher-level thinking skills, make independent decisions, write in a variety of styles, analyze visual sources, sharpen rhetorical skills, and express their creativity. We found that it sharpened student research skills because more readers were evaluating sources as they were posted. The use of a wiki as a database also discouraged plagiarism because more students acted as peer editors as drafts were completed.

The first benefit that I noted was that the wiki allows students to research collaboratively, which is not typical in a college-level class. Students could post articles that were relevant to anyone's topic, which encouraged more discussion and excitement about the research process. The use of a wiki encourages creative and critical thinking by forcing students to analyze their sources and not passively wait for the teacher to declare that a source is credible. Students know that their peers will question their statements, so they put more effort into finding legitimate sources. The most valuable aspect of using the wiki is that it puts control of the research process into the hands of the students. While giving up control of a class project is often risky, the benefit of having students become invested in a project to the point that they own it by determining their own due dates, rubrics, and standards for excellence is worth the risk.

The wiki had personal value to me as a teacher. It allowed me to actually become a facilitator, a role that I have often tried to assume but could not enjoy because I felt overwhelmed by the details of the research process. The wiki allowed me to read and write with my students. I researched and posted sources on my own pages that they could use in their papers. I quickly realized that this type of collaboration did not weaken the research process, nor did it keep students from fully understanding the importance of respecting intellectual property and proper documentation. Students could now see models of documentation on my pages, and they could easily assess one another's work for proper documentation. In the end, the wiki did what all good plans should do—*it lightened the burden of grading*. I was able to check sources over a period of time without having to carry home stacks of printouts, and the final product had been proofread by several other qualified readers—the students—before I began grading it.

Finally, the greatest benefit came in the reactions of the students. While everyone acknowledged that the process was still complex, the students agreed that they had enjoyed working with the wiki. For the first time in eight years, I heard students say that the research paper was *fun*. Imagine that.

Objectives

Students will be able to:

- Generate, gather, organize, and plan ideas for writing
- Select and narrow a topic
- Find and analyze sources, both print and nonprint
- Select and cite appropriate sources in an established documentation style
- Adapt content, voice, diction, and tone to a specific audience
- Revise and edit content
- Use available technology to support the writing process
- Collaborate with peers to complete a project
- Develop rhetorical skills, especially in persuasion (Virginia DOE)

NCTE/IRA standards addressed: 4, 5, 6, 7, 8, 11

Materials/Preactivity Preparation

Before introducing the lesson, you should have clear permission to use a wiki, since it is categorized as social networking and most school district filters block sites of this type. You'll need to do the following:

- Gain written approval from the district to use the wiki both in school and at home as an instructional tool. I worked with the building ITRT, who secured approval for me.
- Secure parental permission for the students to use the wiki at school and at home; include permission to use the students' personal emails, which may be needed to set up their accounts.
- Review several wikis and choose the one that is the best fit for your students and the school. We chose the site Wetpaint (http://www.wetpaint.com/) because it offered the best options for a higher-level class.
- Set all permissions to lock down the wiki from outside contacts.
- Issue electronic invitations to students if they are required to log on to the wiki.

- Create a contract that students sign stating they will not share their account with anyone outside of the class.
- Determine which aspects are not negotiable in the project.

This lesson plan assumes that you have already informed students that a research project will be assigned in the class and that you have a plan to teach the actual research process.

Potential Problems and Troubleshooting Strategies

My first class encountered a few obstacles when first trying to open our Wetpaint wiki site, which was blocked as "social networking" on school computers. To make the wiki available at school, we had to consider the potential for outsiders to find student pages on the Internet and then contact the students personally. We chose to make the site private, which kept it from being viewed through an Internet search, and students signed a contract stating they would receive a failing grade on the project and lose computer privileges for the rest of the school year if they broke the contract. Later classes did not face these issues because the school district moved to Google mail (Gmail) and created a student domain that we now use for the wiki project. The website feature on Gmail is a wiki-like environment with very few differences in design from our original wikis and none of the privacy issues.

You are responsible for setting up the actual wiki and establishing its framework:

- Choose a theme for the project based on the class focus.
- Create an online account for the wiki.
- Create the wiki homepage, which includes an introduction to the project, requirements for students, and a communication thread for class messages.
- Create the other assignment pages: Current Events, Periodical Reviews, Internet Site Reviews, and Book Review.
- Prepare a handout that covers the details of the project so that students have received clear expectations in writing.

Time Frame

This project was taught as a four-part lesson plan for a 90-minute class period on an A/B block schedule.

Description of Activity

Day 1: Understanding the Theme

The first class period involves three collaborative activities. In the first 30 minutes, you will introduce the theme to the class and explain its significance to the project. For example, I chose the theme "Globalization" because I felt that students would be more interested in topics that were current. To introduce the theme, we viewed the film *Did You Know?* by Karl Fisch (about seven minutes long) and discussed the points of the film to develop a definition of the term *globalization*.

For the next 30 minutes, students should work in small groups to answer focus questions and then report their responses to the class. My students worked in small groups to answer the following questions:

- When did globalization begin?
- What other names has the process been called?
- What types of things are globalized?
- What is frequently the precipitating factor in globalization?

The final collaborative activity should help students focus on possible research topics. In the last 30 minutes of class, my students brainstormed for examples that illustrated how globalization is a process that both causes change and reflects reaction to change. For example, we decided that language changes daily in reaction to globalization.

Day 2: Choosing Topics

This class has three objectives:

- In the first 30 minutes, the class should review the final topics generated on day 1 that illustrated how globalization is a process of change.
- Students then choose their topics from the list of ideas. Give students one week to do preliminary research and request a change in topic.
- In the final 30 minutes of class, students should work in pairs to complete two graphic organizers each. The first graphic organizer, possibly a web, should show the relevance of their topics to the theme. The second graphic organizer should generate guiding questions that they will use to direct their research. A K-W-L chart would be most appropriate.

While the list of topics was typical in my class, the perspective was unique in that students had to show how the theme was relevant to their topic. For example, one student chose to research how American fast food is changing other countries, while another student researched how American Muslims have changed America.

Day 3: Setting Assignment Criteria

Students will review the nonnegotiable requirements for the project and make group decisions about those elements that are student controlled.

For the first activity, I spent the first 15 minutes of class explaining the requirements for the assignment:

- Sources: minimum required sources were one book, two Internet sources, two periodicals, and one other source
- Length: five-page minimum, not including the works cited page and outline
- Format: MLA format and documentation; no separate title page
- Research reference text: *The Little, Brown Handbook*, 10th edition (Fowler and Aaron)

For the second activity, students should work for 30 minutes in small groups to develop proposals on the elements of the wiki they control. This process gives students a personal investment in the project and increases the opportunity to create community. Divide the class into five groups:

- Group 1: Propose the number of assignments and the due dates for each part of the project that is negotiable (Homepage, Current Events, Periodical Reviews, Internet Site Reviews, and Book Review).
- Group 2: Determine elements that should be included on each student's homepage.
- Group 3: Develop a grading rubric for each page (Homepage, Current Events, Periodical Reviews, Internet Site Reviews, Book Review, Rough Draft, and Final Draft).
- Group 4: Establish the number and quality of student postings and responses, appropriate editing comments, etiquette, fonts, text size, use of color, and use of Standard English (for example, students could use common "texting" language in posts but not on any of the main pages).
- Group 5: Determine how each task will be graded or weighted based on the time required to complete the task and the complexity of the task.

During the last half of the class, the small groups should present their proposals on the student-controlled elements of the project, and the class should reach a consensus on each element. My class developed the following criteria for their project:

- Homepage must include student's name, broad topic, one graphic (illustration for topic), one video, two quotes, one political cartoon, and a description of topic.

- Current Events Page has two current events, due dates, and works cited entry for each article. Current events could focus on anyone's topic.

- Periodical Review Page has two reviews that focus on the student's individual topic, due dates, and works cited entry for each article.

- Book Review Page includes one review of a book that is central to the individual's research, photo of book, and works cited entry.

- Intro and First Body Paragraph posted and peer edited.

- Final Draft of Research Paper posted.

- Threads: at least two threads started for discussion.

- Ten responses (total) posted to the pages of at least three students over the course of the project.

- Rubrics for each main page, with each grade counting as a daily grade, which could not be accepted late.

Day 4: Previewing the Wiki

Students should spend the entire period reviewing the wiki to determine whether any revisions are needed and to discuss the research process. We reviewed each section of the wiki and made decisions about organization and uniformity in the design. We agreed, for example, that each student should attach drafts to his or her homepage to reduce the potential for clutter that can develop with too many main pages.

Hand out a hard copy of the criteria and due dates that students established the day before for each assignment and answer any remaining questions. Students should review the research process and any expectations set forth for the project as a whole, such as MLA style citations and format or specific concerns about sources such as their books.

Capstone Activity

The final research paper is the culminating activity for this lesson and should reflect the work the student has posted to the wiki. Students will need at least four weeks to complete the entire process and produce a final paper. My class worked on the wiki for six weeks on a 90-minute A/B block schedule.

Assessment

Student-designed rubrics were used to assess the online project (see Handout 15.1 on the companion website). My students received two grades, one for their homepage and one for participation. I also graded each additional assignment separately when they were due.

After developing the wiki, my students worked outside of class on all assignments. I spent about an hour each week grading their online assignments and checking comments to be sure they were appropriate. The ITRT also checked the wiki each week and reported any concerns to me. I did not reprimand students online, but rather talked to the student face-to-face and deleted material I felt was inappropriate. Sometimes it was simply a matter of asking the student to read his or her own words again to prompt a revision. It is important to establish a positive model for communication on the wiki so that students will not lapse into negativity among their peers.

I allowed students to use informal language in their posts and responses. I made the decision to allow students to write freely and even use common texting language so that they had at least one space in which they could express their opinions without judgment.

Connections and Adaptations

This lesson plan connects to the teaching of the research process and can be used in grades 8–12. It can be adapted for 50-minute periods that would cover five to eight class periods. Other uses of the wiki include the ideas listed below:

- Creative projects such as a class anthology of creative writing
- A class project exploring a country, culture, or scientific concept as background to a novel or a literary period
- An author study in which students could write about and react to a number of selections by one author
- An organizational tool for classroom free readings and postings rather than traditional book reports
- A location to discuss and monitor summer reading assignments throughout the summer
- A space to connect classes involved in interdisciplinary studies

Works Cited

Fisch, Karl, modified by Scott McLeod. "Did You Know?" *YouTube*. YouTube Feb. 2007. Web. 1 Feb. 2009.

Fowler, H. Ramsey and Jane E. Aaron. *The Little, Brown Handbook*. 10th ed. New York: Pearson Education, 2007.

Virginia Department of Education. "English Standards of Learning—Curriculum Framework." *Virginia.gov*. Virginia Department of Education, Commonwealth of Virginia, 2003. Web. 1 Feb. 2009.

16 What's in a Wordle? Using Word Clouds to Teach Reading, Writing, and Revision

Beth Ahlgrim
Adlai Stevenson High School, Lincolnshire, Illinois

Context

Adlai E. Stevenson High School, located in the northern suburbs of Chicago, has a student population of 4,345. Approximately 98 percent of our students are college bound. Stevenson offers the standard high school curriculum with different levels of courses: instructional, college prep, accelerated, and AP. Students are required to take four years of English; electives are offered only at the senior level. In each English class, we as a department strive to create stronger readers, writers, and speakers through a variety of activities. How can we help students become better readers and writers through use of visual representation of text? We use vertical scaffolding of skills to help students develop more effective literacy skills as well as be able to participate successfully in our society.

Rationale

In my sophomore English college prep and accelerated junior English classes, students need direct instruction in previewing text, comparing text, and revising their own essays. I teach a very visual generation, so my goal is to achieve a balance between exposing them to print and to nonprint texts while guiding them to make connections. Many of my students believe that previewing a text means simply looking at the cover art and then diving into the novel. Many of them also believe that revision is simply placing a comma in a run-on sentence and calling it a day. I have struggled with peer revision mainly because students simply tell their peers that what they wrote is "fine." So, while teaching writing, I model the importance of thoughtful revision. And while Wordle meets the need to improve students' reading skills, it also helps students revise their compositions. I have discovered that having students create word clouds, or Wordles (a Web-based program that records the frequency of word usage), is time well spent, and the visual replication of text enables students to glean meaning and set a purpose for their reading and revision. While initially working with the program, I realized that previewing text in a one-page document would provide students with a clear understanding of the main idea of the text. I also realized that placing a composition on one page provides students with a valuable snapshot of their *own* writing. What better way to expose intent, main idea, and cohesiveness in published essays and student-generated essays? Students have enjoyed using the Wordles I create as well as creating their own. In the end, their understanding of text and of their own writing has helped them become more aware readers and writers.

Before showing your students the Wordle program and modeling the creation of a Wordle, you need to create one yourself; becoming familiar with the user-friendly program will allow you to troubleshoot any issues that might come up. Experiment with the "Remove common English word" command and the "Keep common English word" command. The biggest obstacle I have faced has involved students not remembering to bring an electronic copy of their essay to class. It's also quite easy to find or create electronic copies of published novel chapters, essays, and poems. If you can, access a class set of computers, or at least enough computers so students can share. Even better is to project the creation of the Wordle through a digital projector. It's a pleasure to watch students' faces light up when they see a text purposefully manipulated.

Objectives

Students will be able to:

- Predict main ideas from a reading passage
- Compare and contrast different sections of a text
- Compare and contrast companion texts
- Establish a focus for reading and analysis
- Identify the use of strong diction versus weak diction in both published and student texts
- Analyse the unity and cohesiveness of their own writing
- Establish a focus for revision

NCTE/IRA standards addressed: 3, 4, 11

Materials/Preactivity Preparation

Creating a Sample Wordle

- You and your students will need access to computers and the Internet.

- Choose a text: a chapter, an essay, a speech, or a healthy paragraph. You can retype the passage if you can't find an electronic version.

- Copy the entire text, whether chapter, essay, or poem.

A novel may be too big and unwieldy to serve your purpose well. Children's stories often work nicely. The first time through, you can create the Wordle yourself and have students watch you complete the steps, or you can let the students create it along with you.

- Open the Wordle homepage and click on "Create."

- Paste your chosen text onto the designated box.

- Click "GO."

- Print out the Wordle.

- Students should follow these steps using their own essays and print enough copies for all members of their revision group.

Time Frame

The reading lesson that accompanies the use of a Wordle will take two 50-minute class periods per reading excerpt(s). The lesson can be used as a prereading, during-reading, or after-reading activity, depending on your goal for the reading assignment. Students can also revisit the Wordle to reflect on their initial observations of the text. For example, when students look at the "Letter from Birmingham Jail" Wordle (see Figure 16.1), they can predict that the main idea of the text pertains to "white" and "negro," allowing them to conclude that King is addressing the issue of race. While reading, they can annotate for the main idea of a "racial divide," and after reading they can see what King was trying to change about race relations in the South. The revision lesson will take one 50-minute class period. The revision lesson should simply inform students about their own strengths and weaknesses as writers. Both lessons require students to reflect on their own learning to enhance future learning.

Figure 16.1. A Wordle of Martin Luther King, Jr.'s "A Letter from Birmingham Jail" (http://www.Wordle.net/).

Description of Activities

Reading Lesson

Before sharing the Wordle with students, I ask if any of them have used word clouds before. Some students may have been exposed to TagCrowd or Many Eyes, other word cloud or graphics programs. I find that many of my students have not heard of Wordle, so I create one using my computer connected to the projector. I choose a piece of text and show them how to copy and paste the text into the Wordle. Students' eyes light up once you click "Go." Clarify for them that the larger a word appears in the Wordle, the more frequently it is used in the actual text. Also, show them the language option, so they can focus on the main idea and cohesiveness of the text by removing common English words.

The day of the lesson, photocopy a class set of the Wordle you have created from a text: novel, short story, or speech. If you are using two texts for comparison purposes, have enough of both Wordles to go around. Directions to the students are simple: "What do you see?" Ask them to share their observations with their classmates while you keep a running list of observations on the board. Once all observations have been made, ask students: "What is the main idea of the passage? How do you know this? Which characters are the focus of the passage?" For a comparison/contrast Wordle: "What is the same? What is different?" Both activities will guide your students' reading and reinforce their understanding.

The Wordle in Figure 16.1 is for the entire text of King's "A Letter from Birmingham Jail." I use this as a prereading exercise so students can get the gist of the letter before we begin to read it, annotate it, and analyze it as a persuasive text. Students can readily see that King's "Letter" focuses on the ideas of "law," "negro," "white," "time," "church," "freedom," and "people," and that King is forceful in his letter with the word *must*. Encourage your students to look at the smaller words too. They carry meaning even though they are not used as frequently. Sometimes a student will point out an observation I have not entertained. When this happens, I know that students are growing as thinkers and that their purpose and intent for reading has a strong foundation.

Next, have students look at their text of the "Letter" and reread it or read it for the first time. I establish my students' purpose for reading from their initial observations of the text in Wordle form. (If you look at the three Wordles included in Handout 16.1 in the supplemental materials, you will be able to compare the three scaffold scenes from *The Scarlet Letter*. With these Wordles, I have determined students' purposes for rereading and analysis of the scaffold passages.)

Then I ask students to annotate their text, using the Wordle as a guide. In the preliminary stages of working with Wordles, it's fine for students to simply focus their annotations on the words found in the Wordle for support of their initial responses. Later, you can guide their reading toward a deeper analysis of text to focus on stylistic analysis, which moves them beyond comprehension issues. While they read, they are answering the question, "How do I know _____?"

You may want to have students work independently first. Once all students have read the passage, ask them to share their annotations. Through the sharing, you will hear valuable conversations revolving around comprehension and inference. You might want to record the annotations on an overhead transparency of the text to ensure all students are receiving the same information and to aid those of your students with IEPs.

Students may not realize they are using various reading skills, so once the class shares as a whole, it's worthwhile pointing out to them the skills they are employing. (Making color-coded annotations on the transparency would serve the students well here if you don't find it too time consuming to constantly switch pens. For the computer savvy, project the text onto a screen and highlight the document as students share.)

You will also readily be able to assess your students' strengths and weaknesses through their small-group discussions. I strongly advise that you try simply to listen to the conversations. Student-centered

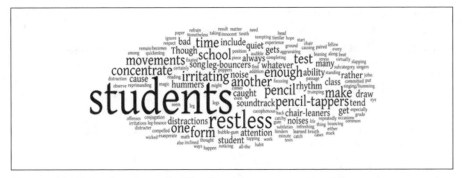

Figure 16.2. Student sample Wordle with common English words removed.

Figure 16.3. Student sample Wordle with common English words included.

learning allows students to own and be invested in their learning, which results in stronger understanding and retention.

Writing Lesson

To use the same technology for a different skill, writing, have students copy and paste their own essays and bring copies to class to share. Students should create two Wordles of their essays: one with common English words removed and one without common English words removed (see Figures 16.2 and 16.3). You might want to divide your class into groups of four, or you could have each student present his or her Wordle to the entire class. If you choose to work as a whole class, each student should print enough copies of both Wordles for every-one. Otherwise, students simply need to print four copies, one for each member of their small group. Students share their Wordles, focusing on one student's Wordle at a time. The owner of the Wordle may not speak during this portion of the activity. The other group members orally share their observations of each Wordle. Ask students to focus on the following for the Wordle with the uncommon words removed:

- Is the essay connected to the prompt? How do you know this?
- Is the essay cohesive? How do you know this?
- By tracing the author's use of specific words, explain how the different parts of the essay are connected.

Direct students to look at their essay by focusing on thesis statement and topic sentences. Do they see a connection between frequently used words and their thesis and topic sentences? If not, they have established a focus for their revision. If so, they have reinforced the fact that their essay is focused, and they can set another goal for their revision.

Next, have students observe the Wordle in which the common words were not removed. The focus of the observations for this Wordle should be diction choices. Ask students to focus their observations on the following:

- Which word is used most frequently? How does this help or hurt the essay? (Responses will probably focus on coordinating conjunctions, overuse of prepositions, and overuse of the *BE* verb.
- Using the Wordle, identify overly used words in the actual text of the essay.

Students can then move on to revision. Have them focus their initial revisions on rewriting sentences that overuse the *BE* verb. You might want to model the revision of these sentences on the board. Students need to see that sometimes they need to rewrite an entire sentence rather than simply remove the *BE* verb and replace it with a "strong" verb.

Students should leave class knowing specifically what they will revise for their next draft. To help students revise successfully, avoid having them target too many issues. If they leave class with two legitimate goals for revision, their chances for success will be good. They can always revise again with a different focus. I have used this technique with great success. Students realize that revision and editing are two different things. Also, by focusing their revision on rewriting sentences, they realize how specific words can strengthen or weaken an essay, and they naturally begin to vary their syntax and word choice.

Assessment

When assessing students' understanding and mastery of this lesson, I use several different tools. Basically it depends on where we are in the school year, the number of drafts I am requiring, and the number of times we have completed a Wordle activity.

I have used both informal and formal assessment. For my purposes here, I have created assessment guidelines for the reading and writing activities I provided in the lesson. Most of the ideas easily can be adapted to other texts, both professional and student created.

The Reading Wordle Lesson

- Check annotations of Wordle and cross-reference to the text: focus mainly on diction annotations. You can either collect annotated copies of the text, or you can circulate the room and assess as students complete the discussions. You might award X amount of points for contributions.

- Have students record predictions and collect them as an exit card. While reviewing the exit cards, you can readily assess students' understanding of the text, the author's intent, and tone.

- After-reading assessment: revisit predictions. Students can complete a self-evaluation to determine whether their predictions were on target. You can also provide a short-answer handout to guide the self-evaluation: Did I correctly predict the main idea? Did I identify proper thematic concepts? Did I make connections between texts? If not, what did I miss? If I was on target, what specifically led me to the correct prediction?

- Comparison: make connections: Students can complete a comparison/contrast list or Venn diagram. You can also extend the lesson by asking why the author would choose to place similar scenes in the novel or story but focus on different characters, time, or place.

The Writing Wordle Lesson

- Students record the focus of their peer's paper.

- The student writer completes a peer response handout: What is the focus of the essay? What words are used too often? Will the frequently used words add or distract from the essay?

- The student writer evaluates peer identification of focus: Were my classmates correct in their identification of the main idea for my essay? [Provide students with some guidelines for their revision.] If so, I need to be careful not to make drastic changes. If not, I need to revise my topic sentences to connect all body paragraphs to my thesis.

- Focus on diction: Students can create new Wordles to accompany each new draft and complete a self-analysis of their own growth as a writer. Guiding questions can easily facilitate and focus students and provide you with helpful feedback: How are my Wordles different? (List differences.) Was this my goal as I created my revision? What word am I ineffectively overusing? What specifically do I need to do to eliminate the overuse?

- Provide small groups with a handout that asks: (1) What is the focus of my peer's essay? (2) What word is most used in the essay? (3) Are my responses to questions 1 and 2 identical?

- You can also require students to revise one another's sentences to eliminate overuse of the *BE* verb. This moves students toward strong verbs, which show rather than tell. You can collect revised sentences to ensure students were on-task and assess them to determine what the focus of future writing lessons should be.

- Students should also turn in their Wordles with their drafts, rough to final. While working in groups, students can annotate one another's Wordles, and you can determine whether they were effectively on-task.

Connections and Adaptations

Initially, I used Wordle only as a prereading lesson, but I soon realized that it's a great way to check for understanding during reading and after. It's also valuable to revisit our initial predictions and reinforce students' comprehension and inference skills. Students see how close their initial observations were to the actual document, allowing for student-centered reflection and self-assessment of skills. To extend the lesson, you could give students portions of a text, have them create the Wordle, and then choose color, font, and shape to further signify and connect to the meaning of the text. For instance, they could focus on the connotation of words and express their findings through font color. You might want to share with the students the universal—or at least Western—symbolism of various colors. You could also have students create Wordles from a specific passage of text and use it as the foundation for a more visual representation. For example, when my class studies the novel *Fahrenheit 451* and students have finished reading the novel, I assign each student a specific excerpt and ask them to create a visual representation of that excerpt. One former student combed through the passage for strong diction choices that would inform his visual. He then placed his diction choices in a Wordle, took a screen shot of it, transferred it to a Word document, and supplemented his word choices with images. His final product initially looked like random words on the page, but he explained that the randomness of the format reinforced the point that Bradbury was making in this passage: "Montag was confused, conflicted, and unaware." This student created an exceptional analysis through a visual representation of a print text that enriched our understanding of the novel.

As far as using Wordle to guide student revision, I have found that revisions are focused and thorough because students are honing in on a specific skill, and they can see what they need to correct in their initial draft. One possible extension of this lesson is to have students create separate Wordles for each paragraph of an essay and then ask a classmate to put the paragraphs in proper order. When students have pieces of a puzzle to manipulate, engagement is 100 percent, and you are meeting the needs of your visual learners as well as your tactile learners.

Overall, the use of Wordle creates an unintimidating forum for comprehension, analysis, synthesis, and revision. Students are very willing to discuss the word cloud because it is accessible, manageable, and fun.

17 Building Rubrics Collaboratively with Google Docs

Sarah M. Zerwin
Fairview High School, Boulder, Colorado

Context

Fairview High School is a large, comprehensive high school on the southern edge of Boulder, Colorado, home to the main campus of the University of Colorado. Our 1,900 students have a wide variety of course offerings from which to choose, including IB, AP, and college preparatory classes. In the language arts department, we offer three strong journalism courses among our range of electives. I used this particular activity in my beginning journalism course, a prerequisite for our two advanced journalism courses: newspaper and yearbook. Both courses are very technology heavy; they each use design and layout software to produce their publications. The newspaper staff also uses Google Docs to submit, respond to, and revise copy for the newspaper. Hence, building some familiarity with Google Docs in the beginning journalism class is key—this prepares students for using Google Docs as a vital component of the workflow for each issue of the newspaper once they join the newspaper staff. This collaborative rubric-building activity formed the beginning of my students' final project for beginning journalism: a journalistic product of their choosing and design, to be completed in small groups or individually, that they would present to the class during our scheduled final exam time.

Rationale

We teach literacy. What that means for our students' futures is not totally clear due to the rapid evolution of communication technology. But what is clear is that our students will need a diverse range of skills to be fully literate in their world—more than just paper-and-pencil literacy (NCTE/IRA standards 1, 6, 7, 8, 12). Yes, they need to be able to write well and read diverse texts effectively. But we must not neglect other critical literacy skills such as being able to effectively read and write a variety of nonprint texts, or to navigate the deluge of information on the Internet to find information relevant to a particular task.

Facility with current and emerging communication technology—such as Google Docs—is one of these critical literacy skills. In the simplest terms, Google Docs provides a free, Internet-based software package akin to what Microsoft Office offers. But the power of Google Docs is more than this; several people can work on the same documents at the same time with all revisions and changes housed in one file that is saved in one place on the Google servers, thereby accessible by any computer hooked up to the Internet. Although Google Docs may not be the exact tool our students will find themselves using in the future to manage collaborative projects (after all, Google Wave is already upon us), students will need to understand technologies that they will use in future academic and workplace collaborative projects. The Partnership for 21st Century Skills (http://www.p21.org/) outlines in its Framework for 21st Century Learning the need for students to be able to communicate and collaborate effectively. Specifically, the partnership calls for students to be able to:

- Articulate thoughts and ideas effectively using oral, written, and nonverbal communication skills in a variety of forms and contexts
- Demonstrate ability to work effectively and respectfully with diverse teams
- Assume shared responsibility for collaborative work

Using Google Docs in the classroom to facilitate collaborative work most certainly works toward these goals.

Beyond the relevance this task has for developing students' literacy skills, this task also plays an important role in assessment. Stiggins argues that students can hit any assessment target they can see clearly and that holds still for them. Involving students in the process of defining those assessment targets is a very effective way to connect students to their learning goals so that their work drives them toward success with those goals. Collaborative rubric building involves discussion between students, and facilitating that discussion with Google Docs captures the discussion as the students are negotiating what their assessment targets should be.

Of course, this kind of discussion could happen with one student at the chalkboard or on the overhead projector and the rest speaking one at a time as the class works through the often laborious process of building a rubric together. But Google Docs has some important advantages; it presents something valuable that we could not achieve without it. I asked my students if it was worth it to use Google Docs to create our rubric and if we got a better rubric in the process. One student responded that "we created a quality rubric in which everyone had a say," and another student reported, "I think it was a similar rubric but took less time to make." A third student said, "everyone can say their idea without being judged or scared." These student responses highlight the value of using Google Docs to involve students in the process of building their own assessment targets. Not only does Google Docs enable a class to build a project rubric together more quickly than without it, but it also enables students to edit the document at the same time, providing space for all students' voices to participate in the negotiation of assessment targets. This might better encourage the participation of students who might feel "judged or scared" in a whole-class discussion setting.

Objectives

Students will be able to:

- Use Google Docs to effectively communicate with their classmates over the creation of a shared document
- Build a project rubric collaboratively, taking into account all students' ideas and suggestions
- Review and examine the conventions of a particular genre of writing (in this case, journalism) to determine clear and high standards of quality
- Form a clear assessment target to guide students' individual work

NCTE/IRA standards addressed: 4, 6, 11, 12

Materials/Preactivity Preparation

- You will need to secure enough computers with Internet access for students to access Google Docs either individually or in small groups—perhaps in the school computer lab.
- You will need some models of the genre of writing that the students will be demonstrating with the project—at least two models for students to do some comparing and contrasting to tease out the standards of quality for that genre as they build the rubric.
  - ◆ Depending on what form the models take, you will need photocopies of the models or a way to project the models in the classroom for the students to examine and discuss together.

- You will need to set up a spreadsheet document in Google Docs where the students will build the rubric together.
  - ◆ This requires you to first create a Google account if you don't already have one. This is free, quick, and easy—click on "Get Started" from www.docs.google.com.
  - ◆ The Google Docs spreadsheet is preferable over the Google Docs word-processing application because the spreadsheet allows up to fifty individuals to edit the document simultaneously. It also offers a live chat panel on the same screen where those who are editing the document can chat with one another as they edit, thereby making it possible for students to discuss on-screen the changes they are making to the document as they work on it.
  - ◆ The spreadsheet you set up can be very simple (see Figure 17.1, a sample from my classroom):

Category	Expectations
[List here the possible categories for the rubric, possibly the Six Traits, or have students come up with the rubric categories on their own.]	[Leave this column blank for the students to complete.]

  - ◆ Google Docs provides some excellent documents to explain how to use all of the Google Docs tools—just click on "Help" once logged in to Google Docs.
- If you want to limit access to the document to only the students in your class, students will need to have individual Gmail accounts, which are free and very easy to set up. This allows you to grant access to each individual student only.
  - ◆ Otherwise, you can set access to the document so that any person who comes across it on the Internet can edit it. You need only to direct students to the URL for the document to access and edit it.

Time Frame

I took three 50-minute class periods to complete this rubric-building task as I describe it below. However, this can certainly be accomplished more quickly, and actual time needed will depend on the scope of the project for which the students are building a rubric. Students will need adequate time to examine models of the product they will be creating (this will vary depending on the complexity of the product) and then time (approximately 30 minutes) to work collaboratively on the Google Docs spreadsheet.

Description of Activity

I used this collaborative rubric-building activity (see Handout 17.1 in the supplemental materials) at the end of a semester-long course for the final project, which was to be a journalistic product of students' choosing and design. Up until this point, we had practiced several types of journalistic writing, and students had worked both in groups and individually on newspaper-style products that required them to report, write, and do the layout for their work with accompanying images using design and layout software. For this final project, students could go beyond newspaper-style journalistic products if they chose two other forms of media such as video, podcasting, Web-based journalism, photo journalism, or magazines. We needed a rubric that would stretch across these different types of media.

I gave the students one class period (50 minutes) to explore journalistic forms other than those we had already produced by setting them loose on the Internet and instructing them to email me a list of links to what they found. I received a wide range of links—from TV news network websites to news parody websites to blogs. This diverse list was exactly what we needed the next day in class to have a discussion surrounding these models of journalistic writing.

The following day, I projected from my computer the list of links I had compiled, and we started taking a look at some of them. With each model we examined, we discussed whether it was an example of journalism, if it was credible, how it might be biased, what the ethical considerations were for each particular example of journalistic writing, and if we considered its content newsworthy.

After students had explored many different forms of journalism and we had discussed and examined the models to tease out their various characteristics, my students were ready to build their rubric to guide their final projects. I set up the spreadsheet (see Figure 17.1) they would work within and prepared to show them how to use it the next day.

The next day, I began by explaining how Google Docs works. It went something like this:

> Google Docs provides free Internet-based software for people to word-process or work on spreadsheets, for example. And since this is all based on the Internet, and the documents you create are saved on the Google servers, you can access your Google Docs documents from any computer connected to the Internet. Google Docs also allows you to share your documents with other people so that they can view or even edit them. I have created a spreadsheet that you can all edit—at the same time—in order to build the rubric for our final project. As you work

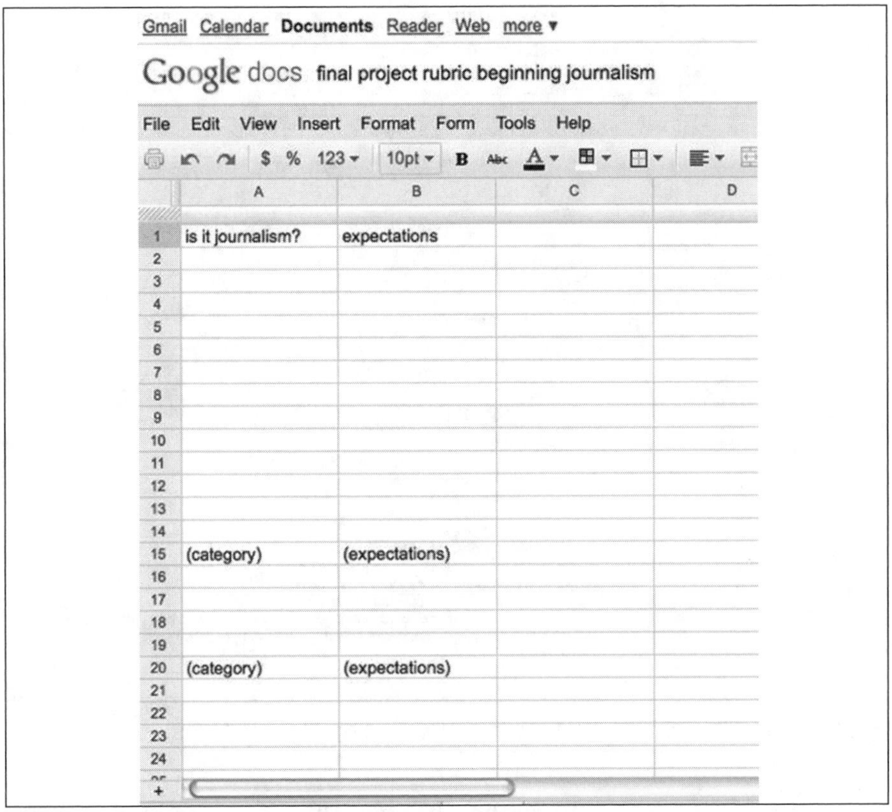

Figure 17.1. Project rubric template in Google Docs.

on this spreadsheet from your own individual computer, you'll be able to see the changes your classmates make to it from their individual computers. And as you work, the document will automatically save your changes. And one more cool thing—you'll see on the right side of the screen a chat box where you can chat in real time with everyone else who is also editing the spreadsheet.

After this, I showed students how to find the spreadsheet on the Internet (I linked to it from my school webpage), indicated to click "Edit this page" in the lower left corner to start adding their ideas to the rubric, and assured them that if this all seemed odd and confusing so far, they just needed to start working with it and it would begin to make sense.

In short, students loved it. After some initial confusion as they stumbled into the document and I rushed about among them answering questions as they worked to figure things out, they settled into the task. They worked with intense engagement, adding their ideas,

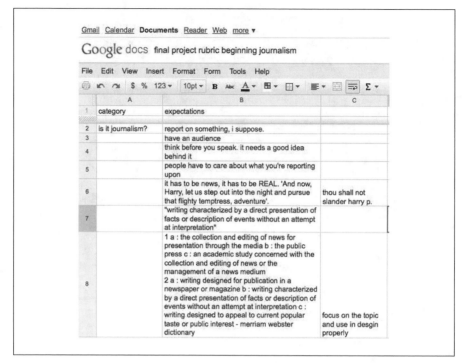

Figure 17.2. Student-created project rubric using Google Docs.

commenting out loud about the changes they saw evolving on the screen, giggling about what they saw showing up in the chat box, and not even noticing as the clock approached the end of class. Figure 17.2 shows what they created.

In this example, you can see how students began to build their list of what makes something journalism to serve as the expectations for the journalistic products they would design for their final projects. They also determined a few other categories they thought their work should be assessed on that are not included in the Figure 17.2 screen shot: organization, clarity, quality, and "having fun"—which they defined as "being excited about your work." I used their categories and expectations to craft a clear rubric that I presented to them the next day for their final approval. Of course, I made a few teacher edits to ensure that the rubric did indeed function as a clear enough guide, and I needed to edit out some of the unrelated banter, such as the Harry Potter comments. To make sure my efforts to build a rubric off of their collaborative work captured their ideas and intentions, we reviewed each category and its expectations, and I asked the class, "Can you live with this? Is this clear? What's confusing and needs to be clarified?"

What I describe here was the first time I had taken this group of students through this process. There was some initial confusion from the students about what I was asking them to do, but I assured them that it would make sense once they got going. And it did. They understood how it all worked very quickly. I also learned a few things as they worked that I'll think about for the next time I teach a group of students how to do this. For one, some students got upset when someone else edited out what they had written. At times, when two students were typing in the same cell at the same time, only one student's work saved to the spreadsheet. These problems can be solved, I think, by making sure students understand how the software works—that others will be editing their work, and that when two people are working in the same spot on the spreadsheet at the same time, not all of what is typed will be saved. I will also ask for a general agreement to edit kindly—it's okay to leave someone else's ideas there if you don't agree with them. Just type your ideas in a different cell.

Another thing I will approach differently has to do with the chat window. I had not previously asked students to set up Google accounts, which would have enabled me to restrict access to the spreadsheet to just the Google accounts I had invited to participate. In the case of invited-only participants, their contributions to the chat window at the side of the spreadsheet would have been labeled with their names. Because I had set the spreadsheet to open access for anyone, the contributions to the chat window from my students were anonymous, and you can probably imagine what that encouraged. There was a running stream of typical teenage silliness in the chat window as they worked on the spreadsheet building the rubric. This is not necessarily bad (they were having fun), but if you want that chat window to be a place for thoughtful discussion connected to the task, there's a better chance of that happening if students' contributions to the conversation are *not* anonymous.

In the end, the rubric was not necessarily of the same character as a rubric designed solely by me. Students wrote their expectations in teen-speak, for example, and the categories were not the exact ones I might have chosen. Even so, the students internalized the assessment targets because they negotiated them with one another, and every student saw his or her voice present in the rubric that guided their work on the final project for the class. Google Docs absolutely facilitated these outcomes effectively and efficiently.

Assessment

The goal of this process is an assessment tool itself. The measure of success here is ultimately how well the collaboratively built rubric guides students toward a strong end product, and how well the rubric facilitates the assessment of student work. We can, however, consider how to assess whether the activity meets the intended goals and objectives of this task. Below I suggest some markers of success toward each of the learning objectives outlined at the beginning of this lesson plan:

- Use Google Docs to effectively communicate with their classmates over the creation of a shared document.
  - Observe students as they work collaboratively on the rubric: Are they all engaged in the task? Are they talking out loud with one another about what they see happening before them on their computer screens? Is the chat window on the screen constantly rolling through conversation between the students as they work? Do students get up to speed fairly quickly with how Google Docs works so that they are able to contribute their individual ideas?
  - Examine the end product: Is there evidence of students responding to what others have proposed—suggestions, questions, other ideas, for example? Do you see evidence that students are building on one another's ideas and suggestions? Were students able to follow the format of the blank rubric and fill in their ideas where requested?
- Build a project rubric collaboratively, taking into account all students' ideas and suggestions.
  - Observe students as they work collaboratively on the rubric: Is anyone complaining that his or her ideas have been erased off the page? Are all students typing and contributing ideas willingly?
  - Examine the end product: Is there enough on the document to suggest that everyone in class contributed something? Is there an overall respectful tone present in what students have written, showing that they value the ideas of their classmates and did not discredit them?
- Review and examine the conventions of a particular genre of writing (in this case, journalism) to determine clear and high standards of quality.
  - Observe students as they work collaboratively on the rubric: Do you hear conversation out loud about the various qualities and characteristics of the type of writing they are focusing on for the rubric? Do students make reference to the models you presented to them? Do students seek resources to help define the genre?

◆ Examine the end product: Does the rubric clearly define quality writing in the genre of focus? Do students list expectations that are specific and detailed? Does the rubric list qualities that are clearly assessable?

■ Form a clear assessment target to guide students' individual work.

◆ Observe students as they work on the project: Do students use the rubric as a guide as they work?

◆ Reflect on how the rubric worked as an assessment tool: Are students able to self-evaluate their finished work meaningfully using the rubric they created? Does the rubric effectively facilitate your assessment of their work? Are you able to communicate feedback clearly to students using the rubric they created?

Connections and Adaptations

This collaborative rubric-building activity is endlessly adaptable. Use this approach to define any kind of writing or project-based activity in the language arts classroom. The key components are models for students to examine and compare in order to tease out standards of quality, and then time to work collaboratively on building the rubric. This can work for writing of all kinds, from portfolio-based projects, to dramatic performances, to film production projects, to multigenre work, to artistic responses, and so on.

The usefulness of Google Docs will only increase as students gain more facility with it. One of my students indicated that he thought they would get better at rubric building on Google Docs the more they practiced it. I hope to work toward making it a practice more seamlessly embedded into the regular workings of my classroom. And Google Docs can be used for so much more than collaborative rubric construction. I've set up a Google Docs page where students can ask me questions about the project as they work, and I answer their questions right on the document that is viewable and editable by the whole class. In this way, we are essentially building our own FAQ document for a particular project. I also built another Google Docs page to collect their feedback on this rubric-building activity. They were able to go to the feedback page at a time convenient for them and quickly and efficiently get their thoughts to me. The possibilities and potential of this kind of Web-based interaction are exciting; what I've outlined here is only a glimpse of how this might work into our regular classroom routines.

Works Cited

"Framework for 21st Century Learning." *Partnership for 21st Century Skills.* Partnership for 21st Century Skills, n.d. Web. 12 Aug. 2010.

"Getting Started Guide with Google Spreadsheets." *Google Docs.* Docs Help. Google, n.d. Web. 12 Aug. 2010.

Stiggins, Richard J. *Student-Involved Classroom Assessment.* 3rd ed. Upper Saddle River, NJ: Merrill Prentice Hall, 2001. Print.

18 Networked Research Reporting: Using Ning to Report Student Research

Joseph J. Geocaris
Adlai E. Stevenson High School, Lincolnshire, Illinois

Context

Adlai E. Stevenson High School, located in the far northern suburbs of Chicago, is home to approximately 4,300 students, more than 90 percent of whom go on to college following graduation. While the majority of our students have Internet access at home, those who do not can take advantage of multiple lab spaces at school available both during the day and before or after school. Our English program consists of a three-year core. Junior-level English highlights argumentative writing and requires a culminating research paper. The following lesson occurs at the end of that research paper unit. I designed the lesson to address course objectives in media literacy, public speaking, and argumentative writing while also working toward my own goal to update the research project to incorporate digital literacy.

Rationale

Social networking sites have proliferated across digital culture. Beyond popular sites such as Facebook, we can see elements of the model present on nonsocial websites like that of General Motors, whose site now contains a social-networking-esque "Owner's Community" with forums on issues such as trip planning and troubleshooting. At first considered a fad in the early 2000s, social networking has rapidly become an important space for literacy activities in our culture. Both my peers and my students use Facebook and similar sites for social purposes such as blogging, chatting with friends, sharing media, and posting pictures. However, social networking can also serve powerful functions in mobilizing groups of people to engage in professional dialogue, to petition, to protest, to raise awareness. Regardless of whether it is a group of English teachers using it for professional development, as on Jim Burke's English Companion Ning, or a high school student using it to organize his or her co-curricular club, the success of a social networking group relies on the same skills most emphasized through research writing, including attention to audience, clarity of purpose, and use of supporting materials. The similarity in these requisite skills between social media composition and assembling a research essay makes the presentation phase of a research paper an ideal time for students to explore social media as a serious writing and publication space. Unlike a PowerPoint presentation, which also allows students to practice these skills, social networking software has a simpler interface with fewer tools, thus forcing students to focus less on proficiency with software and more on the underlying purpose of using it to engage an audience as a topical authority.

Objectives

Students will be able to:

- Identify elements of social networking sites that can be rhetorically adjusted for the purpose of spreading awareness or motivating action among an audience
- Evaluate a social networking group to understand what makes it successful or unsuccessful, through applying effective argumentation and writing concepts
- Apply understanding of writing strategies to a Web-based, interactive, multimodal environment in order to create an effective social networking group
- Apply understanding of authorial credibility to the creation of a personal profile page

NCTE/IRA standards addressed: 4, 5, 6, 11, 12

Materials/Preactivity Preparation

- You will need to arrange for students to have access to a social networking site that allows users to create both profiles and member groups. Although Facebook enjoys immense popularity, that popularity as a social space makes it too distracting for students doing class work (Pascopella and Richardson). Several alternatives are available. In the past, I have used Ning, which used to be a free Web-based program that allows you to create your own social network; Ning is no longer free. Google Groups also performs the needed functions. Then there are sites such as ePals, Youth Voices, and Saywire, which are produced with educators in mind. If you are working in elementary or secondary education, it is critical, due to our legal responsibility to protect students, to ensure that whatever space you choose has adjustable privacy settings that let you control who can see and work on the site. Also ensure that, as network creator, you have privileges to delete any inappropriate content posted to the site.

- Especially if you are the first in your building to venture into social networking, you will want to meet with the individual in charge of your building's computer network. Sometimes this responsibility falls under an assistant principal, and in larger buildings it is a position on its own. Explain the project clearly, including its instructional objectives and why social networking is valuable to your students' learning (please feel free to cite any comments from the Rationale section; the Pascopella and Richardson article also offers valuable insights for this discussion). Some questions you will need to ask this administrator include:

  - ◆ Do we filter Internet sites on our network? If so, will we be able to unblock the social network I have created for my students? (You are likely going to want to have students look at multimedia, so it is also worth asking if it is possible to unblock YouTube for video and Flickr for photos.)

  - ◆ What legal obligations or concerns involving student privacy do I need to be prepared to address when I have students working on a network?

  - ◆ What legal obligations or concerns does the school have regarding intellectual property and copyright for students working on this project?

  - ◆ What are the expectations for use I need to make students aware of? What should be the consequences if students violate these expectations? (Chances are that your students, if they have school passwords, have already signed an agreement for proper use of technology in school, but if they haven't, you will want to work with the administrator to set some clear expectations for your students.)

- You will need to locate samples of both social networking groups that have been successful and those that have been unsuccessful in engaging the public. I found successful groups through searching Google News and EBSCO for "social networking" and "protest" or "movement." At this point, I do use Facebook because it is so widely used. I found failed groups by searching for a topic like AIDS on Facebook, and looking for groups with the fewest members and least activity. I found "A Consortium of Pub-Going Loose and Forward Women," which is in support of the original group that achieved notoriety in building a peaceful protest against the violence directed toward women in India in the spring of 2009 (Schive, Eracleous, and Helena). I like to include a group connected to local issues. This year, I might even use one that students at the high school started in response to recent decisions made by the school administration. But it is absolutely vital to find a failed group for students to look at. One example is "Health Care not SICK care!" (Young). In exploring the failed group's site, students can solidify their impression of what was working in the other, successful groups. My school does not allow access to Facebook, so I have had to take screen shots of each of these groups and post them online for students to study.

- You will need a computer connected to an LCD projection system to give short tutorials, display examples, collect information, and display students' work as they present. The LCD is the easiest way to do these things, but the social networking tools for distributing materials make it possible to do these activities if each student has proximity to a computer screen during these portions of the lessons.

- Students will need access to computers. The lessons that follow are in many ways modeled off workshop and inquiry approaches, which are more effective when students can work in class. However, if school computer access is not possible, but all students have home access, the lessons can be adjusted.

- Students will need a completed research paper that contains at least some element of argumentation.

- You will need to form student editorial groups. These groups consist of students who worked with similar topics on the research paper: environmental issues, educational issues, national politics, to name a few. My students have freedom to choose any topic for their research so long as it connects to a theme I establish: last year's was "Local perspective," and this year's will likely be "Looking to the past to look ahead." As a result, I usually have one "miscellaneous group" made up of students whose topics don't fit with others in the class. I capped the editorial groups at four members and did my best to ensure that at least one student in each group had a higher level of technological skills and could "teach" the others. Forming the groups created a collaborative culture throughout the project and, in doing so, helped to equalize discrepancies in individual student technology skills.

If you are new to the world of social networking, I recommend viewing The Common Craft Show's short video "Social Networking

in Plain English" on YouTube (http://www.youtube.com/watch?v=6a_
KF7TYKVc). This video can also serve as a brief introduction for
students to begin thinking about the purposes behind their social networking activities.

   While Ning's setup wizard makes the network creation process
very easy, you will need to make some decisions about how much
control you will exercise over the network. Remember, though, the
bottom line is that there has to be some trust between you and the
students. You will not be able to monitor all activity all the time.
Therefore, setting clear guidelines and reasonable, immediate consequences is necessary. I listed a set of expectations on my blog within
Ning, as well as consequences for inappropriate use (most of which
were taken directly out of school policy for misuse of technology). I
required all students to respond with an agreement to this policy or
else face removal from the network. This way I was able to be proactive and give students freedom to work without needing me to approve
all content—links, videos, pictures—before it could be displayed, a
process that would greatly inhibit the students' ability to work efficiently. The few infractions I've had came from students' misguided
attempts at humor: foul language or a profile picture with drug-related
innuendo. I simply used my privileges as a site administrator to delete
the content immediately and sent a stern warning to the student. Word
that I took down the content spread fast, and reprimanding one student
right away seemed to quickly solidify the social norms on the network.
The English Companion Ning's "Teaching with Technology" group is a
great forum for getting help and ideas from teachers who have experience with social networking technology in the classroom.

Time Frame

This lesson sequence assumes 50-minute class periods. It involves three
instructional days and two days of work time, followed by presentations to the class. Because of their different levels of typing skills and
of technological literacy, students will work at varied speeds. While I
initially planned on two days for presenting these social networking
groups to the class, I did not count on students voluntarily engaging
in question-and-answer sessions. I often cut these conversations short.
Using a social networking group as a presentation medium forced students to think carefully about engaging their audience. They distilled
their points more concisely and found multimedia artifacts to show the
class. Based on this conciseness, focus on an audience, and skillful use

of supporting media, the audience readily responded to the topics. As a result, my presentations took several days.

Description of Activity

At the start of the research paper process, approximately five weeks before the sequence I'm about to describe, I let students know they would be making their findings public through creating social networking groups. It's important that they conduct the research knowing they will be venturing into the public realm; it tends to increase motivation in the research process.

To start out the process of looking at social networking as a writing space, I post these questions on the digital projector at the beginning of the hour and ask students to think about them for a few moments:

- What social networks are you active on?
- Approximately how many "friends" or connections do you have on each network?
- What groups have you joined as part of your network?
- What are the rhetorical purposes of each group you have joined (e.g., persuasion, action, information, social communication)?

 These questions create the context for the assignment (see Handout 18.1 in the supplemental materials). The first is a basic introduction, but also lets me spot any shifts in students' activities from year to year. I use the second question to illustrate the immensity of the audience accessible through networking sites. Students struggle with the last question, so I have my own Facebook profile with the list of groups I have joined cued up on the projector. I open some of the groups and briefly explain their purposes. This short modeling sets up the day's activities.

After this initial discussion, I introduce the objectives for the day:

1. Students will be able to identify uses of social networking for advocacy and activism.
2. Students will be able to analyze social networking movements as live rhetorical artifacts.

At this point, I assign the editorial groups I have created. The students move to sit by one another and log on to the computers. While the computers are booting up, I explain an editor's job: to work with writers to refine, develop, and compose content. Further, this collaborative process is especially important in online endeavors, where most composing is done in teams. After providing the context for the editorial group, I outline their responsibilities to one another:

- To assist one another in generating ideas and possibilities for each person's project
- To assist one another with technology-related issues such as how to post a link or a photo
- To share relevant materials with group members
- To review and critique one another's social networking groups before they present them to the class
- To respond to the final product each member creates when he or she does present it to the class. They will ask you to either "approve" it and issue a grade, or "hold" the project and have the student revise. The goal of the groups is success for all members.

When I am done explaining, the groups and the computers are all logged in, and I direct students to the Ning network we have been using for most of the year. If you have used Ning before this activity, students will be able simply to log in. If you are starting new, you will need to allow time for students to get to the site, form accounts, and request membership, and for you to approve them. Within the Ning, I use the discussion forum function to post the day's instructions (see Handout 18.2 on the companion website) and any other attachments. Later, students will post their reflections on the day's activity to this forum. Of course, the directions can be given on paper, but a digital discussion forum allows students to see one another's work, respond to it, and use it to extend their own conclusions.

First, students see a list of key concepts we have discussed throughout the year: focus, support, organization, rhetorical effect, audience. The groups' first task is to hypothesize how these concepts might manifest on a social networking group. For the sake of time, I don't ask students to share these hypotheses, although I am sure to check in with each group as they brainstorm.

As the group discussions close, I post the Facebook group "South Africans Abroad" on the digital projector (Steynberg). With screen shots available and posted to the Ning Forum, I have students open it on their screens as well. As a group, we examine this page for how focus, support, organization, rhetorical effect, and audience are present on the site.

- FOCUS: Students should recognize that the focus is to connect South Africans living outside of the country to one another and to keep apprised of important South African issues. They should note that the group's administrators make this clear through the title and the text description.

- AUDIENCE: Students should pay close attention to the "Category" label, the description, the privacy setting, and the "Information" tabs. All of these give valuable insights to the intended audience. In this case, students should see that the audience is expatriate South African citizens who are interested in staying connected to the country's affairs.

- ORGANIZATION: We look at the placement of links, how often the group is updated, how many members are listed as administrators, and how discussion forums are used. We try to answer questions such as whether it is easy for members to engage in discussions and how easy it is to find information within this group.

- SUPPORT: Students should see that videos, pictures, and links to articles or blogs are used to support the site and increase its ability to achieve its goals. They should also notice how wall comments allow members to include links and sources not included by the group administrators. Here we try to note if there is a specific type of information commonly used on the site. Often this site uses politics-related links (although by this book's publication, its focus could have shifted dramatically).

- RHETORICAL EFFECT: Where students tend to struggle a bit is in recognizing the methods creators used to engage the audience and their rhetorical effects. I point them to the text and the comment walls to evaluate tone. Is this a friendly group? Is it focused on debate? Is it contentious? The group's avatar image also is worth looking at to see how the administrators are giving the group a "face." What is the effect of that image on the way members interpret other content?

I explain to students that their goal for today is to compare and contrast the ways three other groups use focus, audience, organization, support, and rhetorical strategies to get their message out; having looked at these groups, they need to come up with a conclusion about what makes for an effective social networking group. Students spend most of the class time in their editorial groups looking at the next three sites and discussing their effectiveness based on the key concepts listed above.

At the end of the hour, editorial groups post their conclusions about effective group composition and design to the discussion forum on Ning where they found the original assignment. I always encourage students not to simply repeat what others have posted, but if they have similar results, to elaborate on the idea by providing examples or further explanation. Between class sessions, I read through these postings and respond where I see fit, often with a question to extend thinking. I rarely respond to all posts. Since these are public discussions, all members of the class also receive any comment I make. There are no grades associated with this lesson.

On the second day, students begin class in their editorial groups. They read through the postings from yesterday's discussion (all of my classes work on the same network, so there will be several responses they haven't seen yet). As they look through their classmates' descriptions of what makes for an effective social networking group, I ask each group to synthesize the discussions into a "Top 5 Guidelines for Composing an Effective Social Networking Group." Each group shares their ideas, and I record them on a Word document that is displayed on the digital projector. We try to resolve any contradictory ideas that come up. For instance, if one group suggests that a good group has a concise description of purpose, and another group suggests that a good group elaborates on its purpose in its description, we try to bring the two ideas together. The result may sound something like "A good group, through its description, provides a necessary amount of information to its intended audience in order to make its purpose clear." I do ask that students elaborate if their guideline is something along the lines of "A good group uses support well." If needed, we will discuss what *support* means and revise the statement into something more specific, like "A good group consistently updates the links and informational materials on its site."

After sharing "Top 5 Guidelines," I pull up the Group Creator template in Ning and show students how to access it. I pause here to allow all students to get to the same place before giving a brief tutorial on how to create the group, insert a link, and load multimedia. Then I give students about 10 minutes to play with the features. Once that 10 minutes is up, we discuss the software limitations they are noticing. This is an important question for any Web 2.0 activity—what is our software and network *not* capable of doing? Only through this knowledge can the designer/writer generate an effective document, or even choose the appropriate programs through which to accomplish his or her goals. On a Word document, I record the constraints we have noticed, adding a few that I know about. We note that on our school's network, YouTube loads very slowly; the "group description" has a word/character limitation; discussion forums and text boxes allow for uploading documents, but the group main page does not. After this discussion, I make a blog post on Ning listing these constraints, and I encourage students to, while they work, add new constraints they run across, or ask questions by using the comment function of my blog.

With knowledge of what makes for a successful social networking group, as well as a functional understanding of the constraints posed by the Ning, students next read through their research papers again, and then work with their editorial groups to form a design plan for remediating the assignment into a social networking group. They need to define:

- The group's purpose
- The target audience
- Resources from their research they might be able to reuse here
- A list of additional multimedia resources they will need
- A plan for use of the wall and discussion forums

Before turning students loose to work, I emphasize to them that the sources they used for the research paper might not be appropriate in a social networking group—that many people will watch a video but not read a ten-page article. They need to do more research! I spend the rest of the class period conferencing with students as they work. The proposals are posted to a forum on the Ning I have set up. Overnight, I respond to each student's proposal with brief affirmative feedback and at least one question.

Assuming I can secure access to a computer lab, the next day is a student work day. I use the proposals to determine which students might benefit most from one-to-one assistance during this time. It's during this work time that students begin to notice that the actual composition does not take long, so I reinforce multiple times through the hour that a successful group requires planning and research for good multimodal support.

The third and final instructional day focuses on creating an online identity that reinforces authorial credibility. One way a social networking group differs from a PowerPoint presentation or an essay is that to participate in the network, the author must have a profile— a page that gives information about the author. A well-constructed profile can enhance the group creator's credibility regarding his or her topic, while a carelessly constructed one can diminish credibility.

To introduce the idea, I again like to start with Facebook. Since Facebook is primarily social, a user has a lot of options for information to include. I tell students that it is not uncommon for people to get in trouble on their jobs or in applying to college based on the information they have posted to their profiles. I ask students to write a brief reflection on the following questions:

- On most networks, you know the people who you connect with. But imagine that someone is being introduced to you through your profile. What would they think about you?

- How many "inside" references or jokes do you have on your profile? Could any of them be misinterpreted?

- Is there anything on here you wouldn't want a parent/teacher/employer to see?

- What, overall, does your profile say about you?

I do not have students turn this in, but I follow up by asking them if they think the same information would be acceptable on a professional site, like our Ning network. I then lead an inquiry discussion, helping students articulate what is different about our Ning network compared to Facebook.

I then pull up my personal page on Ning. I leave it blank for the purpose of this lesson. Together, the students and I examine the information it's possible to post on Ning, and any other tools present on the personal page each of them has. These tools and their appearance change frequently, so I will not list them here. The first year I implemented this lesson, Ning provided lots of "about me" options, including favorite books and favorite movies; this year the personal page is customizable by the network administrator through clicking on the "Manage" tab, followed by the "Profile Questions" application. Then I ask students to help me create a personal page that reinforces my credibility as their classroom teacher and administrator of the Ning network.

Following the group exercise of helping me to create my personal page, I ask students to spend time constructing their own profiles or adjusting the information they have already posted in a way that reinforces their credibility. I ask all students to change their profile picture to something that is more businesslike: for example, a shot of their faces rather than one of their favorite cars.

Again, if I can I secure the lab space for one more day, I do. On that final day, students work the entire period on composing their social networking groups or finishing up their profiles. On this day, I tell students they must work out a plan within their editorial groups for each member to get at least one set of peer feedback. I leave the guidelines for critique open, but tell them to refer back to the criteria we came up with as a class for what makes a group effective (by this time, I have posted onto the Ning the notes I took as we shared "Top Fives"). I also encourage reviewers to test all links and videos on the site. Their homework that night is to email one critique to a member of the editorial group, copying me on the critique.

When the students presented their groups to the class the following week, I had members of the editorial group, who had watched the presenter's work develop, submit a short assessment of the final product as compared to earlier versions, ultimately indicating whether they believed the presenter's group was ready for grading or needed to be held off. I did not have any students vote to hold a grade. If they had, I would have spoken to the presenter after class and given him or her specific suggestions for improvement, along with a deadline to make one last revision.

Students gave short presentations of approximately three minutes. In those three minutes, they used multimedia to address the audience and conveyed a vast amount of information. During question-and-answer sessions, which were added to the schedule on request from the students, the ideas presented through the group were discussed. Students discussed thematic connections between the different presenters. They debated design choice, and how the group might further expand its audience. They connected on personal levels with the topics. It was a fun set of presentations; my only regret was that I had to start cutting them short in order to get through them all.

Assessment

Ungraded formative assessments are integrated into each of these lesson plans: the analysis of the Facebook groups, the Top 5 criteria, the group proposal, the final peer editorial session. Beyond these products, the workshop approach I have described allows for continual, individualized conferencing and assessment. The more freedom students have, the more they will explore the tools. The final presentations to the class are graded, however. For the presentations, I have two sets of criteria: content of the speech and presentation factors. For each of the following points, I give students an E—excellent, S—satisfactory, or R—recommended revision:

Content Evaluation Points
- Explanation of group purpose
- Explanation of design choices
- Rationale for the group

Presentation Evaluation Points

- Use of the Ning to support claims
- Ease of speech
- Eye contact

As you can see from these criteria, I use this project to satisfy a public-speaking curriculum requirement. The criteria can easily be adjusted. I use the presentation component to give students experience in presenting their professional work to a board that has decision power. I do grade the product (aka the group) as well. This is a holistic grade. It is this grade the editorial group can vote to hold off for their member. Having the editorial groups take part in the assessment also helps keep students engaged during presentations.

Connections and Adaptations

I designed this lesson sequence to address several skills in areas of digital literacy and professional communications that students will need as they enter college and the job market. Since I am working with high school juniors, I opted to embrace the full range of complexity. Using networks as publication spaces, however, is an idea that can apply to any course that strongly features writing experiences that allow students to take ownership of and self-direct their composition process. I do not think this type of digital writing workshop environment will generate much investment if students are using it for literary analysis writing. The social networking group provides a space for synthesizing lots of different information and media in order to back up an opinion that the student feels strongly about after conducting in-depth research. Literary analysis writing is often too confined to the text it is analyzing to allow for this level of synthesis, and since it gets its drive from an extrinsic source (aka the text as opposed to the student's own curiosity), it is more difficult to get it to fit well with studies of purpose and audience engagement. The scope is simply too small. The best places to adapt these lessons are in research-driven assignments, or as a method for remediating personal essays. In each of these circumstances there is a strong personal investment from the writer and a wide range of potential audiences, thus making them ideal for the World Wide Web.

One adaptation in the procedure that can make it even more collaborative and more similar to actual workplace projects is to ask the editorial groups to work together to create only one page. In this incarnation, the members of the editorial group select the topic that they believe demonstrates the most likelihood for success in the social networking group format. The group then divides the tasks to build a single webpage. The procedures will remain mostly the same.

I have spent two years using Ning for this project, but I will be using the Google Sites platform next year. Not only has Ning moved to a fee-based platform, but it is also limited in terms of the features it can integrate; in most cases, adding on a new feature requires the user to create a new account. My students have found the platform difficult to work with when working collaboratively as a single group, as well as when they try to integrate news feeds or interactive components from other sites. By contrast, Google presents users with access to a wide variety of tools under a single account. The Sites program is built for collaborative purposes and has more flexibility.

Works Cited

Burke, Jim. "Teaching with Technology." *English Companion Ning.* Discussion Group Forum. Web. 4 Feb. 2010.

Common Craft. *Social Networking in Plain English. YouTube,* 27 June 2007. Web. 29 Dec. 2009.

Pascopella, Angela, and Will Richardson. "The New Writing Pedagogy." *District Administration* 45.10 (2009): 44–46, 48–50. Print.

Schive, Natasja, Hazel Eracleous, and Helena Helena. *Consortium of Pub-going, Loose and Forward Women's Support Group. Facebook,* 23 Dec. 2009. Web. 26 Dec. 2009.

Steynberg, Eddette. *South Africans Abroad. Facebook,* 22 Dec. 2009. Web. 26 Dec. 2009.

Young, Jason. *HEALTH care not SICK care! Facebook,* 14 July 2009. Web. 2009 Dec. 2009 http://www.facebook.com/group.php?v=info&ref=search&gid=90806611983.

Supplemental Resources

Argenti, Paul. "How Technology Has Influenced the Field of Corporate Communication." *Journal of Business and Technical Communication* 20.3 (2006): 357–370. Print.

Gee, James Paul. *What Video Games Have to Teach Us about Learning and Literacy.* Rev. & upd. ed. New York: Palgrave Macmillan, 2007. Print.

Selfe, Cynthia L., and Gail E. Hawisher, eds. *Literate Lives in the Information Age: Narratives of Literacy from the United States.* Mahwah, NJ: Erlbaum, 2004. Print.

Wagner, Tony. *The Global Achievement Gap: Why Even Our Best Schools Don't Teach the New Survival Skills Our Children Need—and What We Can Do about It.* New York: Basic Books, 2008. Print.

19 Photo Essays: Bring Literary Themes to Life

Molly Berger
East Valley Schools/Educational Service District 105
Yakima, Washington

Context

East Valley High School is located in a residential and rural area of the agriculture-rich Yakima Valley in Washington State. Of the 800 students in grades 9 through 12, few have traveled beyond the West Coast and Mexico, so their worldview is limited. Their use of Web 2.0 technologies, although expanding, is largely social. This lesson is part of a senior-level Contemporary World Literature class. The themes of the course focus on developing an understanding of the people of the world as well as exploring great literature.

Rationale

The images my students have of the people of the world are weak, often not even strong enough to form a stereotype. The images come from pictures in social studies texts or films, short stories in language arts classes, and, on occasion, the nightly news. The strongest images are ones of violence because that is what adolescents see in movies and on the news. The literature we read expresses universal themes while illustrating the specific characteristics of a people, place, and time. From class discussions on reading strategies and on selections, it is clear that many of my students do not create a picture in their minds when they read. This assignment is effective in giving them the mental image of the literature they read and in helping them see a connection between the characters and themselves. They begin to see the characters and conflicts as real. Following this assignment, they return to other written texts with more interest and confidence, which results in more thorough comprehension. The project also gives them a context from which to develop Web 2.0 skills for academic purposes.

Objectives

Students will be able to:

- Create a digital photo essay reflecting universal themes from selections read
- Select, crop, and position images to communicate the theme and create impact (audience senses the importance of the theme, remembers it beyond the viewing, and changes thinking or takes action)
- Write and place text that works with the images to communicate the theme and create impact
- Select music that works with the images and words to communicate the theme and create impact
- Use the features of the slide show program to communicate the theme and create impact
- Observe copyright laws

NCTE/IRA standards addressed: 8, 12

Materials/Preactivity Preparation

Technology

- Computers with Internet access, preferably in a lab setting with one student per computer; students can also work in groups with two or three students per computer
- PowerPoint, iMovie, Windows Media Maker, or a similar program
- Sample digital photo essays from YouTube, the Internet, or previous student work
- LCD projector
- Network server (optional)

Teachers should be familiar with searching for and saving images from the Internet and with the software chosen for the project, specifically how to

- Import and arrange images
- Embed music
- Place text
- Set transitions

Knowledge of additional features such as animation is helpful, but the students will often be able to help one another with these features.

To find tutorials, use an Internet search engine (Google, Bing, Safari, etc.). Type in the name of the program and tutorial ("PowerPoint Tutorial"). This will provide many choices. Be sure to check with your technology support for details on the version you are using and any building-specific instructions. Suggested Web resources are listed at the end of this lesson.

Time Frame

As written, this project takes nine class periods and is best spread over three weeks:

Day 1	The power of images discussion
Day 2	Introduction to the prompt and prewriting
Day 3	Computer lab: image collecting
Day 4	In-class evaluation of images; begin writing text and refining storyboard
Days 5–7	Computer lab: image gathering; create the project in PowerPoint, iMovie, or other program
Day 8	"Pitch Your Project," revise project, and continue working
*Day 9	Presentation day

*Between days 8 and 9, allow four to eight days for students to finish the project outside of class.

Description of Activity

Digital photo essays can be created in any class on any topic, but this lesson describes the assignment given in a Contemporary World Literature course for seniors. Before starting this project, the students have read a variety of short stories, essays, and poetry from contemporary authors from Africa, Asia, the Middle East, and Latin America. They have also studied two feature films as literature. This unit transitions then into the study of full-length novels. Films that I have found effective include *Hotel Rwanda*, *The Power of One*, *The Last Samurai*, and *In the Time of the Butterflies* because they engage the students emotionally, are well written, and develop conflict and character thoroughly. For novels, I have used *Things Fall Apart* by Chinua Achebe and *The Joy Luck Club* by Amy Tan because they deal with change and conflicts between generations and cultures.

Throughout the course, I scaffold media literacy skills using the key concepts and questions defined by the National Association for Media Literacy Education (NAMLE) (see http://namle.net/

publications/core-principles/). I use these with print and nonprint texts because I want the students to understand both as means of communicating our thoughts, emotions, and experiences. This background knowledge of both formats is essential for students to create a quality project that reflects the kind of thinking we expect in an English class and that merits the time spent.

I begin the project by showing photo essays on a variety of themes. I find current samples on YouTube or other Internet sites by searching for "photo essay and inspiration." We discuss:

- How effective is the photo essay in communicating its message to its audience?
- How was the message developed?
- What could be done differently to make it effective
  - ◆ to a different audience?
  - ◆ if the theme were changed?

These questions require students to look beyond the surface content and design of the photo essay into the purpose and the craft.

Next, we develop a list of criteria for evaluating the effectiveness of a photo essay. I start with the students in small groups and have them create a list on chart paper so that we can post and view them together. We use these to create a class list, which we then use as a checklist and a scoring guide. I use the computer and a projector to facilitate the collaborative writing process.

After we have drafted our list, I bring up a search engine and type in "photo essay and criteria." We select two or three sites to check and view their criteria to see if we have left out any critical elements. I model the process of this search but have found it is wise to search before class and to preview the sites.

With this preparation, the students are ready for prewriting on the second day. I hand out the assignment prompt and have the students highlight the key points (see Handout 19.1 in the supplemental materials). They ask me for clarification, and I note any aspects they have overlooked. To set the assignment in their minds, I then have them freewrite for 10 minutes on what they are expected to do and ideas they might have. Next, students form small groups of three or four to exchange and generate ideas. To encourage discussion, I use stem sentences such as

Student A:

"One idea I am thinking of is . . ."

Group responses:

"I think this will/won't meet the assignment because . . ."

"One idea you could try would be . . ."

The groups usually move quickly beyond these questions, but these give the conversation direction.

The students next choose to work as an individual or with a partner. Because I have access to a computer lab, have six student computers in my classroom, and most of the students have computers at home, I allow this to be a personal choice. Although larger groups can work, I prefer not to have groups of three or more as it is difficult to engage all in the creating and editing process at the computer.

Next, students begin their plan sheet and storyboard. The plan sheet asks them to list their theme, audience, purpose, specific message, and mood. The storyboard consists of squares on which to sketch the image ideas and lines below for them to make text, music, and technical notes. These can be printed on regular paper, but I like to have the students draw the storyboard on 16" × 20" paper. It gives them a better sense of the project as a whole. At this point, the storyboard is very rough. Students need to dig into the project and then return to the storyboard to develop and refine it.

With this background planning, on the third day students are ready for the computer lab. My students have been to this lab, so they understand how to log in to the computers and how to save their work on the file server under my folder. Before they are allowed to start their work, I review searching for and saving images from search engines. Web 2.0 technology allows us to find images in a number of ways for use in classroom projects. We review fair use and copyright policies for educational purposes and how to cite each image.

If this is new for your students, be sure to plan enough time for them to be successful. I set up a folder on the server labeled "image bank" and require each student or group to contribute ten images. All students can use the pictures in their projects but are not limited to them. This cuts down on the amount of class time used to collect pictures. Be sure to have the students save the picture from the actual file, not from the thumbnail on the search page. The thumbnail photos are too small to project clearly.

After our first lab day, we meet in the classroom to clarify, troubleshoot, and evaluate the images collected. I have found this day essential to moving the students from mediocre to powerful photo essays. From the image bank, I project several of the pictures collected, and we discuss them using the criteria we have developed. I have the students reflect on any additional images they need.

We then begin considering the written text of the photo essay. Reviewing the examples we already viewed, we discuss the power of the words themselves and their placement and format. We consider the importance of word choice and being concise.

To draft their text, students return to the texts we have studied and the reflections they wrote in response to each. I have the students find five powerful quotes from the literature and five powerful statements from their writing. In small groups, they share their lists, looking for common themes. They then combine them and write them on poster paper to hang in the room. As a whole class, we look at the list and circle the words that affect us the most. The students then return to their plan sheets to review and revise their themes and write their text. At this point, we work without the images. Students should focus only on their message.

Next, we return to the storyboard, and students sketch in the placement of texts and images. Many at this point want to get back to the computer, but I emphasize the need to know where they are headed so that their message drives the media rather than the media driving the message.

We have yet to talk about music, photo cropping, transitions, and special effects, but the students need to get their ideas from paper to program. After they have most of the images for their essays and are placing their text, we take time for this. I ask, "When do music, special effects, and transitions add to or detract from a work?" The students begin to see that these techniques must be carefully planned, just like all other aspects of writing.

During the eighth class session, we return to the classroom. The students have their first version or draft complete, and we spend time revising and editing. This activity encourages them to view their work with a critical eye. First, I divide the class into groups with three or four photo essays to review. Each group or individual will "pitch" the project to the whole group. They explain:

- Their purpose, audience, and theme
- What they see as particularly effective in the project
- One quality they would like the group to particularly evaluate

Each student responds with

- Something he or she really likes
- One question
- A response to the writer's question

Following this discussion, I have each group return to the rubric developed by the class and evaluate their own work.

The final revision and publishing of the photo essays is done outside of class time. I give the students time four or five days after the group review to finalize the project. Students can come in before or after school or during lunch or another class period to work, or they can finish them at home.

Assessment

Formative assessment is done informally throughout the unit and is critical to the quality of the final products. I circulate when the students are working to answer questions, redirect them when they are off course, and extend their thinking.

Our final assessment is to share our work. As a class, we plan the presentation day, from where to project the photo essays, to arrangement of seats, to snacks. All the students move their projects to a folder on the file server so that we can easily move from project to project. The students are not allowed to introduce or comment on their projects; the photo essay must stand on its own to communicate the message. I use the rubric developed by the class to give a preliminary score to each project. After the viewing, I have the students write a response to "What did I learn about myself as a student and the writing process in creating this photo essay?" I use these two elements to assign a final grade to the photo essay.

Each semester that my students complete these projects I am amazed by the depth of their thinking. Students who had composed just enough to get by on written essays find their voice. Others express themselves in new ways. All return to their reading with a fresh approach and an increased ability to "picture" the text. They value their ability to experience other cultures vicariously through literature, and they have developed Web 2.0 skills in academic work.

Connections and Adaptations

This lesson can be adapted to student technology skills and the availability of computers. These adaptations can include:

- Creating templates to help simplify the process
- Creating the photo essay as a whole class, collaborating by using one computer and a projector. Break the process down to 15 minutes each day to keep the students focused.
- Extending research papers by having students create a photo essay on their thesis statement
- Having students create a visual poem in the photo essay format
- For advanced students, requiring more use of animation and special effects, as well as requiring more in-depth analysis and evaluation

Work Cited

National Association for Media Literacy Education (NAMLE). "Core Principles of Media Literacy Education in the United States." *National Association for Media Literacy Education*, Nov. 2007. Web. 21 Dec. 2009.

Supplemental Resources

"A Day in the Life of Africa." *Washington Post*. The Washington Post Company, 28 Feb. 2002. Web. 15 Dec. 2009.

"Getting Started: Images Help." *Google Images*. Google, n.d. Web. 15 Dec. 2009.

"The Code of Best Practices in Fair Use for Media Literacy Education." *Center for Social Media*. School of Communication, American University, Nov. 2008. Web. 15 Dec. 2009.

"The Rights of Children." *UNICEF*. Unicef, 20 Nov. 2008. Web. 15 Dec. 2009.

IV Interactive Literature Study: The Paperback vs. the Computer Screen

"To be or not to be . . ." Twittering, Blogging, IMing While Studying *Hamlet*? Is *That* the Pedagogical Question?

Mary T. Christel
Adlai E. Stevenson High School, Lincolnshire, Illinois

I have a shocking confession. As a teacher of literature, I am a "digital dinosaur." I thought my status as an AP teacher shielded me from the expectations, even the pressure, of integrating Web 2.0 technology into teaching the works of fiction, poetry, and drama that would prepare my students for the demands of the exam. The College Board would never "test" my students' virtuosity with Web-based tools like blogs, VoiceThread, Facebook, or Twitter in the rigors of literary analysis. And my students certainly could enjoy a Shakespearean tragedy between the pages of a Folger print edition of the text. For me, the study of literature has been a page-based endeavor, with well-selected detours into the realm of popular culture through the study of film adaptations, contemporary music, or visual art to examine how themes common to literary works are expressed through nonprint forms. I occasionally cast an envious pedagogical gaze toward colleagues who were using iMovie effortlessly and successfully so students could create their own video versions of classic works or craft surprisingly sophisticated movie trailers. Even before the advent of blogs and Nings, colleagues set up email chats to freshen up face-to-face small-group discussion of novels. I tended to fret over the loss of time devoted to training students to use the software. I further fretted over my own lack of expertise and any technology-based activity's success being dependent on a classroom set of laptops that frequently didn't work well or at all. With a background in theater, I never hesitated to bring strategies from my training in creative dramatics to promote greater student engagement, but I was never truly, formally trained in how to successfully integrate technology into my teaching. I certainly sat through enough mandated technology inservice experiences, but they always seemed ill-timed or, if they did provide some intriguing applications, I never seemed to have the time to become comfortable with the program or website. And ultimately and foolishly, I thought the technology was better integrated into writing instruction. Teaching senior electives, I benefited from the technology integration experiences my students had had writing essays and research papers in the standard curriculum that leads them to me.

I embarked on the project of editing this book to immerse myself in what emerging technology, and its related tools, can lend to all facets of ELA instruction by seeing what teachers are accomplishing in the field. Taking cues from various NCTE articles I have read and presentations I have attended, I need to give myself permission to learn along with, and from, my students, as well as from more technologically savvy colleagues.

The study of literature is certainly going to change as a result of the proliferation of various devices that act as digital repositories for text. Whether a reader uses a Kindle, a Nook, or an iPad, the ability to access text has changed dramatically. It is foolish to think that every student will be toting around a digital reader in the near future, but eventually the stacks of paperbacks filling up book rooms will give way to a durable, affordable device that will allow teachers and students a greater range of choice in what will comprise shared and individual reading experiences. And students, those "digital natives" who are more accustomed to reading text on a computer screen, won't find reading a short story, poem, novel, or play on a digital reader that strange; many will prefer it to reading a musty, tattered paperback. They are probably using that device now to read magazines, newspapers, and graphic novels, among other types of out-of-school texts. This expansion of access is no different from the advent of the paperback book when Penguin in the United Kingdom and Pocket Books in the United States introduced that radical publishing format in the 1930s, providing affordable books for the classroom and releasing teachers from the tyranny of textbook editors' selections. So technology will continue to provide teachers and their students easier access to a wide range of reading experiences.

Technology can promote greater engagement with any text, including, I hope, with texts that students find difficult to navigate like those of Shakespeare or Dickens. But it is not enough to rely on slick classroom digital readers to make the act of reading relevant for those students who already carry the capability to text or phone a friend, connect with the Internet, and listen to music or watch a movie or a television program on a single "smart" device in their pocket. Since they are already "programmed" to interact with a variety of experiences using a variety of digital tools, it is then incumbent upon teachers to recognize how many of those tools can be naturally applied to students' engagement with a literary text. The tricky part is making sure that the application isn't merely a gimmick that panders to their reliance on and preference for technology. Teachers need to consider how technology and Web-based applications can help redefine both the text they are reading and the strategies they are applying to that course of study. For students, using technology is like breathing the air—they take it for granted and sometimes don't fully understand what can be accomplished under new or unorthodox circumstances.

As I consider the lessons presented in this section, I envision my use of Web 2.0 tools as first helping students to carefully read the text, then moving them into a keener interpretation, and finally leading them to more meaningful responses to that text that could take many forms, not just a response journal or a traditional essay. Now, this is not an amazing discovery on my part. Overall, this progression certainly mirrors any traditional pedagogy that has been applied to the teaching of literature. For some of us, the application of technology might be relegated to the "dessert" at the end of a unit, something that allows teachers and students to dabble with digital technology, new media, or popular culture. In the past, this would have included screening a film adaptation of a novel or a play, and it would have been considered an "enrichment" activity. It would also have been seen as expendable if time didn't allow. However, the most meaningful application of these digital tools must permeate a unit of study, thereby becoming more organic to the entire process.

The application of online tools can expand how the creative and interactive study of literature appeals to students who learn best through visual and auditory experiences. Luke Rodesiler, for example, introduces his lesson, "Symbolic Analysis of *One Flew over the Cuckoo's Nest*: Literature, Album Art, and VoiceThread," by defining the components of visual literacy and encouraging students to analyze visual images in order to fully understand and appreciate the layers of meaning those images possess. Our natural response to visual images can take the form of a reflex action. We have a tendency to skim the surface of most images, especially since we live in an environment where images crowd our real space as well as our online space. But developing digital literacies does not have to come at the expense of other forms of literacy. They provide yet another opportunity to meld traditional with new literacies rather than at the expense or denigration of more traditional literacy skills.

Abigail J. Kennedy's teacher tips for her lesson on creating book review podcasts remind me that some students don't necessarily welcome the prospect of a "computer project" as part of a classroom experience. I know I have students who resist the idea of "film analysis" because they think it will spoil their pleasure in watching films as a casual, pleasure-driven activity. In their eyes, I am out to ruin their fun. The same notion applies to appropriating the tools and activities that students see as part of their nonacademic life, though various reports and experts' sound bites note that adolescents and young adults are not necessarily embracing the digital tools that adults embrace. For example, Twitter has not taken hold among high school students in the way Facebook has become an obsession. Adolescents tend to be early adopters of new technology trends, but they are quick to discard what adults co-opt, though that wasn't the case when their parents showed up on Facebook. So this might be a caveat: take care to select a tool that has meaning and potency for students, or if it is a tool they have adopted or discarded, provide a rationale that will help them reconsider how that tool can be used effectively or creatively in this new context. For instance, Suzanne C. Linder's lesson on creating tweets for Jane Austen's *Emma* and friends is thoroughly delightful, and I can't wait to have Dante and Virgil "tweet" as they make their way through the *Inferno*.

As I was preparing to write this piece, I came across a segment on *Good Morning America* that reported on parental attitudes regarding students' use of cell phones, as well as parents placing limits on texting and social networking. Forty-three percent of parents responding to the poll thought that students should not use social networking until they were eighteen years old ("How Young Is Too Young?"). That statistic led me to wonder whether some parents will not appreciate having social networking brought into an academic setting. If there is a strong prohibition or embargo on using certain online applications at home, how can educators accommodate and respect the choices some parents make in limiting their children's access with or without adult supervision? This dilemma is similar to the one teachers face when considering the use of R-rated films in the classroom. In some academic contexts and communities, there is little resistance to using those films in a thoughtful and responsible manner, but many teachers are required to send home permission slips to make sure that parents are properly informed and allowed to make choices that are consistent with their values and family policies. Just because we live in an environment in which texting, tweeting, and filing status reports seem ubiquitous to most, we cannot assume that everyone endorses or values those practices. Also, we might be asking students to adopt the persona of a character in a "live" online situation as a way to explore their understanding of a literary character, when we might discourage and disapprove of students adopting pseudonyms and contrived personae to mask their identities online. I guess it comes down to clearly articulating to our students, their parents, and, let's not forget, administrators of our educational purpose in using these tools in a responsible and pedagogically sound context.

Recently I came across a book on one of those "impulse purchase tables" placed at the entrance of Borders or Barnes and Noble, which availed me of a resource for gleaning activities for my own AP class. Entitled *Ophelia Joined the Group Maidens Who Don't Float: Classic Lit Signs on to Facebook* (Schmelling), I initially thought it would be a good addition to the books that piled up on my dining room table as I started this project. Also, I thought it might convince me that the whole Facebook, Twitter, and texting phenomenon heralded the death of sophisticated literary discourse. I must admit that it proved to convince me of the opposite. I have always been a fan of ShrinkLits, those clever little poems that reduce a great work of literature into memorable ditties that capture the essence of plot, character, symbolism, and theme to provoke both a chuckle and a newfound insight into what is essential and eternal about the work. Sarah Schmelling takes the ShrinkLit concept to the next level of cleverness and insight. Her tributes to the works of classical, world, and American literature include author and character profiles, author-sponsored ads, famous characters' playlists, IM chats, news feeds, and "quizzes" of all sorts. The volume includes an introduction penned—or, rather, keyboarded—by William Shakespeare himself, and that made me wonder how the likes of the Bard of Stratford would have embraced the cyber tools that allowed him to engage an audience with tremendous reach and scope. Then, what will literature look like, read like, as our notion of what text is and what a "literary" text is evolves over time and in cyberspace?

The answer to that question came partially with the debut of a quarterly literary magazine in June of 2008. *Electric Literature* (http://www.electricliterature.com) features five short stories in its print incarnation and can be accessed "on paper, Kindle, e-book, iPhone, . . . and as an audiobook" (Lee 1). Its aim is to "revitalize the short story in the age of the short attention span" (Lee 1). The journal's masterstroke is the subscriber's ability to track a story as it evolves on Twitter day by day. Now, Shakespeare's Polonius claimed that "brevity is the soul of wit," but I am hoping that this Twitter-based brevity is not the pervasive future of literature. I am convinced that the novelty of literary production tied to emerging and established microblogging and social networking tools will not overtake the need for the character-rich, intricately plotted narratives that will continue to exist in a variety of formats that provides a wider range of choice and accessibility to the eager reader.

Since I don't want to face extinction as that "digital dinosaur," I am choosing to evolve into a twenty-first-century teacher of literature. The competent or masterful use of Web 2.0 tools might not be tested on the AP exam or by the ACT, but meaningfully applied, these tools can powerfully engage students in reading, analyzing, and appreciating literature on a level that will enable them to interpret poetry and prose using the more conventional analytical tools that a high-stakes test privileges. And naturally, the College Board will need to evolve in this Web 2.0 environment to keep pace, and maybe even set the pace, with the changing nature of literary expression and its analysis. In that case, I will be ready to meet the challenge.

Works Cited

"How Young Is Too Young? Parents Struggle Over Limits." *Good Morning America*. ABC. 21 Feb. 2010. Television. Rep. by Claire Shipman.

Lee, Felicia R. "Serving Literature by the Tweet." *New York Times* 27 Oct. 2009, "The Arts": 1. Web. 28 Oct. 2009.

Schmelling, Sarah. *Ophelia Joined the Group Maidens Who Don't Float: Classic Lit Signs on to Facebook*. New York: Plume, 2009. Print.

Recommended Resources

Albers, Peggy, and Jennifer Sanders, eds. *Literacies, the Arts, and Multimodality*. Urbana, IL: National Council of Teachers of English, 2010. Print.

Darnton, Robert. *The Case for Books: Past, Present, and Future*. New York: PublicAffairs, 2009. Print.

Growing Up Online. Frontline. PBS, 22 Jan. 2008. Prod. Michael Kirk. Web. 12 Aug. 2010.

Kajder, Sara. *Adolescents and Digital Literacies: Learning Alongside Our Students*. Urbana, IL: National Council of Teachers of English, 2010. Print.

20 The *Macbeth* Mystery: An Interactive Approach to Challenging Language

Laura L. Brown
Adlai E. Stevenson High School, Lincolnshire, Illinois

Context

I teach *Macbeth* to my sophomore English class of twenty-five students at Adlai E. Stevenson High School (with an enrollment of approximately 4,300 students) in the northern suburbs of Chicago. These sophomore students come to me having read *Romeo and Juliet* in the ninth grade. They know what to expect from a Shakespearean tragedy but generally know nothing of *Macbeth* specifically. An overarching theme of many of our texts at this level is "ethical action and moral dilemma." We study Bradbury's *Fahrenheit 451*, Orwell's *Animal Farm*, and Martin Luther King, Jr.'s "A Letter from Birmingham Jail." I teach *Macbeth* in the early part of the second semester.

Rationale

Everyone knows how a Shakespearean tragedy is going to end. It's hardly any mystery: we all know that the main character is going to die. The mystery (and the thing that Shakespeare really wants us to pay attention to) is the why. That is where the real mysteries of his tragedies unfold and where we find the important lessons that his plays can teach us. By setting up our study of *Macbeth* as a mystery to be solved, I hope to focus my students on the motivations for the characters' choices and the moral lessons that Shakespeare teaches through this tragedy. The interactive technology, Promethean ActivBoard with Activoters, helps us to examine the language and imagery more closely, use strong visual tools to enhance students' experience with the text, accurately assess students' understanding, promote students' active participation, and respond to students' needs in real time. I also use video material from Discovery Education's United Streaming and BrainPOP to support our understanding of Shakespeare, tragedy, and drama.

Objectives

Students will be able to:

- Annotate text noting meaning, connections, style elements, and language structure and conventions
- Accurately identify important details and infer meaning from them
- Recognize the universal truths of the play and the connections they have to our lives today
- Write an essay that demonstrates an understanding of the important lessons of the tragedy and how those lessons are revealed in the play
- Write an essay that uses appropriate diction, syntax, tone, and content for a particular circumstance and audience

NCTE/IRA standards addressed: 2, 3, 5, 6, 11

Materials/Preactivity Preparation

- A copy of *Macbeth* by William Shakespeare. I use the Cambridge edition.
- Laptop or desktop computer
- Data projector
- Promethean ActivBoard with Activotes and appropriate software; other interactive technology could work (e.g., SMART Board)
- Web video from Discovery Education's United Streaming and BrainPOP
- Mystery assignment description
- A "clue" chosen for each scene (provided)

To prepare to use the ActivBoard, I went through a two-day initial training session with the board and the voters, and continued with occasional help sessions and online tutorials as a follow-up. I learned how to create a "flip chart" (a slide-by-slide presentation), use the annotation tools, and set up and use the interactive voters. Anyone familiar with PowerPoint or Keynote software would find setting up a flip chart lesson to be very similar to these presentation software programs. The software allows you to operate the computer from the board using a special pen that works like the mouse. The annotation tools allow you or the students to highlight and write in various colors on the flip chart slide (or anything else on the computer screen, including documents and webpages). With a click of a button on the toolbar, you can call for a vote, and students can use the voters to enter responses that are then displayed on the board.

The company's teacher resource website, Promethean Planet (http://www.prometheanplanet.com), provides resources, support, and professional development for teachers. This lesson uses the board's most basic tools, so it works for teachers who are only just beginning to use interactive technology. Atomic Learning (http://www.atomiclearning.com/) also provides good tutorials for learning the basics of using the board and its software.

It's important to note that there are many different kinds of interactive technology available, and this lesson is easily adapted to whatever software and hardware you have. While the interactive technology makes this lesson engaging and powerful, you can adapt it to more low-tech alternatives, or use only the pieces of it that suit the available technology.

Time Frame

I usually spend about four and a half to five weeks with Shakespeare. That includes preparing students to read the play, reading the play, and writing the essay. We do most of the reading of the play in class using audio recordings and film versions, as well as performing some of the scenes ourselves. You could shorten the time frame by assigning more of the reading outside of class. I have also spent as much as six weeks with this unit, adding a project in which students create a movie trailer for the play (see Handouts 20.1 and 20.2 on the companion website).

Description of Activity

To set up our study of *Macbeth*, I use some great Web resources to provide basic background. Discovery Education Streaming (http://streaming.discoveryeducation.com/) provides a variety of video content for the classroom, including a great set of videos on tragedy and William Shakespeare by a group called "The Standard Deviants." This is a subscription service and one that I would highly recommend for access to high-quality streaming or downloadable video content for the classroom in all subject areas. Another subscription service called BrainPOP (http://www.brainpop.com/) also offers some video material that provides the basic background for reading Shakespeare.

As we begin reading the play, I set up the problem in this way:

"Why would a man who was a hero in battle, who enjoyed the trust and loyalty of many good friends, who became king of all of Scotland, be overthrown and killed by his own noblemen? And why would a woman who suddenly got all she ever wanted, who was made queen of Scotland, go mad and kill herself?"

The scenario that students receive at the start of the lesson is as follows:

> "Eleventh-century Scotland was a violent and troubled country. Feuding families and clans fought to control trade and territory. The castle was the power base of each rival war-lord (thane). Political murder and revenge killings were commonplace. Marauding Vikings and Norsemen raided constantly.
>
> Macbeth was born into this violent world in 1005, son of the great family that ruled Moray and Ross. His own father was murdered by his cousins. Macbeth married Gruach, granddaughter to a High King of Scotland. They had no children of their own." (Gibson 1993)
>
> Imagine that you are a part of this world, too. Macbeth and Lady Macbeth are dead and you are asked by the new king to investigate their deaths. You are asked to report not only how they died but also why. The new king wants to learn from the mistakes of Macbeth to avoid the same violent end. It is your job to solve the mystery of this terrible tragedy.

 The clues for this mystery are important lines from the play in each scene (see Handout 20.3 in the supplemental materials). As we read each scene in class, a clue is revealed from that scene. I have prepared each clue on a separate flip chart slide with a corresponding image or video clip. The images are paintings, sketches, and photos, and the video clips are from various productions of the play. These can be obtained from image searches on Google, Yahoo!, or Bing; video searches can be found on YouTube or TeacherTube.

Together we annotate the language of the clue using the interactive annotation tools (see Figure 20.1). We highlight key words, paraphrase meaning, and label literary techniques. Annotating is a skill that students find difficult. When they have these interactive tools and strong visual cues to show them the process of annotation, they begin to see its purpose and value. Also, because we are not annotating the entire play but only a small portion of each scene, students find it less intimidating and overwhelming. It also allows us to examine the

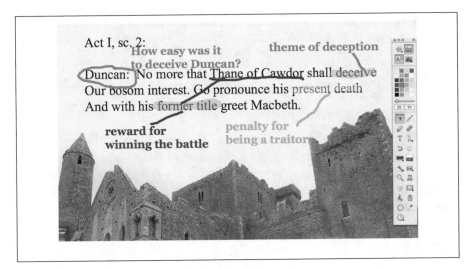

Figure 20.1. Student annotations using interactive tools.

small portion of the text very closely, digging deep into the diction and syntax of each line, rather than spending all our time translating the entire scene and reviewing events.

We also examine the image or video to consider the various interpretations that are possible in the theatrical production. We can annotate the image as well. Students interpret the text of the clues, make and adjust hypotheses regarding the key questions, and write notes in a reading journal—I call it their "detective's notebook." At first, students rely entirely on me to point out the "clue" in the scene, but after the first act or so, I begin to encourage them to guess at what the clue might be. Students begin to develop the ability to pick out the key detail or clue on their own. By the time we get to the final act of the play, students are accurately picking out the key details before the clue is revealed. When we are finished reading the play, the students have all the clues they need to understand why this tragedy happens.

From these clues, students should arrive at the following conclusions:

- Ambition can be destructive. This tragic flaw in Macbeth's character, which was magnified by Lady Macbeth's own ambition, led to his eventual death.

- Evil is seductive and dangerous. The witches tempt Macbeth with the promise of greatness. Their purpose is clearly to corrupt him, and they succeed. The murderous intentions and actions of Macbeth and his wife were evidence of the evil that took over their destinies.

- Nothing is ever as it seems. Macbeth and Lady Macbeth may appear to be one thing but are in actuality something different. Much of the play is about the difference between appearance and reality.

- Guilt and conscience are powerful forces. Both of these characters suffer agonies of conscience as a result of the actions they take to make it to the top.

The visual enhancements, colorful annotation tools, and interactive assessments help students to engage in the language of Shakespeare in new and valuable ways. Students are not passive receivers of information, but are interacting with the text and each day's lesson in ways not possible before.

Assessment

Periodically, in conjunction with a clue, students will perform an interactive assessment. They answer a series of multiple-choice questions that test their ability to interpret, analyze, and make meaning from the text. Each question appears on a slide, and students respond using the handheld voting device. Student responses are then shown in a graph on the board that shows how many students chose each answer (see Figure 20.2). The advantages of this are many. All students are participating—every student answers every question. Students can answer anonymously, providing them with the ability to take guesses safely without the embarrassment of being wrong in front of their peers. I get immediate feedback, knowing exactly how many students understand and how many don't. This allows me to make adjustments in my teaching, immediately responding to what my students most need.

The summative assessment of reading skills at the end of the play involves reading and interpreting not only two scenes from *Macbeth* but also a new scene from *Julius Caesar*. This assessment is designed to determine whether students can apply their newfound skills to a cold reading from another play. The multiple-choice questions are similar to those given during the interactive assessments that students took during our reading of the play.

As a final written assessment, students respond in writing to the following prompt:

> Now that you have the clues, it's time for you to make your report to the king! In a well-developed essay, write an analysis in which you explain the reasons for Macbeth's and Lady Macbeth's tragic end. What lessons can we learn from their tragic story? Use some of your clues as support for your reasons. Be

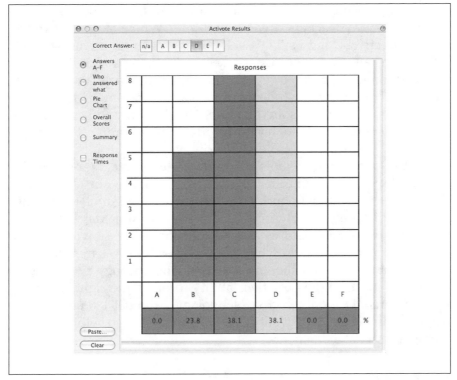

Figure 20.2. An interactive student assessment using ActivBoard's Activote program.

> sure to integrate your quotations smoothly into your writing using appropriate lead-ins. Also, you must cite the lines noting the act, scene, and line number.

(See Handout 20.4 on the companion website for the essay assignment.)

Connections and Adaptations

The mystery strategy is one that can be adapted to any piece of litera-ture in the curriculum at any level, but I think it is particularly well suited to Shakespearean tragedy. Ninth graders could use it with *Romeo and Juliet*; seniors could use it with *Hamlet*. Middle school teach-ers could use it with a text like *The Giver*, where students need to note important details and put them together to draw conclusions about the true nature of the dystopia.

The interactive tools are, of course, useful in many other learn-ing contexts. I use the annotation tools and voters to great advantage when teaching grammar skills. Teaching grammar is always a challenge, and many teachers dread it. Drilling? Whole language? Inductive? Deductive? Linguistic? Whatever approach, it seems students often disengage. The interactive whiteboard is a way to get 100 percent participation in a grammar lesson, and I get immediate and complete feedback showing what students understand. I can make the experience so fun that students are often begging me for another grammar lesson. This interactive tool has transformed my grammar lessons into fun, productive experiences with amazingly positive results.

And because these tools also allow for easy integration of video, websites, and images into instruction, they enhance our close analysis of both print and nonprint text. I can use this tool to improve instruction in the research process: how to use online databases, how to evaluate webpages, and what kinds of sources to use when. But do students know what to do when faced with a real research project? I use an interactive assessment to walk students through two different research projects and assess their ability to make the right choices in their research. Using interactive technology, I can get 100 percent participation and immediate feedback during the lesson to help me find all the right "teachable moments."

Work Cited

Gibson, Rex, ed. *Macbeth*. William Shakespeare. Cambridge School Shakespeare. New York: Cambridge UP, 1993. Print.

21 Podcasting the Traditional Book Review

Abigail J. Kennedy
Pasco High School, Dade City, Florida

Context

Pasco High School consists of more than 1,200 students in a fairly rural, small-townish community. Students are of numerous racial backgrounds, with a fairly large migrant/ESOL population. I've used this lesson with regular and honors students in the English curriculum, as well as with Advanced Placement literature students, using adaptations. This lesson occurs at the end of a quarter (or other form of unit) after many weeks of sustained silent reading (SSR) class periods.

Rationale

The purpose of using podcasting technology for a "traditional" book review is that students (and teachers) are tired of listening to someone "talk" about a book. Adding in the elements of recorded voice, music, and images provides a more interesting presentation of a book and gives the students a more realistic audience. Instead of just presenting to a class full of students and the teacher, their work is viewed by multiple classes across multiple school years, as well as by anyone on the Internet. The promise of this authentic audience elicits more care and engagement from students, their work becomes more original and purposeful, and they evolve into digital authors in their own right.

Objectives

Students will be able to:

- Express their opinions and recommendations of a book of their choice
- Record their own voices and revise their writing, using technology

- Understand how to synthesize oral and visual elements to explain a book
- Reflect on their own interpretations and share them with an authentic audience
- Problem-solve technical difficulties

NCTE/IRA standards addressed: 4, 5, 12

Materials/Preactivity Preparation

- SSR reading time
  - Designating sustained silent reading time, perhaps 50 minutes or more a week, is preferred because it allows for choice and promotes the enjoyment of reading.
- This lesson is essentially a culminating activity after students have read an entire piece of literature—often a young adult novel—of their choice (but you could adapt the lesson with a whole-class book).
- Students need to have read some form of book (fiction, non-fiction), although adaptations can be made for a whole-class novel, poem, newspaper article, etc.
- Technological equipment
  - Computer(s) (Mac preferred)—adaptations can be made depending on the number of computers available. A one-to-one ratio is ideal but not necessary.
  - GarageBand (for Mac), Audacity (for PC)
  - Headset (preferred but not required)
  - Digital camera (if requiring noncopyright images)
- Technological know-how
  - Understand what a podcast is.
  - Review some of the tutorials on your chosen application (GarageBand or Audacity); resources are listed in the works cited (all Perez sources).
  - Be flexible!

Time Frame

Total Time: 5–6 hours

I normally spend about five to six 50-minute class periods on this lesson. On day one, I introduce the podcasting topic, show examples (http://www.turtlesteach.com/, Podcasts), and review the rubric and guidelines. I don't share too many, because my students have already viewed a number of the podcasts during the beginning of the SSR unit, when I initially try to encourage their independent reading. Day two is spent on the actual application—a how-to day, if you will. I show premade tutorials from the Florida Center for Instructional Technology's Laptop Lounge (http://fcit.usf.edu/laptop/index.html) and also do a little demonstration review in the program itself because each tutorial is fairly short and quick. Day three is when I review the how-to and guidelines/rubric. The students then start researching and gathering content. Some even start their scriptwriting. Days four and five are used for actual podcast creation. Each student works individually and I'm able to assist one-on-one. The students often end up helping one another out as well. The final day (day six) can be optional. I like to allow students to watch the podcasts. I often pick only volunteers and sometimes offer extra credit. I also have all students grade the podcasts they view, using the rubric, to help keep them attentive and also to validate the rubric. They then begin to understand the rubric more fully.

On podcast-creation days, it can be helpful to create mini-goals for the students. For instance, the first podcast-creation day could focus on importing pictures and finalizing the script. The second day could focus on recording the voice and adding music. But while giving students a more specific focus each day might be helpful from a management perspective, remember that each student works at a different pace, so keep your guidelines flexible.

As you become more adept at using the application (GarageBand or Audacity), it takes less time to implement this activity. Eventually, it will take only one 50-minute class period to walk students through the program and guidelines/rubric. After that, they need time to work individually. Students troubleshoot and help one another while I spend time one-on-one with individual students. I've found that we are all more productive in this format.

My experience has been with a one-to-one ratio of computers (mobile laptop lab and some desktop computers) using GarageBand. If you have limited access to computers, your time frames will need to be extended. The same will be true if you need to travel to and from a computer lab. It's best to have a headset for each student, because they eliminate background noises when everyone is working simultaneously, but most students tend to be at different phases of their podcasts, so I've been able to get away with having just eight to ten sets. If you have access to quiet areas (such as a backroom, storage room, or outside area), students become more comfortable with recording their voices.

Description of Activity

Before starting the podcast lesson, I have students go through the experience of presenting their books in front of the class. Many students dread this task, and I often have students who will gladly take a zero on the presentation rather than get up in front of their classmates. When I introduce the podcast idea, I explain that I know some of them would prefer to do a podcast and some would choose the oral presentation, but it's my responsibility to give them multiple experiences and opportunities to develop a variety of skills.

During most of this quarter, students read a novel of their choice and keep a weekly reading log (hard copy for the regular students and online for the honors students). I spend a lot of time encouraging them, showing podcasts, and talking up books to help them find something they'd like to read. This is a pro-choice environment with an emphasis on enjoyment! I'm not sure how effective the podcasts would be if students had to do one on a required book. Choice is key to the enjoyment of any activity.

You will most likely hear resistance from students when presenting a "computer" project. Surprisingly, all students don't jump at the chance to work on computers. I've had moans and groans from both the regular and the honors students when initially broaching the topic. Yet, within the same class period, once I've shown them a bit of the program and how they can play with the music, they're anxious to get started (see Figure 21.1). This is one reason I don't spend a lot of time on the how-to; they tune it out and want to start "playing" on the computer. So the key is to be brief with initial direct instruction. Even if you simply play the video tutorials and elaborate on each one a little bit, this will take about 30 minutes and is enough for them to get the gist of podcasting.

I do not allow my students to use copyrighted images or music. If they do, they lose points on their grade and get a guilt trip from me. I am able to set this restriction because my students use GarageBand on Macs (Perez, "GarageBand 06," "Podcasting with GarageBand"). GarageBand provides copyright-free music loops and ways for users to create their own tunes (see Figure 21.2). The Macs also have built-in cameras with the Photo Booth program, which makes it easy for students to take pictures of themselves and of sketches or drawings they have created. Requiring them to take their own pictures and do their own visuals forces students to be more creative and to think outside the box. When I show them examples of previous students' work, they notice that the podcasts with more and varied images are the better products.

Figure 21.1. Students' first exposure to Photo Booth.

This could also be a good opportunity to explain copyright laws and explore how students can legitimately use other people's work while giving credit. However, if you plan to publish the podcasts in some way on the Internet, I suggest you stay completely copyright-free. If your intention is to use the podcasts only within your own school or

Figure 21.2. Student creating her own music in GarageBand.

classroom, I would allow students to use copyrighted materials with appropriate citations at the end of their podcasts.

If you do not have access to Macs, Audacity will get the job done, although you will not be able to use pictures and will have to input your own music into the program (Perez, "Podcasting with Audacity"). It's a little more limiting but still gets the job done. If you use PodOmatic (Perez, "Podcasting with PodOmatic"), you can record your voice directly online (you'll need Internet access) and then upload a single image to go along with it (or upload a movie already made elsewhere). There really are many options, depending on the kind of technology you have available. My work has solely been with Macs, so that's where my expertise lies, but you'll find other options available for PC users.

When students complete their podcasts, they turn them in to me on a flash drive, either one of their own or one they borrow from me. I then post them on my teaching website, where they truly become podcasts since anyone can subscribe to the RSS (Really Simple Syndication) feed. Posting for public access is what makes these recordings true podcasts, not the video/slideshows themselves. Some teachers post the podcasts on their school websites or other Internet sources such as Moodle.

Assessment

My assessment consists of the rubric included in the supplemental materials (see Handout 21.1). I've found that all we need is the final product grade. I have occasionally included a participation grade, but usually this is unnecessary because the students—both honors and regular—are already motivated and use all the time I give them quite productively. You might choose to have students create the script and turn it in, giving you a chance to grade that before moving on. This is a grand idea I've just not found time for.

I have found that spending some time having students watch their own and their peers' podcasts and then grade them on the rubric is a valuable activity. It helps reinforce the purpose of the rubric and the necessity for students to use it as a guideline when working on any project.

Connections and Adaptations

Adaptation for Advanced Placement

Independent Study Project (ISP) is an alternative I've used in my AP Literature and Composition courses. This podcast project is much more in-depth than the lesson provided here, as it explores literary analysis and the "teaching" of literary elements and terms. This also is a step beyond the traditional in-class group presentations students are used to.

Moving to presentation mode with a podcast forces the students to think more creatively and visually. How do they represent a literary term with images? How are syntax and diction explained visually? These are the challenges the AP students face. They work in groups on these projects, and their podcasts are 5 to 10 minutes long rather than the 2 to 3 minutes for the book review podcasts. (See Handout 21.2 on the companion website. Examples also can be viewed at http://www.turtlesteach.com/; click on "Podcasts" and look for any labeled "Lit Review.")

Adaptation for Elementary Level

I truly believe that students of almost any age could accomplish the lesson described in this chapter, but when working with younger students, you might consider having them complete a podcast as a group activity, or have them all podcast about the same book to see the varying interpretations they come up with. (Examples can be viewed at http://www.pascofirewriters.com/; click on "Podcasts.")

Adaptation for Lack of Computers/Technology

I work with young writers at a two-week camp every summer. The campers range from third graders to twelfth graders, all mixed together. While they don't podcast a book review, they create podcasts of their own original writings. One group of campers, inspired by the book *The Best Part of Me* (Ewald), wrote individual pieces about their favorite body part. We then recorded a group podcast for which each student contributed the *best* line from his or her piece of writing. This was a great way to create a podcast with only one computer and headset. Students came up to my computer one at a time and recorded their lines. I took pictures of each student's "body part" and inserted them above the recording of their line. The end result was a group poem of sorts. It took only about 30 minutes and all students were involved. (You can view this podcast at http://www.pascofirewriters.com/; click on "Podcasts"—it's the first one.)

Works Cited

Ewald, Wendy. *The Best Part of Me: Children Talk about Their Bodies in Pictures and Words*. Boston: Little, Brown, 2002. Print.

Perez, Luis. "GarageBand 06: Enhanced Podcasts." Weblog post. *Laptop Lounge Software Guides*. Florida Center for Instructional Technology, 22 Aug. 2006. Web. 15 May 2007.

Perez, Luis. "Podcasting with Audacity." Video blog post. *Laptop Lounge Screencasts*. Florida Center for Instructional Technology, 3 Mar. 2007. Web. 15 May 2007.

Perez, Luis. "Podcasting with GarageBand." Video blog post. *Laptop Lounge Screencasts*. Florida Center for Instructional Technology, 1 Sept. 2006. Web. 15 May 2007.

Perez, Luis. "Podcasting with PodOmatic." Weblog post. *Laptop Lounge Software Guides*. Florida Center for Instructional Technology, 02 Nov. 2006. Web. 15 May 2007.

Supplemental Resources

For examples of both the book review and literature review podcasts, see:

Kennedy, Abigail J. *Kennedy's Krib Podcasts*. Video blog posts. *Kennedy's Krib*, var. dates. Web. 8 Jan. 2010. http://www.turtlesteach.com/.

For examples of open-ended, creative, and original podcasts, see:

Kennedy, Abigail J. "PHS's Podcast." Video blog posts. *PHS's Podcast*, 18 Nov. 2009 and var. dates. Web. 12 Aug. 2010. http://phs.podomatic.com/.

For examples of podcasts from grades 3–12 (Summer Writing Camp), see:

"Podcasts." *[Pasco] F.I.R.E. Writers*. Ed. Abigail J. Kennedy. Tampa Bay Area Writing Project, 1 July 2009. Web. 12 Aug. 2010. http://pascofirewriters.com/.

22 Would Ralph "Friend" Piggy? Using Social Networks to Study Character

Elizabeth H. Beagle
Landstown High School, Virginia Beach, Virginia

Context

Landstown High School is a large, rural public high school in Virginia Beach, Virginia. Close to 2,300 students are enrolled. The school is unique in that it houses the Technology Academy, a school-within-a-school program that aims to equip students with advanced technology skills. Roughly 600 students are enrolled in the Technology Academy. The student population is diverse and includes students from all ethnic backgrounds, as well as a large percentage of economically disadvantaged students. All students are required to take four years of English classes to obtain a diploma. During the 2008–09 school year, students taking English 10 honors classes completed a character study using Ning, the social networking site. Any student taking an English course that requires a character study could successfully complete the assignments outlined in this lesson plan.

Rationale

Every year students are asked to complete character studies of various literary figures. Most of the time this involves some kind of static essay in which the student tries to analyze the motivations of a character. While this type of assignment has value, it generally fails to help students truly analyze a character's motivations and thoughts. One way to help students better analyze character is by using Ning, a social networking site much like Facebook or MySpace. Students are asked to "get into character" as they analyze the character from a first-person point of view. While "in character," the students pretend to be one of the characters by creating a profile, writing blog entries, chatting with other characters on discussion boards, and joining groups. The culmination of the project is to create a digital story analyzing the character studied.

Objectives

Students will be able to

- Analyze character development
- Illustrate an understanding of character

NCTE/IRA standards addressed: 1, 3, 4, 8, and 11.

Materials/Preactivity Preparation

- Piece of literature to be studied (e.g., *Lord of the Flies*)
- Access to a computer and the Internet
- Student email accounts

Before beginning, review with students the elements of fiction, including characterization and plot structure. Students should have finished reading the novel and completed parts 1–3 on Handout 22.1 (found on the companion website). You will then need to set up the class Ning (see Handout 22.2 in the supplemental materials for step-by-step instructions). You don't need expert Web 2.0 skills to do this; it is fairly easy to set up and manage. First, register with Ning (http://www.ning .com/) and create a Ning network. After you've created the site, give the address to your students so they can join the site. They will need email accounts in order to activate and join the class Ning. Once students have joined, the program will ask them to create their profiles. You will need to remind students to remain in character at all times, including during this first step of creating the profile. You will need to find a way to identify specific students online since some will be studying the same character. I instructed my students to use their character name *and* their own name (Piggy/Susan Baker).

Time Frame

When I first taught this lesson, I didn't allow enough time for the students to absorb the novel. Initially, I planned for a two- to three-week activity, but I had to add an additional week to give students time to complete their character studies. The lesson will probably take three to four weeks, including the reading of the novel. The initial lesson (review of character and plot structure) should take 30 to 40 minutes. You need an additional 30 to 40 minutes to explain the project, review samples, and get the students working. The next part of the lesson (reading the novel and completing parts 1–3 on the character study handout) will take place both in and outside of class. When I do this assignment again, I will spend more time on in-class reading. I also think I will have students work together in teams of like characters to complete parts 1–3 of the handout.

Description of Activity

My students and I were about to begin a novel unit, and I wanted a different way to assess their understanding of the literary elements of character and symbolism. I didn't want to assign another essay, yet I knew that I needed them to do more than compile a slide show with a few words and pictures. Furthermore, I was intrigued by the idea of establishing an online community. I believed that many of my students had MySpace and Facebook accounts, so I began to explore the possibilities of these two sites. I joined both sites but quickly decided they were not academic enough for my needs. I discovered Ning at a conference I attended and decided to give it a try.

Ning offered everything I was looking for with a much more academic atmosphere. I was especially excited about the ability to create my own social network that could be managed in a way that allowed me to guard my students' work and identities. I set out to create my class site, called *Lord of the Flies*. I possess intermediate Web 2.0 skills and was delighted to find Ning so easy to use. I am a kinesthetic learner, so I played around a bit and created my own page. In a little over an hour, I had created the class site and felt comfortable enough to present it to my students (see Handout 22.2, Screen Shot 1 in the supplemental materials).

To begin, I held a mini-lesson to review the elements of fiction, paying special attention to character and symbolism since these were the two elements I wanted to focus on. After the mini-lesson, I distributed the texts and the character study handout (see Handout 22.1). Then I took an informal survey to find out how many of the students had a MySpace or Facebook account. I wanted to see how many of my students were familiar with social networking. The results were not surprising. Most students did indeed have one or both. Next, I reviewed my expectations for this activity and showcased the class site, including my own page (the one I created while learning how to use the site). I also shared the rubric with them to ensure that everyone understood what was being assessed. I was pleased to discover that the students were excited about this project.

Over the next couple of weeks, we read *Lord of the Flies* and held many class discussions about the reading. Students worked in teams to analyze symbols found in the novel. During this time, students completed several activities that helped them analyze the symbols, with the ultimate goal of creating a slide show to illustrate their understanding of the symbol they studied as a team. Additionally, students complete parts 1–3 of Handout 22.1. I felt it was important for them to create these pieces before logging on to the site; I was afraid that if I allowed them to join the site too soon, they would get carried away with the glitz of the technology and not spend enough time analyzing their character.

After students created their slide shows and completed parts 1–3 of Handout 22.1, I took them to the computer lab to join the class Ning, create their profiles, and begin their personal pages. Again, I was pleased to see their excitement. In the first 45 minutes of our lab time, most students completed the profile, uploaded several photos, completed their "About me" paragraph, and worked on their blogs (see Handout 22.2, Screen Shot 2 on the companion website). We went to the lab one more time for an hour and a half to complete the project. I encouraged students to work at home as well.

While students worked on developing their pages, I was pleased to see that they went beyond the responses asked for on the handout. For example, I required them to complete four blog entries. The first one had to deal with the conflicts the character experiences. Students did an excellent job of describing the conflict from the character's perspective. Furthermore, some of the students made comments on one another's blogs while remaining "in character." (See Handout 22.2, Screen Shot 3.)

Another benefit of the Ning is that it was easy to determine whether students understood the complex relationships in the book. One of the first tasks students were asked to complete was to send a friend request to other characters. This activity was very telling; if a student pretending to be Piggy "befriended" Jack, I had a clear indicator that that student didn't understand the relationship between these two characters. Additionally, students were instructed to join groups— The Hunters or Ralph's Gang. By joining the right group, students indicated their understanding of how the characters interacted with one another. A student pretending to be Ralph shouldn't be joining The Hunters, because Jack (the leader of the hunters) and Ralph are enemies. After joining the appropriate groups, students were encouraged to correspond with one another while "in character." A member of The Hunters posted this entry:

> Jack: Guys, focus. We obviously will be here awhile. We must search for food. It is important to our survival.

This was an appropriate post because, as we know, in *Lord of the Flies* Jack is focused on finding food, and as the leader of the hunters, he has to keep his group focused. The dialogue on the site between the group members was further proof of their understanding of characters' motivations and decisions.

The culminating assignment was the slide show, which I used to evaluate students' understanding of the symbols we had identified in the novel. I put students into groups of four to complete an assignment about a specific symbol. Each group analyzed a different symbol. Using Windows Movie Maker, students demonstrated how the symbol (e.g., the fire, Piggy's glasses) was used to create or develop the theme. For the most part, students did a good job with this, but ultimately I felt that I was asking them to do too much, analyze too many aspects of the same novel. I didn't feel as though their work on the slide show was of a particularly high quality; it was too disconnected from the main character study assignment. In the future, I will amend the assignment to have students create a slide show that analyzes the character they studied.

After students completed this project, I asked them to reflect on their work. Some of the questions included:

- What did you think of this assignment?
- How do you think this assignment helped you understand the characters in *Lord of the Flies*?
- Do you think using Ning helped you understand the characters better? If so, how? If no, why not?
- On a scale from 1 to 10, with 1 being very easy and 10 being very difficult, rate the difficulty level of using Ning.
- Explain what you have learned about your assigned character and how this assignment helped you expand your understanding of the character.
- What did you like about the assignment? Not like?
- What do you think needs to be changed to make this assignment better?

Overall, students enjoyed the project and felt that because they were asked to become a character, they had a better understanding of the characters' motivations. They also enjoyed working in teams to complete the symbol analysis. They *really* enjoyed the social aspect of the project. I got very few complaints. The main complaint came from those students who do not have computer access at home. The only suggestion students offered for improving the project was to include the creation of a slide show about their characters. In general, students felt they had learned more about the characters than if they had been asked to write an essay.

To view the class site and explore actual student work, go to http://lhslordoftheflies.ning.com/.

Assessment

Students were assessed on their knowledge of their assigned character and their analyses of their symbol. I used several elements of the project to determine their understanding:

- I reviewed and scored their preparatory work on the handout (parts 1–3).
- Then I used a rubric to score their overall project.
- I also used a rubric to evaluate their teamwork on their symbolism slide shows.

Connections and Adaptations

I created this lesson to study character and symbolism in *Lord of the Flies*; however, this lesson easily can be adapted to study any character in any piece of fiction. Since I taught this lesson last, there have been two new developments with Ning. The first is that now users can upload videos directly to the site. This would have been extremely useful for my students, who could have stored their videos on the site instead of on our school network. The other new development is that students must activate their registration with a real email address. When I first taught this lesson, one could use a "dummy" email account, which made things easier since students cannot access their personal email accounts at our school.

Next time around, I will give students more time to work together in character teams, and I will require that each student create a slide show about their character. The slide show will serve as a culminating activity to demonstrate mastery of character study. All in all, this was a fantastic lesson that inspired real learning in my classroom, and one that I am eager to re-create this coming year.

23 Dear Emma, Just Tweet Me: Using Microblogging to Explore Characterization and Style

Suzanne C. Linder
University of Illinois Laboratory High School, Urbana, Illinois

Context

University of Illinois Laboratory High School (Uni) is a small public high school for gifted students on the campus of the University of Illinois. The approximately 300 students who attend Uni have a demonstrated history of succeeding in school and are generally motivated, interested, and engaged in their schoolwork. The school has a very progressive computer usage policy and does not use any filtering software. This lesson was written for use with *Emma* in Sophomore English but has also been adapted for use in other courses.

Rationale

My students frequently complain that the language of nineteenth-century novels is too flowery and dense to be enjoyed by a modern audience; however, when asked to imitate the language, they demonstrate a keen ear for stylistic features and often enjoy the light mockery that is allowed through imitation. One clever student transposed Austen's description of Emma to a bowl of fruit through pastiche: "The orange, handsome, vibrant and sweet . . ." Through pastiche and transposition,

students are able to see the similarities between the rigid social structure in a novel of manners and the equally rigid (although invisible
until examined) social structure of high school. This lesson capitalizes
on students' expertise in the nuances of social dynamics and familiarity with and interest in social networking software in order to explore
character development and experiment with style. Additionally, the
networked nature of the software allows students to easily publish
their writing to be read by and quickly responded to by other students
and extends the possibility for interaction beyond the classroom.

Objectives

Students will be able to:

- Identify and experiment with unique features of Austen's
  writing style
- Increase knowledge and real-world technical skills by using
  social networking technology to assume the persona of a literary character
- Explore, evaluate, and make predictions about character
  development through assuming the persona of a literary
  character

NCTE/IRA standards addressed: 3, 5, 6

Materials/Preactivity Preparation

- Computer lab or classroom set of laptops
- Computer with projection equipment
- Jane Austen style sheet handout (see Handout 23.1)
- Historical tweets examples (see Handout 23.2)
- *Emma* by Jane Austen (or alternate novel)

Preparation Steps

1. Sign up for your own Twitter account (either as yourself or as
   a character from the novel) to familiarize yourself with what
   is involved in the sign-up process and how sending a tweet
   works.

2. Familiarize yourself with the Jane Austen style sheet and add
   additional stylistic elements or examples as you see fit.

3. Duplicate any handouts required.

Twitter is a Web-based social networking application that allows members to broadcast 140 character messages ("tweets") to their followers. A number of people have become popular on Twitter by impersonating celebrities or literary characters and sending tweets from those characters. This lesson asks students to compose tweets from literary characters as a way to explore characterization and style in *Emma*. If you are unfamiliar with Twitter, you might read David Pogue's "Twittering Tips for Beginners," which both explains how Twitter is used and gives advice for someone unfamiliar with the service.

Although you should become familiar with Twitter to help students get started on the project, the lesson draws on students' knowledge of and expertise with social networking software, so it is not essential that you be the expert. In fact, if you are nervous about using unfamiliar technology, you might ask a student to serve as the IT person for the class. It is more important that you be able to assist students with identifying and imitating the stylistic elements of the literature than act as a technological guru.

Time Frame

This lesson can be completed in three 50-minutes sessions in class, or the discussions included can be contracted to only a portion of three periods. After the historical tweets activity has been introduced, I ask students to send tweets for at least a week, but if they are really enjoying the activity, they can continue through the remainder of their reading of the novel.

Description of Activity

This activity begins with identifying the formal characteristics of Austen's language (litotes, appositives, compound subjects, antithesis, compound-complex sentences, etc.). On the first day of class discussion (after we've read the first chapter of the book), I ask students to revisit the first paragraph of *Emma* and read the passage aloud; then I ask the class what they notice about Austen's writing style in this opening paragraph. The first thing students notice is that the entire first paragraph is one long sentence; after that, they often comment on Austen's use of the semicolon. With a little prompting, they are able to articulate that her character descriptions are longer than those of other authors they have read ("handsome, clever, and rich, with a comfortable home and happy disposition"). Once they have exhausted the examples in the first paragraph, I ask them for additional observations they may have made about writing style in their reading of the full chapter.

As this discussion of literary style takes place, keep track of stylistic features in a way that allows students to view the list, and name and define the literary terms for the observations they make (for instance, my students can frequently recognize that Austen uses the "not un-" construction but rarely know that it is called *litotes*). Once the class has named and defined the literary terms for their observations, you might add more of your own (refer to the Jane Austen Style Features sheet, Handout 23.1, on the companion website for specific features and examples).

Toward the end of the period, I test comprehension and begin to introduce the idea of pastiche by asking students to write a descriptive sentence about themselves that follows the stylistic format of the first sentence of the novel (e.g., "Ms. Linder, regal, witty, and gracious, with a rambunctious class and saintly disposition . . ."). Depending on time, I ask students to share aloud their sentences or, if time is running out, I collect the sentences to check for comprehension.

This is the definition of pastiche that I use:

> *Pastiche* is a French word for a parody or literary imitation. Although the intent is often humorous (ranging from witty satire to gentle, affectionate ribbing), the writer of pastiche sincerely imitates the style, technique, and themes of a writer or work they wish to parody (so there is an element of tribute or homage, as well as parody). The reader should be able to recognize distinctive features of the author's style in the pastiche.

Finally, I instruct students to continue to keep their eyes and ears open for unique features of Austen's writing style as they read further into the novel. As they read, they should add notes to the style sheet or keep their own notes.

Once students have read at least through Chapter 8 of *Emma*, I introduce the idea of historical tweets. Before class, I visit the Historical Tweets website and preview current entries. These tweets from famous historical figures are quite funny and popular with students. All of the past tweets are archived, so you can pull up a specific tweet that you think will work for your class, or you can use the historical tweets included in Handout 23.2 in the supplemental materials. These have been produced by the authors of the Historical Tweet website specifically for inclusion with this lesson. This class period will work best in a computer lab (or in the classroom with laptops) but could be completed in a classroom with a computer hooked up to a projection system.

I begin this class session by asking students what important events have occurred recently in the text (Mr. Martin has proposed; Harriet has refused after much prompting by Emma; Emma and

Mr. Knightley have had a strong disagreement about Emma's role in Harriet's refusal; Emma is increasingly convinced of Mr. Elton's affection for Harriet, particularly because he has offered to take the portrait of Harriet to be framed). I remind students (or introduce the idea if it hasn't come up in our discussion) that *Emma* is a novel of manners and, as such, is not overly plot driven but, rather, concerned with the drama of everyday life and the minutiae of social interaction. The events that have occurred over the last few chapters are seismic in the world of *Emma* and give the characters much to think and gossip about. My students have no trouble connecting the drama in the social world of *Emma* to the kind of drama that occurs in the social world of high school and can easily recognize how Emma and Harriet can spend so much time analyzing the behavior of Mr. Elton. (Another good way to illustrate this connection is by using scenes from the movie *Clueless* [1995] directed by Amy Heckerling.).

I transition to introducing the historical tweets portion of this lesson by asking if any students are familiar with Twitter. Usually at least one student is a Twitter user, and I ask that student to explain to the class how the social networking site works. If no one is familiar with Twitter, I briefly explain that it's a "microblogging" service that allows people to update their followers throughout the day with information contained in "tweets" of no more than 140 characters. I

then project the Historical Tweets website or share the historical tweets included on Handout 23.2 (the convention of "@username" indicates that the tweet is in response to or directed at another user). I discuss with students where the humor in historical tweets comes from (primarily from historical anachronisms and the transposition of historical characters into a modern setting; additionally, these tweets are reacting to well-known events that are implied but not described—e.g., to get the joke, the audience for the tweet has to understand the historical context without having it explained in the tweet).

I then move on to ask students what specific challenges writers face when they are allowed only 140 characters to communicate their thoughts (some possible answers are that language must be precise and writing clear; extraneous and long words have no place in a tweet; tweets should be about an event that is easy to reference or imply and should make sense without extra contextual information; declarative sentences or questions work well). This is a particularly entertaining conversation to have while reading *Emma* as my students are often frustrated with the length of Austen's sentences and descriptions. I use their frustration with Austen as a motivation for this lesson—they will

be reducing *Emma* down to its essence and cutting out all those extraneous words. Additionally, pastiche allows students to gently make fun
of the material they are reading in class, which I take full advantage of
with this lesson.

   Once the class has an understanding of tweets and a familiarity with the humor in historical tweets, I have students open the
word-processing software on their computer and practice writing a
140-character tweet about their day so far to get a sense of length.

   Once students have had a few minutes to experiment writing a
tweet about their day, I ask them to try their hand at writing a historical tweet from the perspective of a character in *Emma*. They should refer
to their Jane Austen style sheets for guidance in writing a tweet that
sounds like language a character in Austen would use; however, they
will have to do some creative composing in order to communicate a
full thought in 140 characters. At this point, obvious and rich character
choices are Emma, Harriet, Mr. Elton, Mr. Knightley, and Mr. Martin, but
the Misses Martin, Mr. Woodhouse, and Miss Bates would be interesting
to hear from as well. Here are two example tweets that I show students
as models; the first is from Harriet and the second is from Mr. Martin:

> @hsmith
>
> Think I have done the right thing in writing a letter today.
> @ewoodhouse assures me of it. But do still wonder.

> @martin
>
> Am astonished at the letter I received today. @gknightley
> assured me all would proceed amiably. Perhaps I should have
> read that book?

The last in-class session should take place in a computer lab or a
classroom with laptops after students have read Chapters 9 and 10. I ask
students to choose which character from *Emma* they would like to send
tweets from, register for Twitter, and send a test tweet. As students
register for Twitter, they should begin to follow one another, and you
should follow all of them so that you can read their tweets (Twitter will
automatically prompt users to choose people to follow, but you might
need to keep track of the user names students choose so that they can
find one another). I allow more than one student to represent the same
character, but Twitter will require them to choose unique user names.
These user names should still communicate which character they are
representing, and they should turn in to you their real name and their
Twitter user name for record keeping and identification purposes.

I circulate the classroom and help students who run into challenges registering for Twitter. If you are not comfortable with this job, or if you have a number of students who are struggling with this task, you might employ students who are familiar with Twitter to help people sign up. Alternately, if you have a very computer-savvy class, you can ask them to sign up before class starts and save some in-class time.

As students complete their registrations, I encourage them to follow one another and begin sending tweets. As their classmates send tweets, their screens will quickly fill up with messages from *Emma* characters that they can respond to. They should respond to those tweets, continuing to stay true to events in the text and working to employ aspects of Austen's writing style (by this point, they should have read through Chapter 10—Mr. Elton writes a charade, Emma claims she has "little intention of ever marrying," and Jane Fairfax is introduced into the story).

I find that students start out trying hard to compose witty, Austen-esque tweets and, as the class period continues, move toward interacting with the other characters from the novel. They find being mentioned in other characters' tweets to be motivating, and that leads to interaction between the characters. I read along with the tweets they are posting and occasionally have to remind students to continue to experiment with Austen's style, keeping their characters' comments consistent with the behavior of the characters in the book.

At the end of the period, I assign students to log in to Twitter once a day over the course of the next week to read their classmates' tweets, and to send at least five more tweets.

The lesson can end here, or it can be extended to more social networking interaction on a Ning (see "Connections and Adaptations"). If you choose to end the lesson after the historical tweeting activity, move on to the reflection activities in the "Assessment" section of the lesson. However, if time and resources allow, you can expand this activity to re-create the social structure of Highbury on your own Ning.

Assessment

I create a character on Twitter to participate alongside my students and use that character to interact with students, but also to keep track of who is posting, give praise to students who are writing particularly witty tweets, and prompt students who aren't tweeting as much as I would like. More minor, older characters are good for teachers to take on—Mr. Woodhouse, Isabella Knightley, and Mr. John Knightley all work well. I keep a simple checklist in my grade book of who is tweeting and how frequently. When the activity is finished, I ask the following reflection questions and use the data I gathered about students' tweeting behaviors, plus their answers to the reflection questions, to assess their work on this project:

Reflection Questions

1. What realizations and observations about the social world of *Emma* did you have while transposing it to social networking software?

2. Do you see any similarities between the social world of *Emma* and the social world of high school? If yes, what are they?

3. What did you learn about Jane Austen's writing style through imitation? Did you find it difficult to imitate her style? If so, what was challenging?

4. What writing skills do you feel you employed in composing your tweets?

5. What technical skills do you feel you employed in composing your tweets? Did you feel as though these activities helped you improve those skills?

6. What did you enjoy about the historical tweets activity?

7. What did you find challenging or frustrating about the activities?

Connections and Adaptations

- Assign students a chapter from *Jane Fairfax: The Secret Story of the Second Heroine* by Joan Aiken as a model of a pastiche.

- While this lesson is designed with *Emma* as the focus, it would work just as well with other novels. I have a colleague who asks students to tweet one message from Dante to Beatrice for every book of the *Inferno*; I have used this lesson with Emily Brontë's *Wuthering Heights*. The possibilities are endless.

- Ning is a Web-based social networking platform that allows users to set up their own password-protected social network (like Facebook but limited to a group that you select). You can have students create profiles for characters from the novel on a Highbury Ning and continue their transposition and pastiche in that arena.

Works Cited in Lesson

Aiken, Joan. *Jane Fairfax: The Secret Story of the Second Heroine in Jane Austen's* Emma. New York: St. Martin's Griffin, 1997. Print.

Austen, Jane. *Emma*. New York: Bantam, 2004. Print.

Clueless. Dir. Amy Heckerling. Perf. Alicia Silverstone, Paul Rudd. Paramount, 1995. Film.

"Ning." *Ning*. Ning, Inc., Oct. 2005. Web. 17 Dec. 2009.

Pogue, David. "Twittering Tips for Beginners." *New York Times Online*. The New York Times Company, 15 Jan. 2009. Web. 17 Dec. 2009.

"Twitter." *Twitter*. Twitter, 2006. Web. 17 Dec. 2009.

Work Cited in Supplemental Materials

Beard, Alan, and Alec McNayr. *Historical Tweets*. *HistoricalTweets.com*, 17 Dec. 2009. Web. 17 Dec. 2009.

24 Symbolic Analysis of *One Flew Over the Cuckoo's Nest*: Literature, Album Art, and VoiceThread

Luke Rodesiler
University of Florida

Context

This lesson was developed for use with juniors and seniors in an English language arts elective offered at South Lyon High School (SLHS), a suburban high school in southeast Michigan. The curriculum was designed to engage students in examining contemporary literature and tracing shifts in thinking and expression in the latter part of the twentieth century. This lesson was developed to support our exploration of symbolism while reading Ken Kesey's *One Flew Over the Cuckoo's Nest* and to invite students to participate in digital conversations around media.

Rationale

VoiceThread is an online tool used to hold conversations around media. It supports PDFs, Microsoft Word, Excel, and PowerPoint files, images, and videos. Users can navigate through uploaded files and provide comments by typing out text, uploading audio files, using a webcam, using a desktop microphone, or making a telephone call. Users can also doodle or draw on the media while recording a comment. The robust features provided online at http://voicethread.com/ make VoiceThread an ideal medium for various projects that require students to read, write, speak, and represent in contemporary classrooms.

While many digital tools are impressive and eye-catching, it is the degree of participation a tool like VoiceThread allows that proves most beneficial for the English language arts classroom. In recent years, online tools and applications, including wikis, blogs, and social networks, have helped to foster a participatory culture that moves us from literacy practices of individual expression to a more collaborative effort (Jenkins et al. 4). This cultural shift requires educators to "devote more attention to fostering what we call the new media literacies: a set of cultural competencies and social skills that young people need in the new media landscape" (Jenkins et al. 4). The skills Jenkins describes, including networking, negotiation, and appropriation, can be developed when teachers invite students to explore media using participatory tools like VoiceThread.

In addition to new media literacies, this lesson speaks to the value of visual literacy, prompting students to "read" visual images and find symbolic meaning in the colors, objects, expressions, positioning, and spacing displayed in album artwork, texts from popular culture that many students encounter on a regular basis. The visually literate "must be able to decode imagery—look at it, perceive meaning, and make decisions based on what they see" (Metros and Woolsey 81). Furthermore, visual literacy includes the ability "to articulate to others your perception of what the image communicates and listen to others' responses" (Way 39). As with those who possess more traditional literacy skills, the visually literate do not merely happen upon these abilities; however, it seems that visual literacy is often overlooked in education. In the twenty-first century, when multimedia texts incorporating still and moving images are prominent, we must provide students with opportunities to enhance their ability to read and discuss texts of all varieties. The National Council of Teachers of English (NCTE) has worked to promote "nonprint" fluency, and this lesson supports that cause.

Objectives

Students will be able to:

- Analyze symbolic meaning in visual and print-based texts
- Evaluate the analyses of their peers
- Use new media tools to participate in digital conversations

NCTE/IRA standards addressed: 3, 6, 8

Materials/Preactivity Preparation

- *One Flew Over the Cuckoo's Nest* (for the exploration of symbolism)
- Computers with Internet access (for locating album art and creating VoiceThreads)
- Desktop microphones (for recording analyses)
- Headphones (for listening to tutorials and voice-over recordings)
- LCD projector and screen (for teachers to model VoiceThread's vast features)

Though this lesson accounts for visual literacy and invites students to participate in digital conversations around media, print-based literary works are truly at its core. *One Flew Over the Cuckoo's Nest* is referenced here, but I do encourage you to use any literary work that is heavy on symbolism and fits your curriculum. Before implementing the lesson, you should identify symbols in the work for classroom exploration, regardless of the selection.

In preparation for exploring color communication with students, familiarize yourself with *Color in Motion* (Cortés), an interactive site that can assist students in making sense of color symbolism, located online at http://mariaclaudiacortes.com/. Additionally, in preparation for addressing basic visual elements, you will want to locate album artwork that exemplifies the elements introduced. Some examples are provided in this lesson, but countless others would also work.

You should also familiarize yourself with the features of VoiceThread and set up a K–12 account to provide a safe, secure location for students. Once the class account is set up, you might consider creating a sample analysis to model what a thorough analysis using VoiceThread's robust features looks and sounds like.

To assist students in preparing their own analyses, review the tutorials provided at the VoiceThread website ahead of time and decide which ones to share with students when introducing VoiceThread.

I also encourage you to begin organizing sites for students to use as they begin searching for symbolic artwork. Artists' websites, commercial sites like Amazon, and search engines like Albumart are all recommended resources since each typically provides high-quality images.

Time Frame

Students' comfort level with symbolism and their familiarity with the VoiceThread interface will likely dictate the time required for this lesson. For my particular context, this lesson was crafted for five 60-minute class periods.

Description of Activity

Activity 1: Exploring Symbolism in Literature

Discussing symbolism in *One Flew Over the Cuckoo's Nest* can seemingly begin at any page. From the opening scene, readers are introduced to a host of motifs evident in the elaborate descriptions of machinery, the detailing of hands, and the close attention paid to size. Each recurs throughout the novel and represents greater ideas that help to inform the novel's major themes. In a similar fashion, individual symbols pop up at various points. For example, R. P. McMurphy's boxers, adorned with big white whales, and his aces and eights tattoo—the "Dead Man's Hand"—hold symbolic meaning as they suggest a fateful future for McMurphy. Because the symbols are so prevalent, you will have no difficulty addressing symbolism throughout the novel.

When prompting students to analyze motifs and symbols in literature, it's helpful to provide students with a chart like the one available in Handout 24.1 (in the supplemental material), which has been adapted from the work of my SLHS colleague Tim O'Dowd. This can help students to organize their thoughts and make sense of the symbolic nature of the motifs that run throughout the text. Additionally, the following questions might be used to help students think through prominent symbols in Kesey's novel:

Guiding Questions

- When describing McMurphy's underwear, Chief Bromden notes that they are adorned with "big white whales" (76). What do we know about "big white whales" in literature? Given what we know about McMurphy, why is it fitting that Kesey would make this association?

- In the same scene where we are exposed to McMurphy's boxers, Chief Bromden describes McMurphy's tattoos, one of which consists of "aces and eights" (77). This poker hand is more famously known as the "Dead Man's Hand" since notorious gunman Wild Bill Hickok was reportedly holding this hand at the time of his death. Given this insight, what meaning might this hold for McMurphy? Explain the symbolism in McMurphy having this particular tattoo.

- McMurphy is widely recognized as a Christ figure in Kesey's novel. What Christ-evoking symbols do we see in his characterization and in the novel more broadly?

- Symbolism can even be found in McMurphy's name: R. P. McMurphy. What are RPMs? Given what we know about what McMurphy is bringing to the ward, why are these symbolic initials so appropriate?

Activity 2: "Reading" Colors

In addition to helping students read symbols in literary works, this lesson prompts students to "read" visuals to discern symbolic meaning. Color surely holds great meaning in a visual, so helping students explore color communication is a reasonable starting point.

To transition from thinking about literature to thinking about the symbolism in color, I encourage you to reflect with students on passages that indicate colors being associated with particular characters. For example, Nurse Ratched and the color white and McMurphy and the color red quickly come to mind. Conversations about Kesey's purposeful use of color should help to contextualize this activity for students.

To further students' thinking about color symbolism, I have found *Color in Motion* by Claudia Cortés to be an excellent resource. The site, located at http://mariaclaudiacortes.com/, provides an overview of color communication, including the traits associated with various colors, meanings tied to colors in different cultures, complementary colors, and what each color typically represents. I have found the "Stars" section of the site useful for introducing basic color symbolism. Likewise, the site's "Movies" section provides animation to further illustrate symbolic associations for each color.

After students have grasped the symbolism of colors reviewed in the "Stars" and "Movies" sections of the site, you might then opt to make use of the site's "Lab" to gauge students' understanding of color communication. Depending on time constraints, you might choose to provide students with a more interactive experience by assigning the site's "Project 1: Direct a Scene," which requires students to create scenes based on a word that represents a color of their choice as modeled in the site's "Movies" section. When creating the scene, students can add and position figures and select and manipulate props. As a low-tech feature, scenes can be printed and compiled to create flipbook animation.

If time is limited, the Lab also offers "Project 2: Star Manager." This gives students a chance to test their color symbolism knowledge by matching colors to titles of fictional productions. For example, red, often recognized as a "hot" color associated with romance and aggressiveness, might be fitting for a title like *Love and Hate*, but it is less likely to be associated with a title like *Ocean Breeze*. Students can check their scores on the site, which provides the correct answers. In this way, this project can help you gauge students' understanding of color symbolism in an efficient manner.

Activity 3: Introducing Basic Visual Elements

After exploring color communication, I have found it useful to engage students in thinking about other basic visual elements that help viewers make meaning of images. Because album artwork is used in the symbolic analysis, the culminating activity of this lesson, familiarizing students with album artwork now is beneficial.

Share a number of album covers with students to illustrate how expressions and the purposeful positioning of people in an image can convey meaning. In each case, you could share the artwork via LCD projector, prompting responses from the class as to the meaning or feeling implied through facial expressions and/or positioning, and playing a track from the album to support student responses. For example, Johnny Cash's *American IV: The Man Comes Around* (2002) depicts a profile shot of the legendary singer's somber face amidst darkness, positioned looking downward. One listen to the album—perhaps Cash's cover of Nine Inch Nails' "Hurt"—immediately supports the melancholy feeling projected by the positioning of Cash's head and his grave expression. Another possible example comes from Pantera, a Texas-based metal band. The artwork of *Vulgar Display of Power* (1992) shows a fist connecting with an unfortunate victim's face, projecting brutal, aggressive vibes. Fittingly, the band's aggressive sound—evident on a track like "Walk"—matches the feel of the artwork.

You might also opt to address scale as a visual element that influences meaning-making. The manipulation of scale or the apparent size of objects in an image to convey feeling can be demonstrated with album artwork as well. To create a sense of allure and mystery, for example, scale can be pushed to the extreme, limiting the exposure of an image's subject to the viewing audience, as with the cover of British recording artist Adele's *19* (2008) and *Dangerous Magical Noise* (2003) by The Dirtbombs, a Detroit-based rock band. Scale can also be manipulated to reduce the size of figures in an image, helping viewers feel the sense of isolation suggested in the visual. For example, the artwork for *The Marshall Mathers LP* (2000), Detroit-based rapper Eminem's second major release, presents a shot of the artist by himself on the steps of a house that is shot from such a distance that he is rendered nearly insignificant amidst his sizable surroundings.

After introducing basic visual elements that influence meaning for viewers and sharing examples, prompt students to find their own examples of concepts employed in the artwork accompanying their favorite albums.

Activity 4: Introducing VoiceThread

Most videos at http://voicethread.com/ are useful for introducing VoiceThread. With an LCD projector, you can open this activity by projecting the "What's a VoiceThread anyway?" video from the Voice-Thread Browse page. This video provides students with a brief introduction to the medium. To capture VoiceThread's usability, "1 minute VoiceThread" is a short video that might comfort anxious students by efficiently demonstrating the simplicity with which VoiceThreads can be created. Additionally, "The Doodler!" is a brief tutorial demonstrating the way students can draw on any uploaded documents. Depending on the context, you might share all three videos as a class, instruct students to explore the videos at individual computers, or use a combination of whole-class and independent viewing.

Once students understand what a VoiceThread is, you can rely heavily on "play" as an instructional technique. Following the videos, you will need to distribute individual account information to each student. With students logged in, you can then prompt students to explore the features available through VoiceThread. Encourage students to upload various types of files and to comment on uploaded files in multiple ways. Though many school districts enforce policies limiting phone usage, you might consider prompting students to explore the phone feature by calling in a comment. Understandably, some of you might cringe at this suggestion, but some students may need to use this feature after school hours if computer microphones are not accessible.

After students have explored VoiceThread, make time to demonstrate how VoiceThreads are shared, and remind students that commenting on the work of others is done by following the same process used when adding commentary to their own VoiceThreads.

Activity 5: Culminating Activity

Once students have investigated symbolism in a literary work, thought about color and other basic elements when reading visuals for greater meaning, and explored VoiceThread as a medium for holding conversations around media, they are prepared for the culminating activity. The final activity calls for students to analyze album art and draw symbolic connections between the art and a character, relationship, or theme in the literary work at hand. Students must apply what they know about symbolism to connect two seemingly disconnected pieces of art—one print, one visual. To assist students in this process, and to provide them with an opportunity to develop the participatory skills necessary for effective communication in the twenty-first century, students conduct their analyses via VoiceThread. As indicated previously, this digital medium allows students to audibly record their analysis, use a doodling function to highlight or emphasize particular features of a visual, share their work with a real audience, and receive audible feedback from their peers in the form of analysis extensions or alternative perspectives. Because VoiceThread is an online tool, allot plenty of time for work to be conducted in class to avoid access issues that inevitably arise. See Handout 24.2 in the supplemental materials for a sample assignment sheet.

Assessment

Assessment of students' understanding of symbolism and characters, relationships, or themes in a literary work can be done through class discussions, completion of the motif chart (see Handout 24.1), written responses to select questions, and each student's symbolic analysis created using VoiceThread (see Handout 24.2). I evaluate the depth of a student's analysis, which might include accounting for multiple elements in the visual used, including colors, expressions, and positioning. Likewise, the clarity of connections between the artwork and the identified character, relationship, or theme should be considered.

You can also assess students' ability to use VoiceThread as a participatory tool. Students' effective use of available features, including uploading images, doodling efficiently to highlight relevant features, and commenting in a clear, audible fashion should guide such assessment.

Finally, you can assess students' contributions to the class as a learning environment through the commentary students provide for one another. Are students extending the analysis or providing alternative perspectives? Are they moving beyond the superficial to provide useful feedback? Such questions can guide you through this portion of the assessment.

Connections and Adaptations

Though *One Flew Over the Cuckoo's Nest* was the text used in my classroom, this lesson can be used for class study of any literature rich in symbolism. Common high school novels that immediately come to mind include *The Great Gatsby, Lord of the Flies,* and *The Bluest Eye.*

Studying symbolism and exploring album artwork is just one way to draw connections between art and literature. In a course that features world literature, for example, students might examine literature-based art, including artistic renditions of creation stories based on Genesis, or perhaps the range of art inspired by Dante and *The Divine Comedy.*

The use of VoiceThread in the classroom is not limited to making connections between art and literature. As a digital tool that allows users to upload images and record voice-overs, VoiceThread is an effective medium for creating and sharing digital stories. With the option to upload digital media, including videos and images, VoiceThread also proves to be quite useful for media literacy education. It can be used to help students collaboratively analyze advertisements, commercials, videos, and more.

Works Cited

Cortés, Claudia. *Color in Motion.* Color in Motion, n.d. Web. 5 May 2009.

Jenkins, Henry, et al. "Confronting the Challenges of Participatory Culture: Media Education for the 21st Century." *Project New Media Literacies* (supported by The MacArthur Foundation). Annenberg School for Communication and Journalism, n.d. Web. 30 April 2009. http://www.newmedialiteracies.org/files/working/NMLWhitePaper.pdf.

Kesey, Ken. *One Flew Over the Cuckoo's Nest.* New York: Penguin, 1996. Print.

Metros, Susan E., and Kristina Woolsey. "Visual Literacy: An Institutional Imperative." *Educause Review* 41.3 (2006): 80–81. Print.

Way, Cynthia. "Visual Literacy: Concepts and Strategies." *Focus on Photography: A Curriculum Guide.* International Center of Photography, n.d. Web. 5 May 2009.

25 Macbethbook: Synthesizing Research and Literary Analysis to Create a Social Networking Environment

Natalia Barker
Vanderbilt University

Context

Walhalla High School is a small rural high school in upstate South Carolina. Over the years, it has implemented literacy initiatives to accommodate the changing needs of its students, including necessary improvements and additions of technology tools and instruction. In designing the English II (tenth-grade) curriculum in the last several years, the department has focused on integrating a variety of technology into instruction and assessment. Decisions regarding this inclusion are based on the nature of students' interactions with technology in their own lives, and we have worked to develop classroom experiences that are authentic to the way students live with technology. Although we've kept the core content the same, various writing assignments have become publishing opportunities in Web 2.0 environments, digital stories have taken the place of printed narratives, and hypertext bibliographies have strengthened students' understanding of the importance of sources and their relationships to one another. This inclusion is necessary to bridge students' personal experiences with 21st century literacies on the Web and their reading and writing experiences in their course work. In addition to developing a relevant connection between students' academic and personal lives, we have been able to strengthen writing and reading skills both on the Web and in print and to initiate skill development necessary to interacting as responsible and educated digital citizens.

Rationale

> It's time to ensure that the way students learn with technology agrees with the way they live with technology.
>
> Harter and Medved

Students' literacy practices have extended beyond activities of traditional reading and writing to include technology. In addition to using the computer as a tool for reading, writing, and meaning-making, school-aged generations are using it to connect to others in their town, in their state, in their country, and even across the world. As builders and members of a variety of communities, students are interacting on a daily basis with elements of traditional reading and writing and elements of technology-based multiliteracies to explore ideas, create meaning, and share with others.

By honoring the way students "live with technology," teachers can develop strategies for optimizing "the way students learn with technology," and one comprehensive method for doing this is to develop an online learning environment (Harter and Medved). Such an environment can extend the classroom learning community outside of the time and space confines of the school day and into the unlimited spaces of the virtual world. Students' experience with social networks such as Facebook, MySpace, and Twitter gives them the reference point needed to make such a network appropriate for a classroom. The opportunities for reading, writing, and communicating through various modalities in these networks are abundant, and teachers can use a similar network to help students make connections between their literacies outside of school and their literacies inside of school.

Applying these guiding principles to the study of *Macbeth* allows students to experience social networking from a metacognitive perspective. As they build and interact within Macbethbook, a mock version of a social network, they have the opportunity to analyze the multimodal components of these networks, as well as the characteristics of identity, literacy, and community within these networks, ultimately equipping them to evaluate their personal experiences and interactions in mainstream social networking environments. When their school experiences with social networking are layered with the synthesis of research and literary analysis, students are able to apply these school experiences to their independent learning and personal experiences with social networking, thus creating an authentic experience with audience, purpose, and writing that creates an enduring understanding of literature and composition.

Objectives

Students will be able to:

- Describe and analyze features of a social networking profile
- Use multiple modalities to compose a mock version of a networking profile
- Synthesize research with literary analysis to demonstrate an understanding of a literary work (*Macbeth*)
- Work collaboratively in a Web 2.0 setting

NCTE/IRA standards addressed: 1, 3, 4, 5, 6, 7, 8, 11

Materials/Preactivity Preparation

- Set up an online space for creating the profile page before the lesson. I suggest setting this up in Wikispaces or a similar sharing host. Explore this in plenty of time to have space unlocked or approved by your school's technology specialist.
- Have a computer and LCD projector set up for demonstrations. Preparing a model page ahead of time is helpful.
- Make sure students have access to computers.
- Students will need to work in pairs, so you will need to pair them up beforehand or allow/approve partnerships.
- The class will need a literary text and/or research topic to base the page on. In this example, the text is *Macbeth* and the research accompanying it is focused on the students' choice of political figures. In my class, the research was conducted in partnerships that extended into the lesson. Students need to have completed their research before you initiate this lesson.

Hosting services such as Wikispaces can be accessed for free and from any computer with Internet access, and can provide most of the text- and image-editing tools necessary for page creation. It is essential that you provide a model, and it might be helpful to begin it before introducing the lesson and develop it a step ahead of the students throughout the process. Use an LCD projector to demonstrate changes and explain problems and your solutions for them. Collaborating with the entire class on elements of your model page will help students develop skills and problem-solving techniques for creating their own pages.

Students can apply their personal experiences with social networking to the creation of the network page, but they need a space in which to do that. Using Wikispaces in my class worked well because we used it throughout the year for different purposes, including collaborating on page creation in other projects. The new page appears without layout, so students are introduced to an understanding of spatial considerations instead of simply plugging text and pictures into predetermined spaces. By setting up a collaborative environment for the project, you provide students with a space in which they can collaborate to make the most of their individual skills and have support in problem solving during the page's creation.

Providing ample computer time is necessary for the success of the project. If students do not have computers with Internet access at home, they will need time during class and before or after school to work on this project. Debrief any lab attendant or media specialist on the details of the lesson and other activities associated with it so students can get support from them if needed.

Time Frame

The lesson on page creation spans two 90-minute class periods for the initial setup and continues periodically for whatever amount of time you determine students need. You might need to make additional time available for students with limited home computer and Internet access or limited experience with social networking. As students build and revise pages beyond the scope of this lesson, you might need to provide mini-lessons to help them troubleshoot technology and composition problems.

Description of Activity

Day 1: Profile of a Profile Page

To begin the lesson, I post a warm-up activity on the board and provide markers for students to write their responses on the board. The activity simply asks for the characteristics of a Facebook, MySpace, or Twitter profile page. We open the lesson by discussing their responses, adding to their comments, and creating categories for the characteristics they have named. We then discuss two major aspects of social networking profiles that are essential for their understanding and will later guide their creation, adding their responses to the collection on the board:

1. How is a social networking profile composed to develop an identity of its subject?
2. How do others interact with an individual's profile using various modes of communication?

Transitioning to the literary text, I ask students to extend their understanding of our initial discussion and the two main ideas to *Macbeth*, brainstorming with a small group about what a profile page for a main character of the play might be like. Assigning characters to groups is helpful in eliminating overlap, but overlap can also show different perspectives on the same character. I provide chart paper to the groups for them to develop their ideas as a list or a mock-up.

After sharing these ideas and posting the chart paper on the wall, I ask students what they think we are going to do. I collect their responses and add them to the characteristics and examples of profile pages we have already compiled, and present them for a full view of the purpose of the lesson. Responses will vary, but ultimately students glean that we will integrate the reading of *Macbeth* with norms of social networking in some way.

Transitioning from the setup to the creation of the page relies on your modeling. I project my model, provide some reading and thinking time, and ask students to identify their assignment. We look at a social networking model so students can pick out information from wall postings. Together we verbalize the overall product from the lesson: a social networking profile based on *Macbeth* and the research they have completed on a contemporary political figure who has faced an ethical dilemma. Once that has been decided on, students help me identify the various topics we have discussed in examining the model. As they evaluate the model (see Handout 25.1 in the supplemental materials) and identify what is missing, I make an addition-and-revision list for my own page. Revisions might include changing font size, style, and color to better project the character represented. I then choose a simple revision and open the edit mode of the page to demonstrate how to make the revision, showing students that editing the space is fairly easy.

Day 2: Profile Page Workshop

As part of an earlier research unit and precursor to the Macbethbook activity, I had assigned students to research a contemporary political figure who has faced an ethical dilemma. Now, using those figures and their research, I ask students the following:

- If [researched figure] had a Facebook page, what would it say?
- Who would post on it?
- How would he or she present himself or herself?
- What music, video, or picture elements are appropriate for this person?
- How active would he or she be in this kind of community, and why (i.e., consistent activity vs. sporadic activity)?

Answering these questions leads us to make links from the politicians to characters in *Macbeth*. As students discuss and brainstorm these ideas with their partner, I pass out computers from the mobile laptop lab. Once every partnership has a computer, I again pull up Wikispaces and walk students through setting up their profile pages for a character from *Macbeth*. From there, I allow at least 45 minutes for workshop time on the pages, circulating to troubleshoot issues and make comments. While circulating and assisting, I look for signs of trouble between collaborating pairs and encourage ways for them to work together. I also encourage pairs to assist each other with technology skills to help them troubleshoot and solve their own problems.

In later lessons, students will integrate their research and understanding of the play by having their profile subject interact with the characters and events of *Macbeth* on their profile page. To begin their synthesis, I wrap up the lesson with an exit slip. Students, still in pairs, determine which of the characters from *Macbeth* is most like the political figure they researched and which is the least like that politician. Then the pairs separate the two characters and write a letter to their political figure from that character. As they leave class, students staple the responses together and turn them in for feedback. Before the next lesson, I read the letters and provide feedback on how their responses can work into their page creations. I also provide feedback on the pages themselves using the discussion tool in the digital environment.

Assessment

Day 1

The assessment of day 1's activities is based mostly on informal discussion and response. In brainstorming or sketching out a sample profile for a character from the play, students demonstrate their understanding of the ideas presented in discussion and their understanding of the play. In creating the revision-and-addition list for your model page, students use their viewing skills to evaluate the embodiment of the ideas discussed in earlier points of the lesson.

Day 2

The page-creation workshop day should be informally assessed for how the student partnerships have begun to integrate their understanding of social networking into the composition of the page. You should provide feedback from the workshop day directly onto the pages using a discussion or comment tool. The exit slips from the second day will provide you with a view of the students' synthesis of information about the play and the research they conducted on a contemporary political figure. Although it does not assess the day's work specifically, this activity acts as a preassessment of how the partnerships might have the various figures interact within the virtual space in later lessons. (For a sample rubric, see Handout 25.2 on the companion website.)

By the end of this process, students will have created a page that satisfies several assessment ends. First, the page should convey an understanding of the literary text on which it is based. Second, it should convey a synthesis of ideas gleaned from the literary text and from the research students conducted. Third, these ideas are developed through a variety of multiliteracy practices to create a multimodal composition that integrates text, video, audio, and image to demonstrate understanding.

Connections and Adaptations

Although *Macbeth* is the central text for this lesson, any literary text can be substituted as the central focus. This project incorporates a previous research assignment as an additional source to integrate, but any supplemental text or experience can act in its place. For example, students could read appropriations of a text along with the original play, noting the differences and similarities on their profile pages. The same can be done with film appropriations and adaptations, as well as multimedia connections such as thematically similar songs, films, or alternative texts. Developing interactions between students' profile pages is also an option. Students could respond in the discussion tool or edit one another's pages from the persona of their own character's profile. The appropriateness and adaptability of this lesson for the middle grades depends on how experienced the students are with social networking sites.

Work Cited

Harter, Dennis, and Justin Medved. "Curriculum 2.0." *YouTube*. YouTube, 11 Sept. 2007. Web. 5 Dec. 2009. http://www.youtube.com/watch?v=4xBYSdMK1LU.

26 A New Media Pilgrimage: Chaucer and the Multimodal Satire

Paul Joseph Stengel
Teachers College, Columbia University

Context

This unit was first taught at Joseph A. Foran High School in Milford, Connecticut. Foran High is one of two high schools in the district and consists of more than 1,200 students in grades 9–12. Although the project can be applied to most texts, I used it to focus on Geoffrey Chaucer's *The Canterbury Tales*. After we study the literary techniques used by Chaucer, I ask each student to create his or her own tale of satire that focuses on high school culture.

Rationale

Traditionally, Foran High's World Literature course evaluates student literacy based on each student's ability to demonstrate analysis of canonical pieces of work through classroom discussion, homework assignments, and unit essay exams. As an extension, this unit challenges each student not only to identify and discuss the rhetorical devices used by Chaucer, but also to attempt to use these devices to produce a satirical tale that takes advantage of audio-, image-, and software-production tools.

Objectives

Students will be able to:

- Participate in an online community using learning management tools to collaborate with peers, reflect on progress, and add to a personal portfolio of work

- After guided practice, identify literary elements within the "The Pardoner's Tale" and the "The Wife of Bath's Tale" and analyze the meaning of each excerpt, as well as participate in discussions in class and online
- Transmediate text through a writing process that requires drafting a satire first as prose, then as poetry, and finally as a storyboard to be recorded with images
- Use information resources to select visual images to enrich the satire's recorded word

NCTE/IRA standards addressed: 6, 8, 12

Materials/Preactivity Preparation

Learning Management Style

The analytical discussions and milestone blogs featured in this lesson depend on Moodle, Wikispaces, or any learning management system that allows for collaborative writing, group discussion, and a personal reflection blog. For this lesson I used Moodle, but that doesn't mean that Moodle is best for every classroom. When choosing a learning management system (LMS), think about pedagogical purpose, ease of setup, and student privacy.

It is important to keep in mind that each learning management system comes with a set of features that will influence your pedagogy. When choosing an LMS, think about how you will use it in your class and what features will enhance your teaching style. Learning management systems such as Blackboard are designed to work best out of the box for lecture and file sharing. Moodle is one of the few learning management systems that has been designed to provide many flexible constructivist tools, but it is worth considering whether these tools behave in a way that complements your teaching style and learning expectations. Using Wikispaces gives you a blank slate to build and organize your learning environment to fit your teaching style, but by nature it is a wiki and therefore designed for equal contribution from all users.

Depending on your time and resources, LMS software setup should be a consideration. Wikispaces is the easiest and least expensive to set up. Simply by navigating to the company website, anyone can set up a free course wiki ready for use the same day. Moodle typically requires installation on a server and maintenance of software tools, although some websites do offer free Moodle classrooms to teachers.

You might want to speak with your information technology team to learn more about district policies for storing student work and information on a third-party site like Wikispaces or a free Moodle classroom. Also, consider reading "Insidious Pedagogy: How Course Management Systems Affect Teaching" by Lisa M. Lane for more information on choosing an LMS that matches your teaching style and purpose.

Storyboards

Each student will use the wiki environment to build the second draft of his or her satire. Within a two-column storyboard, students will add poetry to the left column and corresponding image(s) to the right column. A new row will be established for each stanza or transition.

Computers with Microsoft Photo Story 3 or VoiceThread Account

Photo Story is an application that runs on a computer, whereas VoiceThread is a Web-based application. Both allow users to load and sort images into a workspace and record audio to be played along with the images. Photo Story provides panning, zooming, and other features that can enrich a narrative.

Headphone with Microphone

Each student will need a pair to record and play back his or her satire with the Photo Story software.

Theoretical Texts

You might want to read *Multimodal Composition* by Cynthia L. Selfe for additional resources, as well as *Slide:ology* by Nancy Duarte. Both authors discuss the strategic use of multimodal affordances to design and produce enriching multimodal texts. I highly recommend Sheridan Blau's *The Literature Workshop* for the close reading activity.

Time Frame

The length of time you'll need for this unit varies depending on experience. For inexperienced classrooms, the lesson could take up to seventeen 45-minute class periods. For experienced classrooms, the lesson might take up to twelve 45-minute class periods. Because of the time commitment involved, this "lesson" truly is more of a unit.

Any LMS will do for this unit as long as it includes a wiki, blog-like functionality, and discussion area. If you and the students are currently experienced with a specific LMS, by all means use it for this activity. Otherwise, you should schedule one or two classes in a computer lab to give a basic tutorial on Wikispaces or Moodle. This is a great opportunity to have students work on an "easy" assignment such as creating a profile page or writing their first journal entry. Make sure students practice all activities you will expect for this unit, including linking to webpages and uploading files. To manage the cognitive load, the first activity should not be a textual analysis activity; rather, the challenge should lie in navigating the learning management environment.

You should also investigate whether your district supports Photo Story or a similar program. Although Photo Story is free, it does require some setup, and you might find an online solution such as VoiceThread to be easier to manage. For software programs like Photo Story, I've found it to be a good idea to coordinate in advance with the IT department of the school or district to make sure all required software is available on the computers planned for use. Additionally, since some videos can be large, it is important to facilitate a method for students to save finished video files in a safe place that can be accessed over time.

Since much of this assignment relies on production, keeping students on-task between deadlines can be challenging. Within the LMS, I establish common areas that students can reference during the unit. Here I post an online Google calendar of daily assignments due. I also provide copies of assignment directions and rubrics, along with any materials I present during mini-tutorials. Additionally, students are required to keep reflective blogs; some entries are based on prompts and others are open-ended. These entries correlate with milestones throughout the production of the final assessment. The blog entries are helpful for keeping students on-task, and entries provide another form of data to consider when thinking about ways to improve my lessons. All entries for this lesson are part of a course portfolio of student work.

Description of Activity

Close Reading Workshop

Typically, I teach this unit after our class has had some experience with close reading and textual analysis of literature. At this point, students must be able to study examples of new literary devices within a text and identify new examples on their own. We begin our first day with concepts such as frame story and satire, and read "The Pardoner's Tale" for examples of symbolism, archetype, and satire. I ask students to take notes during our discussion and finish the reading at home. For homework I ask students to post questions about the reading on our course discussion board and to attempt to provide an example of a literary device used in the story that was not covered in class.

Occasionally, inexperienced students complete assigned work within the asynchronous environment using informal language and highly stylized fonts that are hard to read. My advice is not to punish these students. Instead, speak with each student individually to reinforce the project goals and evaluation systems. If a majority of the class demonstrates informal effort, a mini-lesson on netiquette might help everyone.

We continue this process of reading and analysis over the course of two or three 45-minute periods. In groups of three, we discuss "The Pardoner's Tale" and "The Wife of Bath's Tale." We spend class time discussing the most interesting posts from the night before as well as reading new sections of each tale. I use methods from Sheridan Blau's *The Literature Workshop* to facilitate discussion both in class and online. Blau's book is an excellent resource that provides a methodology for students to tap into what they know as individuals within a group setting as a way to analyze texts, with you as facilitator of the process rather than sole knowledge provider. Once students demonstrate competence at finding examples of symbolism, archetype, and satire in the two tales, I ask them to turn their critical eye on the other texts and the world around them. First I might ask: "What are examples of satirical texts popular in today's culture?" Students often shout out *"The Simpsons"* and *"The Daily Show."* Then I ask: "What systems in American high school culture can be satirized? What symbols and archetypes exist?" Answering this might require students to revisit "The Pardoner's Tale" or "The Wife of Bath's Tale," but typically this question is made easier by the extensive knowledge base available for students to reference among the posts on the discussion board. I ask students to research peers' posts and reference these posts if applicable in their own post responses to the preceding questions. This exercise begins the process of developing ideas for tales to be written and produced using Microsoft Photo Story.

The Writing Process

Once the close reading process is complete, students write their top three tale ideas on a designated wiki page that is linked to the common area of the LMS. I also share this link in the Google calendar and mass email it using Moodle's mail tool. To avoid too many tales written about the same topic, I approve one of the three tale proposals and organize the tales within the frame of the story. I strongly suggest that you write the frame narrative for the satire yourself to bring continuity to the student work and to demonstrate to students a dedication to the project. Writing the frame narrative helped me become more reflective about the tale-writing process for future classes. For homework, I ask students to find their tale assignment listed on the wiki and task them to brainstorm the first draft of their tale in a portfolio blog entry. I usually give students a word minimum for this task. As needed, I differentiate this task by allowing students to draw six to ten frames that develop the initial tale, or to select an image from the Internet to use as a catalyst for writing.

During the next class session, I distribute the directions for the final multimodal assignment as well as a rubric. Then I review the content of the handouts and give students a class period to begin transforming their first draft into a poem that contains all the elements required on the rubric. This assignment can be completed in the classroom on paper or in a computer lab. Students will eventually create a two-column storyboard and place all poetry in the left column (see Handout 26.1 in the supplemental materials). This storyboard will be created on a wiki page, and a link to the storyboard will be added to the main page of the LMS site. Depending on what we've done in previous units, I might give students a mini-lesson on stanza construction, literary devices, and sound devices in poetry. Ideally, these were covered during the textual analysis of Chaucer's *Canterbury Tales,* and students only need to call on that information to try it in their own narrative poem. Students might need more than one class period and a homework assignment to complete this task. If so, I typically give them the sixth classroom session and two nights to complete the assignment. For the seventh classroom session, I begin to introduce students to image searching on the Internet.

Databases and Fair Use

The second week of the unit, each student begins collecting images for the project, and I provide an orientation on online search methods. It is worth coordinating this effort with the school librarian, who may be of great help. Whenever I teach a lesson that requires online searching, I work with the school librarian to provide students with the latest databases available. I find that if I share the project description and rubric with the librarian, he or she is able to find databases that are helpful to students. The Free Media Library at Penn State is also helpful in finding media for free use. Of course, the use of images from the Internet requires a discussion regarding copyright law. Some librarians are able to give this talk; otherwise, you can access many resources online that offer information about proper citation and use of media in student projects. For homework, I ask students to continue searching for images to place on the right side of their wiki storyboards. I also remind each student that images selected should align with the descriptive language written in their poem. Students should save the image files to a portable drive to be accessed at home or on campus. If students don't have access to a portable storage device, then I encourage them to save the direct links to images to a wiki page or text file for later reference. I remind them to collect all citation information from image sites to aid them in building a works cited page for their project. It is important to note that image files will eventually need to be saved to the computer for Photo Story to process the images to be included in the workspace. At this point, we have reached a major milestone, and I ask students to write a blog entry on the process of writing their poem and searching for images to further enrich the meaning of their satire.

Creating the Multimedia Satire

We spend the final four days of this unit working on arranging images, recording audio, and composing a multimodal satire on high school culture. I consider this a good time to invite a representative from the school district IT department to work with me to troubleshoot any issues with the software or hardware. Photo Story is relatively simple, but I usually like to have someone around during the first class session to help me troubleshoot issues with items such as recording and playback volume, file extensions, and directory permissions. I encourage students to experiment with the special features of Photo Story during the ninth and tenth day of class. We discuss how strategically using the special features of the software with thoughtfully selected images can emphasize the symbolism or irony, or draw the audience's attention to key aspects of the story. To keep students on-task, on the tenth day I might also ask them to write a short blog entry on their progress and offer special after-school hours to answer any questions and to help with work on projects. Once students have completed their projects, I publish the final draft of their storyboards online along with video presentations. I ask students to add the link of their final project to their portfolio and write a blog entry that evaluates the unit we have just finished, as well as the work they completed. Many students enjoy the creative elements of this assignment but find the process of completing a long-term project to be very challenging. Overall, this assignment allows students to produce a multimodal narrative that requires new skills that many consider worthwhile practicing. Samples of student work can be found at http://www.learningspiral.org.

Assessment

Students are evaluated on each section of the unit leading up to the final project. I evaluate the written responses on the online discussion board on a three-point scale that focuses on the amount of recall, analysis, and textual support with line numbers each answer contains. Student answers typically become richer as grades are assigned using the Moodle scoring tool within the forum. I also evaluate student blog reflections based on descriptive language and synthesis of ideas.

After completing the storyboard, I ask students to partner up to complete a peer evaluation of one another's work. This peer evaluation focuses on the following:

- Does your partner have a cohesive satirical narrative on an approved topic?
- Are the images chosen relevant to the stanzas provided?
- Are all of the required literary elements present in the poem?

 I use a rubric to grade the final project (see Handout 26.2 on the companion website). I provide the rubric in advance and frequently revisit it with the class throughout the unit. On the final day of the project, each student is required to highlight and label each rubric element present in his or her storyboard. This allows me to evaluate even failed attempts at completing complex tasks such as properly using literary devices, and it serves as a final self-check for the student. Essential items of a model project include:

- A narrative poem that conforms to the definition of a satire, thus remarking on some human weakness, vice, or folly present in high school culture
- Contains examples of all required literary devices studied such as irony, allusion, archetype, symbol, etc.
- The structure of the poem is thoughtful, including a prologue to establish the setting and content of the tale within the narrative frame
- Each slide image is clear, and there is evidence of thoughtful planning, composing, and arranging of images in sequence with audio
- Effective use of multimedia to establish theme through point of view, panning, zooming, and transitioning
- A citation slide providing careful MLA citation and respecting all copyright

Connections and Adaptations

The activities described in this unit can be purposefully used in many ways in core language arts curricula. Any language arts class that asks students to critically analyze literary devices present in a work can use this lesson to guide students through a collaborative analysis that leads to the production of a project with attributes common to the text studied. For instance, a poetry unit might culminate with a music video that incorporates images that enhance the meaning of student-drafted lyrics or lines. You could also ask each student to choose a poem and record a personal reading of it along with personally selected images that capture the descriptive language, symbolism, and metaphor of the poem.

A composition class might create a visual argumentative essay, or a descriptive essay, using only images and the Photo Story software. As an initial assignment for the school year, I like to have students use the software to record a technology autobiography. From these autobiographies, we learn much about our own experiences, strengths, and weaknesses regarding technology, and it provides our class a starting point for supporting one another throughout the school year.

Students with more advanced media production skills might want to manipulate transitions, add video, lay down audio tracks, and save the final project as a different file type. Advanced students might find Microsoft Movie Maker or Apple iMovie excellent software package alternatives to Photo Story.

Works Cited

Blau, Sheridan D. *The Literature Workshop: Teaching Text and Their Readers.* Portsmouth, NH: Heinemann, 2003. Print.

Duarte, Nancy. *Slide:ology: The Art and Science of Creating Great Presentations.* Sebastopol, CA: O'Reilly Media, 2008. Print.

"Free Media Library." *Media Commons at Penn State.* Penn State, n.d. Web. 4 Jan. 2010.

Lane, Lisa. "Insidious Pedagogy: How Course Management Systems Affect Teaching." *First Monday* 14.10 (2009): n. pag. Web. 7 Feb 2010.

Selfe, Cynthia L. *Multimodal Composition: Resources for Teachers.* Cresskill, NJ: Hampton Press, 2007. Print.

Supplemental Resources

"iMovie '09: What Is iMovie?" *iLife*. Apple Inc., n.d. Web. 4 Jan. 2010.

Learning Spiral. Paul Stengel, n.d. Web. 4 Jan. 2010.

Microsoft Photo Story 3 for Windows. Windows XP. Microsoft Corporation, n.d. Web. 4 Jan. 2010.

Moodle Tutorials. Moodle Tutorials, n.d. Web. 4 Jan. 2010.

"Choose a Tour." *Wikispaces*. Tangient LLC, n.d. Web. 4 Jan. 2010.

Windows Movie Maker 2.1 Download. Windows XP. Microsoft Corporation, n.d. Web. 4 Jan. 2010.

Index

Note: page numbers in *italics* refer to illustrations.

Editors

Mary T. Christel has been a member of the English department at Adlai E. Stevenson High School in the northwest suburbs of Chicago since 1979; she teaches AP literature classes as well as courses in media and film studies. She has published *Seeing and Believing: How to Teach Media Literacy in the English Classroom* (2001) with Ellen Krueger, as well as edited *Lesson Plans for Creating Media-Rich Classrooms* (2007) with Scott Sullivan. Christel has served on various committees and boards focusing on the promotion of media literacy in the language arts curriculum, including the National Council of Teachers of English, the National Telemedia Council, and the National Board of Professional Teaching Standards.

Scott Sullivan is an assistant professor of secondary education at National-Louis University. He is also the manager for university partnerships at the Academy for Urban School Leadership. He has taught in middle school, high school, and graduate school in urban and suburban settings. Currently, he is active in school reform, teacher training, curriculum, media, and school turn-arounds. He is the father of four fabulous children, Grace, Emmett, Ellie, and Georgia, and husband to one wonderful wife, Dawn, whose support makes his work possible.

Contributors

Andrew D. Adams has taught English language arts at Lauren Hill Academy in Montreal, Québec, for the last six years. He is always searching for different ways to bring digital photography and comic books into his classroom to engage his students in creative writing assignments. Many of these projects have been turned into publications that are in school libraries throughout Montreal. Adams has presented at city-wide and provincial conferences and he was featured as part of a video series on innovative classroom practices. He is a graduate of McGill University in education and also holds a BA in history from Concordia University, Montreal.

Beth Ahlgrim began her career in 1986 at a private school on the northwest side of Chicago. Working at Adlai E. Stevenson High School since 2002, she teaches Sophomore English and Junior Accelerated English. Ahlgrim earned her BA in English education from St. Mary's University, Winona, Minnesota, and her MA in English literature from DePaul University. She is presently pursuing National Board Certification and an MA in educational leadership, Type 75.

Natalia Barker taught various levels and areas of literature in her five-year experience at Walhalla High School in South Carolina before relocating to Nashville to earn an MEd at Vanderbilt University. Her academic interests focus on using students' out-of-school digital literacies in the classroom to create authentic and relevant learning experiences with literature, research, and multimodal composition. The lesson featured in this book is her first publication.

Elizabeth H. Beagle has been a high school teacher in Virginia Beach, Virginia, for the last seventeen years. She earned her BSS in education at Old Dominion University. She works with adolescents in grades 10 and 12, always looking for ways to use electronic texts to engage students while helping them develop the literacies fundamental to their future. She has also worked with students on creating digital portfolios and is currently helping to steer her school system toward a K–12 digital portfolio assessment program. Beagle has written several articles on portfolios and has presented nationally on portfolios and 21st century literacies.

Molly Berger is currently the instructional improvement coordinator in Educational Service District 105 in Yakima, Washington, where she works with media resources and professional development. Previously, she taught language arts grades 7–12 for thirty years, primarily in the East Valley School District in Yakima. She earned a BAEd in speech/drama/English/journalism and an MAEd focusing on literature and film from Central Washington University. She is National Board

Certified in English Language Arts/Adolescence and Young Adulthood. Berger has written for *English Journal* and state journals and has presented workshops at the state and national levels on media and language arts instruction.

Laura L. Brown has been an English teacher at Adlai E. Stevenson High School in Lincolnshire, Illinois, since 1987 and has been a leader there in technology integration since August 2000 through her work with a staff development program called the "PowerRangers." This award-winning program provides technology resources, training, and support for teachers so they can make the most effective use of these tools in the classroom. Brown has shared her work at numerous workshops and conferences and has also published a lesson plan in *Lesson Plans for Creating Media-Rich Classrooms* (2007).

Anna Meyers Caccitolo began working in Chicago's western suburbs at Lyons Township High School in 2002. She has been teaching English for the past ten years, focusing mainly on ninth graders and junior accelerated literature, sophomore interpersonal communications, and various speaking electives. Meyers Caccitolo was a catalyst in creating the interpersonal communications curriculum when it debuted in 2005. She earned her BA in English from the University of Illinois at Urbana–Champaign and her MA in curriculum and instruction from National-Louis University.

Belinha De Abreu is an assistant teaching professor at Drexel University's College of Information Science and Technology. She earned her PhD from the University of Connecticut in curriculum and instruction with a focus on media literacy education. Her research interests include new digital media literacies, young adults, and teacher training, with a focus on the impact and resultant learning of media watched and used by K–12 students. She has most recently published "Middle Schoolers, Media Literacy, and Methodology: The Three M's" in *Issues in Information and Media Literacy: Education, Practice, and Pedagogy* (2009).

Mark B. Dolce is a former grant writer and teacher who is currently writing under contract to Event 360, Inc., the nation's top producer of large-scale fundraising events benefiting nonprofits throughout the country. He earned a BA in English and film studies from Indiana University–Bloomington and an MAT from National-Louis University in Evanston, Illinois. Dolce also contributed to *Lesson Plans for Creating Media-Rich Classrooms* (2007).

Joseph J. Geocaris has taught in the communication arts department at Adlai E. Stevenson High School since 2004. His teaching load has included accelerated, regular, and instructional versions of ninth-grade and junior English. He earned his BA in English from Eastern Illinois University and his MA in new media studies from DePaul University in Chicago. He has presented on issues related to technology and literacy on both local and national levels.

John Golden is currently a curriculum specialist for high school language arts in Portland, Oregon. He is the author of *Reading in the Dark: Using Film as a Tool in the English Classroom* (NCTE, 2001) and *Reading in the Reel World: Teaching Documentaries and Other Nonfiction Texts* (NCTE, 2006). Golden has delivered presentations and led workshops around the country to help teachers use film actively in the classroom as a way for students to improve their reading, analytical, and critical thinking skills.

Mindy Hawley is a curriculum specialist for grades 6–8 language arts in Portland, Oregon, where she leads professional development programs for teachers in a wide range of formats. She also collaborates with teacher teams to create curriculum that supports reading and writing instruction in the middle grades. Previously, Hawley taught middle school for fifteen years, including eighth-grade language arts and social studies, self-contained sixth grade, and sixth-grade language arts and social studies.

Katherine Higgs-Coulthard has enjoyed teaching writers of all ages through her experiences as a classroom teacher for South Bend Community Schools, adjunct faculty at Saint Mary's College, and director of the Michiana Writers' Center. Currently she freelances as a teacher consultant for schools wishing to increase students' motivation to write.

Heather A. Ingraham has been teaching at Niles North High School in Skokie, Illinois, since 1992. A graduate of the University of Notre Dame (BA in the Program of Liberal Studies and in English) and the University of Chicago (MAT in English), Ingraham teaches sophomore literature and composition, an at-risk group of sophomores, and Advanced Placement English. She coached swimming for many years and now assists the chess team. A native of Los Angeles, Heather is working on hiking each of California's fifty-eight county high points.

Chris Judson has been a member of the English department at Concord High School in northern Indiana since 1995, where he teaches AP English Language and Composition as well as other composition and journalism classes. He earned a BA at Grace College in Indiana in English education with a minor in journalism and an MS in secondary education at Indiana University. He is a National Writing Project fellow (1997) and a recipient of a Lilly Endowment Teacher Creativity Fellowship Program grant (2009) for his proposal "40 Plays in 40 Days." He discusses using technology for learning on his website http://www.bashinged.com/.

Abigail J. Kennedy is a National Board Certified Teacher in Pasco County, Florida. She teaches English IV (including honors), AP literature, yearbook, and multimedia, and adjunct teaches at Pasco-Hernando Community College and Pasco eSchool. Kennedy is an Apple Distinguished Educator, a Master Digital Educator, and a teacher consultant for the Tampa Bay Area Writing Project. She reviews YA novels for the journals *SIGNAL* and *The ALAN Review* and is a recipient of NCTE's High School Teacher of Excellence Award, FCTE's Teacher of the Year, and

NCTE's Media Literacy Award. Her BS is in telecommunications from the University of Florida, and her MA is in English education from the University of South Florida.

M. Elizabeth Kenney is a graduate of the Great Books program at the University of Notre Dame and holds an MA in the teaching of English from the University of Chicago. She has taught at Adlai E. Stevenson High School since 1989, where she has had adventures in teaching American and British literature, world literature, AP English, and, most recently, film and media studies. Kenney also contributed to *Lesson Plans for Creating Media-Rich Classrooms* (2007).

William Kist has been researching classroom uses of new media for more than fifteen years. His profiles of teachers who are broadening our conception of literacy were included in his two books, *New Literacies in Action: Teaching and Learning in Multiple Media* (2005) and *The Socially Networked Classroom: Teaching in the New Media Age* (2010). A former high school English teacher and curriculum supervisor and currently an associate professor at Kent State University, Kist remains active as a filmmaker and musician and earned a regional Emmy nomination for Outstanding Music Composition.

Suzanne C. Linder teaches Sophomore English, Current Topics in Social Justice, and Gender Studies at the University of Illinois Laboratory High School. During her tenure at Uni High, she has traveled with students to Mississippi and Greece, converted a car to run on waste vegetable oil, and produced a documentary on being labeled gifted. She earned a BA in English and theatre education from Calvin College in Michigan and an MA in speech communication from the University of Illinois. She frequently contributes lesson plans to readwritethink.org, and in 2004 she was selected to participate in a Fulbright Hays Seminar to New Zealand.

Michele Luchs is currently the coordinator of English language arts for the Ministry of Education of Québec, Canada. She has taught English and media studies at the high school level and to preservice teachers at McGill University. She wrote the media competency for a new provincial K–11 ELA curriculum and has trained teachers around the province in media production and analysis in ELA. She coedited the Rainbow of Dreams series, and directed and edited a series of films in innovative teachers' classrooms, including that of Andrew Adams. She was a member of NCTE's Commission on Media from 2001 to 2008.

Louis Mazza received his BFA in media arts from the Minneapolis College of Art and Design and his MAT in visual art from the University of the Arts. Mazza teaches media arts and media literacy at the Arts Academy at Benjamin Rush in Philadelphia, Pennsylvania. Through the practice of photography, filmmaking, and graphic design, his students learn how to create messages and communicate their ideas effectively while gaining valuable insight into the construction of the visual environment that surrounds us. Mazza regularly exhibits his visual art and photography and practices graphic design for educational and nonprofit organizations. He has been a high school educator since 2006.

Susanne Lee Nobles has taught English at Fredericksburg Academy in Fredericksburg, Virginia, since 1995. Working in an independent school with a 1:1 laptop program, Nobles has been able to teach it all, from yearbook to writing fundamentals to world literature, while exploring the powerfully collaborative and reflective nature of a laptop classroom. She currently teaches Introduction to Genres and AP Literature and Composition and has written about both in the *English Journal* and *Kappan* magazine. She is pursuing her PhD in English with a focus on new media and professional writing at Old Dominion University.

David P. Noskin has been a member of the English department at Adlai E. Stevenson High School since 1985, where he formerly served as the director of the Communication Arts Division and currently teaches Sophomore and Junior English. He earned a BS at the University of Wisconsin–Madison in English/speech education and an M Ed at National-Louis University in English education with an emphasis in writing instruction. Noskin earned his PhD in curriculum and instruction at the University of Wisconsin–Madison, where he taught courses in English education. He has published several articles for *English Journal*.

Neil Rigler teaches in the English department at Deerfield High School, located in the northern suburbs of Chicago. He teaches Senior English, American Studies (interdisciplinary English and social studies), and media studies classes on film and television. He earned a BS in psychology from Duke University and an MA in English, as well as an MS in education, from Northwestern University in Evanston, Illinois. He is a fellow of the Institute for Writing and Thinking at Bard College. Rigler has published several articles and presented at the NCTE Annual Convention on various topics, including technology, media literacy, and revisiting homework practices.

Luke Rodesiler is currently a doctoral fellow studying English education in the School of Teaching and Learning at the University of Florida, where he also teaches preservice English teachers. A former high school English teacher at South Lyon High School in southeast Michigan and a teacher consultant of the Red Cedar Writing Project at Michigan State University, his work has appeared in various academic journals, including *English Journal*, *Classroom Notes Plus*, *Screen Education*, and *Computers and Composition Online*. Rodesiler's research interests include teacher education and the use of popular media and technology in the teaching of English.

Vicki Luthi Sherbert began her career as an educator in 1985. She taught second and third grades in Clay Center, Kansas, for sixteen years, and in 2001 she began teaching sixth, seventh, and eighth grades in

Wakefield, Kansas. She earned BS and MS degrees in elementary education at Kansas State University and is a PhD candidate at Kansas State in curriculum and instruction. Sherbert serves as co-director of the Flint Hills Writing Project Invitational Summer Institute, providing professional development and leadership opportunities to educators of all content areas and grade levels from kindergarten through postsecondary.

Paul Joseph Stengel is an educational technologist for Columbia University, where he works every day with faculty as a consultant and project manager for the purposeful use of Web technologies in the classroom. Additionally, he is working toward an advanced degree in instructional technology and media at Teachers College, Columbia University. His current research interests include designing sustainable online communities of practice as well as multimodal case study environments for professional development. Previously, Stengel worked as a language arts teacher at Joseph A. Foran High School in Milford, Connecticut, where he experimented with online learning technologies in his classroom.

Brian Turnbaugh teaches global studies and media literacy and composition at Community High School District 94 in West Chicago. He has contributed pieces to the Bill of Rights Institute's *Media and American Democracy* (2005) and to NCTE's *Lesson Plans for Creating Media-Rich Classrooms* (2007).

Sara Wilcher Zeek teaches college composition and AP Literature and Composition at Lord Botetourt High School in Daleville, Virginia. She is also an adjunct at Dabney S. Lancaster Community College, Clifton Forge, Virginia. She earned a BA in English and an MALS in interdisciplinary studies from Hollins University, Roanoke, Virginia. Zeek is a National Board Certified Teacher and a teacher consultant for the Blue Ridge Writing Project, Blacksburg, Virginia. Her most recent publication was a poem in the *Virginia English Bulletin*.

Sarah M. Zerwin is in her fourteenth year as an educator, twelve years in the high school classroom and two years teaching methods classes to preservice teachers. She currently teaches language arts and journalism at Fairview High School in Boulder, Colorado. She earned a BA in English literature at the University of Colorado at Boulder, an MS in education at the University of Illinois at Urbana–Champaign, and a PhD in secondary literacy at the University of Colorado at Boulder. She is working on a book from her doctoral dissertation about teaching literature to reluctant high school readers.

This book was typeset in Palatino and Helvetica by Precision Graphics.
The typeface used on the cover is Cosmos.
The book was printed on 50-lb. Opaque Offset paper by Versa Press, Inc.